Undergraduate Topics in Computer Science

Series Editor
Ian Mackie

Advisory Board
Samson Abramsky, University of Oxford, Oxford, UK
Karin Breitman, Pontifical Catholic University of Rio de Janeiro, Rio de Janeiro, Brazil
Chris Hankin, Imperial College London, London, UK
Dexter Kozen, Cornell University, Ithaca, USA
Andrew Pitts, University of Cambridge, Cambridge, UK
Hanne Riis Nielson, Technical University of Denmark, Kongens Lyngby, Denmark
Steven Skiena, Stony Brook University, Stony Brook, USA
Iain Stewart, University of Durham, Durham, UK

'Undergraduate Topics in Computer Science' (UTiCS) delivers high-quality instructional content for undergraduates studying in all areas of computing and information science. From core foundational and theoretical material to final-year topics and applications, UTiCS books take a fresh, concise, and modern approach and are ideal for self-study or for a one- or two-semester course. The texts are all authored by established experts in their fields, reviewed by an international advisory board, and contain numerous examples and problems, many of which include fully worked solutions.

More information about this series at http://www.springer.com/series/7592

Joseph Migga Kizza

Ethics in Computing

A Concise Module

 Springer

Joseph Migga Kizza
Department of Computer Science
University of Tennessee
Chattanooga, Tennessee, USA

ISSN 1863-7310   ISSN 2197-1781   (electronic)
Undergraduate Topics in Computer Science
ISBN 978-3-319-29104-8   ISBN 978-3-319-29106-2   (eBook)
DOI 10.1007/978-3-319-29106-2

Library of Congress Control Number: 2016939119

Printed on acid-free paper

This Springer imprint is published by Springer Nature
The registered company is Springer International Publishing AG Switzerland

Preface

The overwhelming growth of technology, and its ability to give us unlimited powers that make us able to do things unthinkable just a decade ago, are creating equally both excitement and bewilderment. Tremendous technological advances have been registered across the board from telecommunication to computing with jaw-dropping developments. Along the way, these developments are creating unprecedented convergence communication and computing platform technologies that are reaching into all remote corners of the world, bringing the poor and less affluent on a par with the rest of the developed world. These new technological developments have created new communities and ecosystems that are themselves evolving, in flux, and difficult to secure, with questionable, if not evolving, ethical systems that will take us time to learn, if any remain constant at all. Because of these rapid and unpredictable changes, I found my previous editions, including the epic *Ethical and Social Issues in the Information Age*, becoming really voluminous to accommodate and include as many of the changes as possible. Without losing my focus and flavor of the previous editions, I am selectively reducing the content of those editions to a small, compact, and concise module edition. In this small edition, my message is still the same: that a time is coming, if not already here, when we, as individuals and as nations, will become totally dependent on computing technology. Evidence of this is embodied in the rapid convergence of telecommunication, broadcasting, computing, and mobile devices and the miniaturization of these devices, and their ever-increasing storage capacity, speed of computation, and ease of use. These qualities of these devices have been a big pulling force drawing in millions of new users every day, sometimes even those unwilling. Other appealing features of these devices are the increasing number of applications, apps, as they are often becoming known, and that they are wireless and portable. Whether small or large, these new gizmos have become a centerpiece of an individual's social and economic activities, the main access point for all information, and the empowerment of the device owner. Individuals aside, computing technology has also become the engine that drives the nations' strategic and security infrastructures which control power grids, gas and oil storage facilities, transportation, and all forms of national communication, including emergency services. These developments have elevated the cyberspace ecosystem as the most crucial economic and security environment of nations.

The rising trend in cyber attacks, many of them at lightning speed, affecting millions of computers and other electronic-bearing devices worldwide and in the process causing billions of dollars in losses to individuals and businesses, may be an indication of how unprepared we are to handle such attacks, not only now but also in the future. It may also be a mark of the poor state of our cyberspace defensive abilities and the lack of the will to develop these abilities. We need to develop protocols and build facilities and capabilities that will diminish the effects of these menacing activities, if not eliminating them all together.

It is encouraging, however, to hear that governments, legislative bodies, and law enforcement agencies around the world have started to act. One hopes that as these governments prepare defensive stances, they will also take steps to protect the individual citizens. As we look for such defensive strategies, the technological race is picking up speed with new technologies that make our efforts, and the existing protocols on which these strategies are based, obsolete in shorter and shorter periods. All these matters illustrate the speed at which the computing environment is changing and demonstrate a need for continuous review of our defensive strategies and, more importantly, the need for a strong ethical framework in our computer, information, and engineering science education. This need has been and will continue to be the focus of all my writings on this topic, and it is and remains so in this concise edition.

Chapter Overview

The concise edition is divided into 12 chapters as follows:

Chapter 1   **Morality and the Law**, defines and examines personal and public morality, identifying assumptions and value of the law and looking at both conventional and natural laws and the intertwining of morality and the law. Together with Chap. 3, Chap. 1 gives the reader the philosophical framework needed for the remainder of the book

Chapter 2   **Ethics and Ethical Analysis,** builds upon Chap. 1 in setting up the philosophical framework and analysis tools for the book discussing moral theories and problems in ethical relativism. Based on these and in light of the rapid advances in technology, the chapter discusses the moral and ethical premises and their corresponding values in the changing technology arena.

Chapter 3   **Ethics and the Professions**, examines the changing nature of the professions and how they cope with the impact of technology on their fields. An ethical framework for decision making is developed. Professional and ethical responsibilities based on community values and the law are also discussed. Social issues including harassment and discrimination are thoroughly covered.

Chapter 4   **Anonymity, Security, Privacy, and Civil Liberties**, surveys the traditional ethical issues of privacy, security, and anonymity and analyzes how these issues are affected by computer technology. Information gathering, databasing, and civil liberties are also discussed.

Chapter 5   **Intellectual Property Rights and Computer Technology**, discusses the foundations of intellectual property rights and how computer technology has influenced and changed the traditional issues of property rights, in particular, intellectual property rights.

Chapter 6   **Social Context of Computing**, considers the three main social issues in computing, namely, the digital divide, workplace issues such as employee monitoring, and health risks, and how these issues are changing with the changing computer technology.

Chapter 7   **Software Issues: Risks and Liabilities**, revisits the propoerty buyers' rights and producers's responsibility and accountability with a focus on computer software. The risks and liabilities associated with software and risk assessment are also discussed.

Chapter 8   **Computer Crimes**, surveys the history and examples of computer crimes, their types, costs to society, and strategies of detection and prevention.

Chapter 9   **Cyberbullying**, discusses the growing threat and effects of repeated deliberate harm or harassment to other people by using electronic technology that may include devices and equipment such as cell phones, computers, and tablets as well as communication tools including social media sites, text messages, chat, and websites.

Chapter 10   **New Frontiers for Computer Ethics: Artificial Intelligence, Virtualization, and Cyberspace**, discusses the new frontiers of ethics in the new intelligent technologies, virtualization technologies, virtual realities, spaces, and the implications of our participation, cyberspace, and the Internet, and how these new frontiers are affecting the traditional ethical and social issues.

Chapter 11   **Ethical, Privacy, and Security Issues in the Online Social Network Ecosystem**, discusses the new realities of global computer social network ecosystems; global linguistic, cultural, moral, and ethical dynamisms; and their impact on our traditional and cherished moral and ethical systems.

Chapter 12   **Elastic Extension Beyond the Traditional Computer Network: Mobile Systems and Intractable Social, Ethical, and Security Issues**, begins by presenting a rather frightening view of the quickly evolving mobile telecommunication and computing technologies; their unprecedented global reach and inclusion; the unparalleled social, financial, and cultural prowess; and the yet to be defined social, moral, and ethical value systems.

Audience

The book satisfies the new **ACM/IEEE-CS Computer Science Curricula 2013 (CS2013) Social and Professional Practice (SP)**, a draft of which is found at http://ai.stanford.edu/users/sahami/CS2013/strawman-draft/cs2013-strawman.pdf. The CS2013 focuses on the need for any computer science undergraduate to understand the basic cultural, social, legal, and ethical issues inherent in the discipline of computing. To do this, they need to:

- Understand where the discipline has been, where it is, and where it is heading
- Understand their individual roles in this process, as well as appreciate the philosophical questions, technical problems, and aesthetic values that are important in the development of the discipline
- Develop the ability to ask serious questions about the social impact of computing and to evaluate proposed answers to those questions
- Be aware of the basic legal rights of software and hardware vendors and users and also appreciate the ethical values that are the basis for those rights

Students in related disciplines like computer information and information management systems and library sciences will also find this book informative.

The book is also good for computer science professionals who must practice the principles embedded in the CS2013 curriculum based on understanding:

- The responsibility that they bear and the possible consequences of failure
- Their own limitations as well as the limitations of their tools

The book is also useful for anyone interested in knowing how ethical and social issues such as privacy, civil liberties, security, and anonymity, and workplace issues such as harassment and discrimination, are affecting the new computerized environment.

In addition, anybody interested in reading about computer networking, mobile computing, social networking, information security, and privacy will also find the book very helpful.

Acknowledgments

I appreciate all the help I received from colleagues who offered ideas; criticisms, sometimes harsh; and suggestions from anonymous reviewers over the years. Special thanks to my dear wife, Dr. Immaculate Kizza, who offered a considerable amount of help in proofreading, constructive ideas, and wonderful support.

Department of Computer Science and Engineering   Joseph Migga Kizza
University of Tennessee
Chattanooga, TN, USA

Contents

Morality and the Law

Learning Objectives

After reading this chapter, the reader should be able to

1. Learn to make sound moral reasoning.
2. Learn about moral values and ideals in a person's life.
3. Learn about the relationship between morality and religion.
4. Distinguish between morality and etiquette, law, and the professional code of conduct.
5. Learn what it means to have moral principles, the nature of conscience, and the relationship between morality and self-interest.

Scenario 1: With Stem Cell Research We Can Grow Just About Anything Human!

The parliament of the Republic of Kazini passed legislation, and the president signed into law, authorizing its citizens and scientists working on Kazini territory to carry out stem cell research to the best extent possible only limited by the physical resources. Scientists in Kazini have spearheaded such research and have made major breakthroughs in recent years.

Stem cells abound in bodies, but as human bodies age, the number of these cells and their potential and functions start to diminish as well. Embryonic stem cells that are found in the early stages of the body's development have the ability to divide indefinitely in culture and can therefore, at least in the laboratory, develop into virtually any cell type in the body.

The scientists in Kazini and their counterparts from around the world believe in the great benefits of stem cell research, especially embryonic stem cells. Many newspapers and scientific journals, not only in Kazini but also

(continued)

© Springer International Publishing Switzerland 2016
J.M. Kizza, *Ethics in Computing*, Undergraduate Topics in Computer Science,
DOI 10.1007/978-3-319-29106-2_1

Scenario 1: (continued)
from other countries, have written stories of limitless benefits, the most imme-
diate being the replacement of insulin-producing cells in the pancreas, dam-
aged muscle cells, and dead nerve cells due to strokes, spinal injury, and
degenerative diseases that include Alzheimer's and Parkinson's. It may also
lead to the development and replacement of liver cells destroyed by a hepatitis
and other liver diseases.
*   Dr. Don Rogan, a brilliant young scientist, is the director of Kazini Clinical*
Research Laboratory, the leading research nerve center in Kazini. Rogan is
convinced that the legislature's action is morally wrong. However, his
Laboratory has been chosen for funding and his dedicated scientists and staff
are excited by the legislature's actions. They had lobbied hard for the passage
of the bill. Now they see a ray of hope for millions of people not only on Kazini
but also around the world. Rogan is facing a personal dilemma.

Discussion Questions

1. What options does Rogan have?
2. If you were Dr. Rogan, what would you do?
3. Is Dr. Rogan bound by the legislation?

1.1   Introduction

Whether you believe in a supreme being or you are an atheist, you acknowledge the existence of human life because you are alive. You are alive because someone nurtured you and protected you from all adversities. Whoever did so followed a set of rules of conduct that kept both of you alive. Such shared rules, written or not, play a vital role in all human existence.

Human beings do not live randomly. We follow a script—a life script. In that script are hundreds of subscripts we follow both for survival (e.g., eating and sleeping) and for specific tasks. For example, when you meet a stranger, you follow a subscript different from the one you follow when you meet a long-lost friend. If you are hungry, the subscript you follow is different from the one you use to overcome anger. Within each subscript are variations we introduce to suit the situation. For example, when meeting an old friend, some people cry and others jump up and down, but both responses remain within the same subscript of meeting an old friend. The most important purpose of all these subscripts is human life, our own as well as others.

Believing in human life implies that we also believe life has a purpose. And because no one wants to live a life of pain, every human being believes in happiness as a purpose for life. To be happy, we need those conditions that create happiness, namely life, liberty, and property. Each condition is embodied in each of the three basic human survival subscripts: morality, ethics, and law. In this chapter, we discuss morality and law, and in Chap. 2 we discuss ethics.

1.2   Morality

Morality is a set of rules for right conduct, a system used to modify and regulate our behavior. It is a quality system in human acts by which we judge them right or wrong, good or bad. This system creates moral persons who possess virtues such as love for others, compassion, and a desire for justice; thus it builds character traits in people. In particular, morality is a survival script we follow in our day-to-day living. According to Wikipedia [1], morality has three different definitions:

- A descriptive definition according to which morality means a set of rules (code) of conduct that governs human behavior in matters of right and wrong. An example of the descriptive usage could be "common conceptions of morality have changed significantly over time."
- A normative and universal definition that is more prescriptive and refers to an ideal code of conduct that would be observed by all rational people under specified conditions. An example is a moral value judgment such as "murder is immoral."
- A definition of morality that is synonymous with ethics. Ethics is the systematic philosophical study of the moral domain. We define and discuss ethics in the following chapter.

In each one of these definitions, morality concerns itself with a set of shared rules, principles, and duties, independent from religion, applicable to all in a group or society, and having no reference to the will or power of any one individual whatever his or her status in that group or society. Although moral values are generally shared values in a society, the degree of sharing these values varies greatly. We may agree more on values such as truth, justice, and loyalty than on others. To paraphrase Shakespeare, life is but a stage on which there is continuous acting from the subscript of morality. Every time we interact in a society or group, we act the moral subscript that was developed by that society or group for its members over time.

Because morality is territorial and culturally based, so long as we live in a society we are bound to live within that society's guidelines. The actions of individuals in a society only have moral values if taken within the context of this very society and the culture of the individual. A number of factors influence the context of morality, including time and place.

1.2.1   Moral Theories

If morality is a set of shared values among people in a specific society, why do we have to worry about justifying those values to people who are not members of that society? In other words, why do we need moral theories? What do moral theories have to do with the moral subscripts? If you write a script for a play, you want both the audience and the cast to understand the message of the play. If you can find a way to help them get that message and believe it, then you have put credibility in the script. This is where moral theories come in. According to MacDonald, moral theories "seek to introduce a degree of rationality and rigor into our moral deliberations" [1]. They give our deliberations plausibility and help us to better understand those values and the contradictions therein. Because many philosophers and others use the words *moral* and *ethical* synonymously, we delay the discussion of moral theories until we discuss ethics.

1.2.2 Moral Decision Making

Every human action results from a decision process. Because every human action follows a subscript, the decision-making process follows a subscript as well. A decision is morally good if the result from it is good. A good moral decision embodies nearly all moral theories and usually takes into consideration the following points:

1. All the facts surrounding the situation, taking into account the interests of all parties involved, and
2. The moral principles involved and how they will affect all others involved

Combining points 1 and 2 implies there must be reasoning and impartiality in any moral decision. Moral and ethical theorists have outlined four ways of ensuring reason and impartiality in moral decision making, as follows:

1. The use of the rational intuition of moral principles, which helps us perceive moral principles such as the notion of justice and deciding what is good.
2. The use of reason to determine the best way to achieve the highest moral good.
3. The ability to distinguish between primary and secondary moral principles. Primary moral principles are more general; secondary principles are more specific and are generally deduced from the primary ones.
4. The rational calculation of the consequences of our actions. The calculation should tell us whether the action is good or bad depending on the consequences [2].

Nearly all moral theories embody one or more of these themes.

1.2.3 Moral Codes

The *Internet Encyclopedia of Philosophy* defines moral codes as rules or norms within a group for what is proper behavior for the members of that group [2]. The norm itself is a rule, standard, or measure for us to compare something else whose qualities we doubt. Moral codes are often complex definitions of right and wrong that are based upon well-defined group's value systems.

In a way, moral codes are shared behavioral patterns of a group. These patterns have been with us since the beginnings of human civilization and have evolved mainly for the survival of the group or society. Societies and cultures survive and thrive because of the moral code they are observing. History has shown failures of societies and cultures such as the once mighty civilizations and great empires of the Babylonians, the Romans, and the Byzantines, probably because their code failed to cope with the changing times.

Although different cultures have different codes, and we have established that morality is relative to time, there have been some timeless and culture-free (moral) codes that have been nearly universally observed. Such codes include this partial list created by the astronomer Carl Sagan [3]:

1. *The Golden Rule*: "Do unto others as you would have them do unto you."

   Versions of the Golden Rule in Different Religions[1]
   BUDDHIST: Hurt not others in ways that you would find hurtful.
   CHRISTIAN: All things whatsoever ye would that men should do to you, do ye even so to them.
   CONFUCIAN: Do not unto others what you would not have them do unto you.
   HINDU: This is the sum of duty; do naught unto others which if done to thee would cause thee pain.
   ISLAMIC: No one of you is a believer until he desires for his brother that which he desires for himself.
   JAIN: In happiness and suffering, in joy and grief, we should regard all creatures as we regard our own self.
   JEWISH: Whatever thou hatest thyself, that do not to another.
   SIKH: As thou deemest thyself, so deem others.
   TAOIST: Regard your neighbor's gain as your own gain, and your neighbor's loss as your own loss.
   ZOROASTRIAN: That nature alone is good which refrains from doing unto another whatsoever is not good for itself.
2. *The Silver Rule*: "Do not do unto others what you would not have them do unto you." Great men like Mahatma Gandhi followed this rule almost to the letter.
3. *The Bronze Rule*: "Repay kindness with kindness." This rule is widely observed because of its many varying interpretations. Some people call it the "carrot-and-stick" rule. However you interpret it, it seems to support the vendetta syndrome.
4. *The Iron Rule*: "Do unto others as you like, before they do it unto you." This rule, if followed by a leader, can create dictatorships. It seems to say, "He who is on the floor cannot make rules" or "Do it if you can get away with it."
5. *The Tin Rule*: "Pay homage to those above you and intimidate those below you." This is what many call the bully rule.
6. *The Nepotism Rule*: "Give precedence in all things to close relatives, and do as you like to others." This rule legitimizes corruption.

---

[1] http://web.engr.oregonstate.edu/~mjb/cs419h/Handouts/VisEthics/visethics.pdf

Because most of these rules seem vindictive, corruptible, dictatorial, and abusive, Sagan proposes the following as what seems to be a good culture-free and timeless universal set of moral codes:

1. Be friendly at first meeting.
2. Do not envy.
3. Be generous; forgive your enemy if he or she forgives you.
4. Be neither a tyrant nor a patsy.
5. Retaliate proportionately to an intentional injury (within the constraints of the rule of the law).
6. Make your behavior fair (although not perfectly) clear and consistent.

Other timeless, culture-free, but less widely practiced and less universally accepted codes are those observed by small groups of people with similar interests (e.g., religious and professional groups). Examples of such moral codes include the Native American Ten Commandments, the Jewish and Christian Ten Commandments, and the Unix Users Group Ten Commandments, as outlined here:

1.2.3.1 Native American Ten Commandments [4]

1. Treat the Earth and all that dwell thereon with respect.
2. Remain close to the Great Spirit.
3. Show great respect for your fellow beings.
4. Work together for the benefit of all Mankind.
5. Give assistance and kindness wherever needed.
6. Do what you know to be right.
7. Look after the well-being of mind and body.
8. Dedicate a share of your efforts to the greater good.
9. Be truthful and honest at all times.
10. Take full responsibility for your actions.

1.2.3.2 The Christian Ten Commandments [5]

1. I, the Lord, am your God. You shall not have any other gods besides Me.
2. You shall not take the name of the Lord, your God, in vain.
3. Remember to keep holy the Sabbath day.
4. Honor your father and your mother.
5. You shall not kill.
6. You shall not commit adultery.
7. You shall not steal.
8. You shall not bear false witness against your neighbor.
9. You shall not covet your neighbor's wife.
10. You shall not covet anything that belongs to your neighbor.

1.2.3.3 Unix Users Group Ten Commandments (The Manual, Ex. 20, Verses 1–21) [6]

And lo did Unix[2] speak these words upon the reboot:

1. Thou shalt use no other operating system than Unix.
2. Thou shalt not make unto thee a false operating system. Thou shalt not program them for I am the Unix and a jealous O/S.
3. Thou shalt not take the mark of trade of Unix in vain, or thou shalt be sued.
4. Remember thy password, and keep it secret.
5. Honour thy parent shell, for if it should die, thou shalt not live long (unless thou hast dissociated thyself).
6. Thou shalt not kill (l)-9 any process, for surely they shalt becometh zombies or defunct.
7. Thou shalt not commit hacking, else thou shalt eat quiche.
8. Thou shalt not use other users' data, for thou shalt be referred to the Data Protection Act, 1984, and sued (again).
9. Thou shalt not create Trojan horses, worms, viruses, or other foul beasts of false programming.
10. Thou shalt not rm -rf thy neighbor's home, nor covet his disk space allocation, nor his workstation account.

The purpose of moral codes in a society is to exert control over actions of members of the group resulting from emotions. Observance of moral codes in most societies is almost involuntary because members grow up with these codes, so they tend to follow them without questioning. In some societies, observance is enforced through superstition and in others it is enforced through folklore and customs. In Chap. 3, we show that professions need to have codes to which their members adhere for them to be ethical and moral in their day-to-day professional activities.

1.2.4 Moral Standards

A moral standard is a moral norm, a standard to which we compare human actions to determine their goodness or badness. This standard guides and enforces policy. Morality is a system that, in addition to setting standards of virtuous conduct for people, also consists of mechanisms to self-regulate through enforcement of the moral code and self-judge through guilt, which is an internal discomfort resulting from disappointment in self-mediated conscience.

---

[2] Let Unix be a trademark of AT&T.

1.2.5 Guilt and Conscience

Moral guilt is a result of self-judging and punishing oneself for not living up to the moral standards set for oneself or for the group. If individuals judge that they have not done "good" according to moral standards, they can activate the guilt response, which usually makes them feel bad, hide their actions from both self and others, and find a fitting punishment for themselves, sometimes a very severe punishment. This internal judgment system is brought about because human beings have no sure way of telling whether an action is good or bad based independently on their own "standards." Individual standards are usually judged based on group standards. So individuals judge themselves based on group standards, and self-judgment comes into play whenever one's actions fall short of the group's standards.

The problem with guilt is that it can be cumulative. If individuals commit acts repetitively that they judge to be below moral standards, they tend to become more and more withdrawn. This isolation often leads individuals to become more comfortable with the guilt. As they become comfortable living with the guilt, their previous actions, which were previously judged below standards, begin to look not so bad after all. Individuals become more and more complacent about the guilt and begin to look at the whole moral system as amoral.

Guilt can be eased by encouraging people to focus on the intentions behind the actions. Sometimes the intentions may be good but the resulting action is bad. In such a case the individual should not feel so guilty about the action. Besides looking for intentions of actions, one should also have the will and ability to forgive oneself. Self-forgiveness limits the cumulative nature of guilt and hence helps an individual to keep within the group.

Our moral code, and many times the law, lay out the general principles that we *ought* not do this or that because it is wrong to do it. The law also tells us not to do this or that because it is illegal to do so. However, neither system specifically tells us whether a particular human action just committed is an immoral or illegal act. The link must be done by the individual—a self-realization. It is this individual inner judgment to tell us that the act is right or wrong, lawful or unlawful, that we call our *conscience* . Additionally, conscience is the capacity and ability to judge our actions ourselves based on what we set as our moral standards. The word *conscience* comes from the Latin word *conscientia*, which means *knowing with*. It is an "inner voice" telling us what to do or not do. This kind of self-judgment is based on the responsibility and control we have over our actions. Conscience is motivated by good feelings within us such as pride, compassion, empathy, love, and personal identification. Conscience evolves as individuals grow. The childhood conscience is far different from the adult conscience because our perception of evil evolves with age. The benefits of conscience are that the actions done with good conscience, even if they end up being bad, do not make one guilty of the actions.

Fr. Fagothey [11] writes that conscience applies to three things:

1. The intellect as a faculty for forming judgments about right and wrong individual acts
2. The process of reasoning that the intellect goes through to reach such judgment
3. The judgment itself, which is the conclusion of this reasoning process

We have seen in this section that morality does not belong to any individual, nor does it belong to any society or group of people. Thus, it cannot be localized. However, those parts of the moral code that can be localized become law.

1.2.6   Morality and Religion

Religion, in contrast to morality, draws much from the divine. Most religious belief systems include or are built around the idea of divine will and divine judgment. However, many of these systems usually correspond to a moral code of conduct, and because of this, many religions claim that religion and morality are intimately connected.

Issues for Discussion
In Roman Catholicism, morality derives from God because God created man and nature and that the ultimate sanction for immorality is the loss of a relationship with God. How does your religion relate to the morality of your society?
How do both Atheism and Pantheism relate to morality?
What values are essential for a person that would allow him/her to starve rather than to steal?

1.3   Law

According to *Merriam-Webster's Dictionary*, a law is a binding custom or practice of a community; a rule of conduct or action prescribed or formally recognized as binding or enforced by a controlling authority; the whole body of such customs, practices, or rules [7]. Black states that law is an art we can create and model, and contemporary critics define law as an instrument of exercising power [8].

Bryan Bourn combines both these definitions of law and describes it as both an art and an instrument for exercising power [8]. He bases his definition on the fact that law on many occasions strives forcefully to create something desirable without following a precise and exact process or formula that can be reproduced (thus the art component). Fr. Fagothey defines laws as a rule and measure of actions directing them to proper ends. It obliges us to make our conduct conform to the norm of morality. He goes on to divide law into two types:

1. Physical law, which directs non-free irrational beings to uniform action toward their ends by inner necessity of their nature, that is, imposing physical necessity
2. Moral law or natural law, which directs free rational beings toward their ends by imposing obligations on the free will—thus imposing moral necessity

However one defines law, whether as a rule, an injunction, an art, or an exercise of power, there is always a component of force that must be obeyed with the purpose of creating something desirable for the community that the law is intended to serve. This goal is achieved through the reign of equal justice for all in the community. We tend to obey two types of laws: the natural and the conventional.

1.3.1   The Natural Law

Natural law is an unwritten but universal law. It is a theory that an eternal, absolute moral law can be discovered by reason and is derivable from reason. It is distinct from the law of nature, applies to all rational creatures, exists independently of human preferences and inclinations, and is applied cross-culturally. According to James Donald [9], natural law "follows from the nature of man and the world, and consists of rights like the right to self-defense and the right to individual property. So naturally it is 'higher' than any other conventional law enacted by a human authority like a government because no conventional law has jurisdiction over natural law." Natural law has been known since the time of Plato and Aristotle (ca. 500 BC) but has its clear formulation and definition in the writings of Thomas Aquinas, a thirteenth-century philosopher and theologian [1].

Natural law is the anchor of our rights of self-preservation, liberty, and property. Before organized human societies, humans existed because of natural law. It secured the environment in those human settlements for those activities that sustain life, beginning with hunting and progressing through business and commerce. Even today, there are human societies that exist without conventional law. Present-day examples include those states with collapsed governments because of political strife. People in these states, even in the absence of a central governing authority and a functioning legal system, are still living their lives, many of them happily. Although they may not enjoy all the pleasures of life, they have a way of protecting life, liberty, and personal property. Ironically, there are even states that supposedly live with organized authorities resembling government yet have no rule of conventional law; they are surviving on natural law.

The existence of natural law has been debated for centuries. In fact, there are many who do not believe in natural law and are always advocating the supremacy of conventional law. Thomas Hobbes, the famous English philosopher, argued that the nature of man is not such that one could deduce natural law from it, that the natural law so deduced does not place any significant limits on the powers of civil law, and that social order is a creation of state power [1].

1.3.2 Conventional Law

Conventional law is a system created by and for human beings, usually in public deliberations such as a council of elders or representatives in national legislatures. It derives from that part of the moral code that is enforceable and varies from society to society and from culture to culture. Although history and experience have shown that natural law has been used as the basis for some conventional laws, and there are examples such as the English Magna Carta and the U.S. Constitution and Bill of Rights; judgment is not based on natural law [9, 10]. In day-to-day judgment, decisions are based on facts and the matching of facts to words, not on natural law.

Conventional law takes two forms: (1) declarative, which simply restates what the natural law declares, such as forbidding murder, theft, etc., and (2) determinative, which fixes ways of acting in accordance with natural law, such as in contracts, taxes, traffic, and other types of laws. Conventional law has a long history of evolution from natural law. Some of the outstanding examples follow [11]:

1. *Law of nature.* Originating from the Roman *jus gentium.* The Romans developed *jus gentium* from a mosaic of nations that formed the Roman Empire. *Jus gentium* was a common factor of all laws of all nations in the empire. When the empire collapsed, the resulting states developed this *law of nations* into the modern European legal system.
2. *English common law.* A result of centuries of unwritten precedents and decisions of common courts, statutes, and acts of the English Parliament.

The English common law gave birth to the modern English and American law.

1.3.3 The Purpose of Law

Both conventional and natural laws exist to protect the life, liberty, and property of the group covered by these laws. According to Fr. Fagothey [11], laws are needed for the following reasons:

1. The ignorant need instruction and control by the wise
2. Earthly penalties are required for the safety of society
3. Concerted action demands teamwork and leadership
4. Society must meet changed conditions harmoniously

1.3.4   The Penal Code

Laws are always useless unless there is a right to punish and an enforcement mechanism is in place. The penal code is a system of set rules prescribing punishment for unlawful acts. In a way, the penal code is that enforcement mechanism. The punishment system consists of three functions [11]:

1. *Retributive*—by paying back the victim for the crime committed, reestablishing the equal balance of justice, and reasserting the authority.
2. *Corrective*—by trying to improve the offender; in other words, rehabilitating the offender back into society.
3. *Deterrent*—by trying to prevent similar actions in the future by the offender, and indeed the offender community, that is, forewarning the offender community by the state, which is the law maker.

The enforcement is different in criminal and civil cases. In criminal cases, the punishment may lead to denial of certain individual rights for a period of time. The period of incarceration depends on the nature and types of violations. In civil cases, punishments are usually damage awards to those whose rights were infringed upon.

1.4   Morality and the Law

Conventional laws of a society are determined by the moral beliefs of that society. Many people disagree with this statement. In fact, there are two views. The proponents of natural law believe that conventional laws are valid if they meet certain standards of morality, whereas opponents of natural law, usually referred to as legal positivists, do not believe in the validity of conventional laws based on morality [11]. Whatever your camp, both morality and the legal system serve the purpose of keeping society stable and secure. They are both used in making judgments about people's actions, and such judgments are justifiable by reason. Although morality and the law seem to have a common purpose and the means to achieve the stated purpose, the implementation of these means to achieve the purpose is different. The following are some of the major differences:

1. *The process of making codes and laws*: Laws are enacted by authorities such as councils of elders and assemblies of the people's representatives. Moral codes, however, are developed not by one central authority but by all members of a society, over a period of time, from experiences and reason.
2. *Enforcement*: Laws are enforced by the authority that enacted them or representatives of that authority, such as judges and courts, and security forces such as the police. However, morality is self-enforced, not enforceable by courts, nor is it enforceable by any authorized security force. There is no moral or ethical court to judge moral wrongdoers. For example, no one can impose penalties for not obeying the Ten Commandments.

3. *Nature of punishments*: Unlawful acts are punishable by penalties that depend on the type, nature, and civility of the action. If it is criminal, it may result in incarceration, and if it is civil, it may result in payment of damages. However, if the act is judged to be immoral, the judgment is usually based on the individual's perception of that society's morality, and the penalties imposed are also individually based.
4. *Conflict resolution*: Laws are used to resolve interpersonal conflicts in a society. However, morality is mostly used to harmonize intrapersonal conflicts.
5. *Types of judgment*: Morality passes judgment on a person's intentions and character based on what is in your heart. Although courts do not always ignore a person's intention or state of mind, the law cannot normally govern what is in the person's heart.

Because of these differences, it is correct to say that in any society not all laws are based on the morality of that society. Because morality is a higher and superior system, there is only a small area where the two overlap, and there are many times when the two conflict. Let us look at examples. In February 1997 came the startling news of the results of a bold genetic engineering experiment. The Roslin Institute in Edinburgh, Scotland, reported that a team of researchers led by embryologist Dr. Ian Wilmut had successfully cloned two identical sheep. Wilmut's team beat the odds predicted by researchers around the world by taking a mammary cell from an adult sheep, preparing its DNA to be accepted by the egg from another sheep, moving the egg's own DNA, and replacing it with the DNA from the adult sheep by fusing the egg with the adult cell. The fused egg began to grow normally to form an embryo, which scientists then implanted into another sheep, and that sheep later gave birth to a cloned lamb they named Dolly.

Although the experiment was done purely for animal reproduction, many scientists saw the potential for drug manufacturing and replacing human parts. Animals could be used to produce pharmacologically useful proteins for manufacturing drugs, literally making animals serve as drug factories. Animal clones could also be used to "manufacture" animal parts with human characteristics that could later be used in human transplants.

The cloning experiment created substantial legal, ethical, and moral problems. In many countries, it is not illegal to clone human beings, but because of the potential for abuse, such countries are already scrambling to enact laws that will make such an act illegal. Moral and ethical issues also need to be addressed. For example, what will prevent an unethical scientist from cloning a person he or she loves, or a person on whom to experiment, and what will stop governments strapped by lack of labor from cloning thousands of their best living human beings who have exhibited extraordinary intelligence or skills?

In the rush to create ourselves, we may end up creating monsters that could destroy us, because although the physical characteristics of clones will be similar, behavior characteristics will be as unpredictable as ours! Wilmut acknowledges the potential for misuse of this scientific breakthrough [10]. It is a daunting moral dilemma for which the society must find solutions.

Imagine seeing someone drowning and calling desperately for help while you simply look on and enjoy the show. Your action is not only repugnant, but immoral, and depending on whether the laws of deliberate indifference apply to you, your action may even be illegal. In another example, authorities in some societies fight teen violence by imposing a night curfew on the teens. In such societies, it is illegal for teens to venture out after curfew hours, although it is not immoral. Another good illustrative example is free speech. Consider a situation that occurred on a college campus in which a list of male students, posted by a group of female students led by a faculty member, warned that those male students were potential rapists. Such an act is repugnant, yet it is legal to post such a list. Consider also the trade in pornographic images both in print and on the Internet. These images not only degrade the men, women, and children depicted, they also contribute to other related crimes such as rape. In most cases, however, trading in such images is legal.

These examples illustrate that even though both morality and conventional law are integral parts of human life, they do not cover the same domains. There are hundreds of similar cases where the legal system, although protecting civil liberties, unintentionally obscures morality.

Issues for Discussion
Name a few of what you consider to be unjust laws and sometimes unjust legal systems that imprison innocent people.

1.5   Morality, Etiquettes, and Manners

Etiquette refers to a code of behavior, a set of norms of correct conduct expected by a society, group, or social class. It is a generally expected social behavior. These rules of the code or the set of norms are usually unwritten, but aspects of these may reflect an underlying moral code.

Manners are unenforced standards of conduct or cultural norms that show that an individual is "refined" and "cultured" with a society or group. These norms codify or set a standard for human behavior. However, in contrast to laws that also codify human behavior, manners, just like morality, have no formal system for punishing transgressions other than social disapproval.

Issues for Discussion
Lapses in etiquettes, the consequences of which may vary depending on the audience, occur when least expected. Discuss these consequences and how etiquettes are related to the moral code of the group.

Discuss your own situations that involved such lapses. What does society expect from the offending individual?

Exercises

1. How do morality and law relate to each other?
2. What is moral relativism?
3. What is the connection between law and art?
4. Why is reasoning so important in morality?
5. Is morality evolutionary or revolutionary? Discuss.
6. Happiness is human. Discuss.
7. What is the role of education in moral behavior?
8. Show how and why the following rules are culture free:
    (i)   The Golden Rule
    (ii) The Bronze Rule
    (iii) The Iron Rule
9. If you were charged with creating a "new" human society, what moral code would you design and why?
10. We tend to live a moral script every day. Reflect on what is in your script.
11. Morality is time sensitive. Discuss.
12. Study the Native American Ten Commandments and the Christian Ten Commandments. Without comparing them, discuss the common thread between them.
13. How does guilt help to shape our moral journey?
14. Discuss the interplay between guilt and conscience.
15. What roles does the conscience fill in decision making?
16. Natural law is universal. Discuss.
17. What is the law of nature? Discuss why it is different from natural law.
18. What role does each one of the following have in our lives?
    (i)   Conventional law
    (ii) Natural law
    (iii) Law of nature
19. Can there be a common morality? Why or why not?
20. Is common morality possible in cyberspace?
21. Discuss the possibility of common morality in the age of globalization.
22. What is the effect of globalization on morality?

References

1. MacDonald C. Moral decision making: an analysis. http://www.ethics.ubc.ca/-chrismac/moral.decision.html
2. Moral relativism. Internet Encyclopedia of Philosophy. http://www.utm.edu/research/iep/ni/m-ration.html
3. Sagan C (1993) A new way to think about rules to live by. Parade, November 28, p 12
4. The Native American ten commandments. http://www.indians.org/prayer/ten.html
5. The Christian ten commandments. http://www.avenue.com/v/ktheten.html
6. The Unix ten commandments. http://www.pipex.net/people/jasonh/command.html

7. Merriam-Webster's Dictionary. http://www.merriam-webster.com/dictionary/law
8. Bourn B. Law as art (with apologies to Charles Black). http://www.usinternet.com/bdbourn/black.html
9. Donald J. Natural law and natural rights. http://catalog.com/jamesd/rights.html
10. Kalota G (1997) Scientists report first cloning ever for adult mammal. New York Times, February 23, sec. 1, p. 1. http://search.nytimes.com/search/daily/bin/fastweb?search/
11. Fagothey Fr. A (1959) Right and reason, 2nd edn. Tan Books, Rockford

Further Reading

Conclusion: words, not laws, should be the weapons. The Ethical Spectacle, November 1995. http://www.spectacle.org/1995/concl.html
Edel A, Flower E, O'Connor F (1989) Morality, philosophy, and practice: historical and contemporary readings and studies, 3rd edition. Random House, New York
Johnson DG (1994) Computer ethics, 2nd edn. Prentice Hall, Englewood Cliffs
Kizza JM (ed) (1996) Social and ethical effects of the computer revolution. McFarland, Jefferson
Macer DRJ (1994) Bioethics for the people by the people. Eubios Ethics Institute, Christchurch, pp 74–91. http://bio.tsukuba.ac.jp/-macer/BFPSE.html
Objective morality. http://www.percep.demon.co.uk/morality.html18
Shepard J, Micheal GG, Virginia WG. Teaching business ethics through literature. Online J Ethics. http://condor.depaul.edu/ethics/gerde.html

Learning Objectives

After reading this chapter, the reader should be able to

1. Analyze an argument to identify premises and draw conclusions.
2. Illustrate the use of ethical argument.
3. Detect basic logical fallacies in an argument.
4. Identify stakeholders in an issue and our obligations to them.
5. Articulate the ethical trade-offs in a technical decision.
6. Evaluate professional codes of ethics for the ACM (Association for Computing Machinery) and other organizations.

Scenario 2: Should We Clone Humans?
Professor John Wesley is a brilliant scientist with an enviable track record of medical successes. In the last 5 years, he has carried out a dozen high-risk medical operations successfully and has become a must-have on talk shows. He is a sought-after speaker on medical matters, and he is gifted on all reasonable subjects. He has led pioneering research in cloning and has been contemplating cloning some human replacement parts, if he can only get a human body to give him a convincing push.

Mrs. Joan Kaggwa is a well-known and successful entrepreneur, a wonderful wife, and a philanthropist. She is a president of several local and national charity organizations. She sits on the boards of several national and international corporations. For the last 21 years of her marriage, she has worked hard for her family and community. Two years ago, however, her only son, a young man nearing his 18th birthday, was killed in an automobile accident. He was the apple of his parents' eyes. The family was devastated by the death.

(continued)

© Springer International Publishing Switzerland 2016   17
J.M. Kizza, *Ethics in Computing*, Undergraduate Topics in Computer Science,
DOI 10.1007/978-3-319-29106-2_2

Scenario 2: (continued)

For a while now, Mrs. Kaggwa has been following the cloning stories that have appeared on television and in the newspapers, but without seriously giving them much thought until the day of her son's death. Then, with her instance, and to the annoyance of her husband, the family agreed to keep their son's body with Infinite Life Corporation, a company that keeps human frozen bodies in liquid nitrogen for years. Mrs. Kaggwa hoped that someday science would bring her son back. Her prayers were answered, at least according to her, one Sunday morning when she was going through the Sunday paper just before church. A small article caught her eye. The article was about a planned cloning experiment by a young scientist. During the following 2 weeks, Joan made calls that led her and her husband to the waiting room of Professor Wesley to discuss the cloning of their beloved, but dead, son.

Discussion Questions

1. *Are there justifiable reasons that lead people to clone their loved ones?*
2. *Is Mrs. Kaggwa justified in wanting to clone her son?*
3. *Do you think the Kaggwas' son, if successfully cloned, will be the same as the dead son? Why or why not?*
4. *What compelling reasons can Professor Wesley give to justify cloning the Kaggwas' son?*
5. *Do you subscribe to such reasoning?*
6. *What are the pros and cons of human cloning?*
7. *Animal cloning is now routine. Why has there been no organized opposition to it?*

2.1   Traditional Definition

Fr. Austin Fagothey, in *Right and Reason* [1], traces the origins of ethics from the Greeks. He observes that the Greeks' desire and curiosity to learn about themselves, the human life, and society led to the examination of all human conducts, a part of philosophy called ethics. Ethics is, therefore, a study of right and wrong in human conduct. Ethics can also be defined as a theoretical examination of morality and as an equivalent of the "theory of morals." Other philosophers have defined ethics in a variety of ways.

Robert C. Solomon, in *Morality and the Good Life* [2], gives a traditional philosophical definition of ethics as a set of "theories of value, virtue, or of right (valuable) action." Johnson elaborates on Solomon's definition by defining ethics as a set of theories "that provide general rules or principles to be used in making moral decisions and, unlike ordinary intuitions, provides a justification for those rules" [3].

The word "ethics" comes from an ancient Greek word *eché* [2], which means character. Every human society, whether civilized or primitive, practices ethics because every society attaches a value on an individual's actions, on a continuum of good to bad, right to wrong, according to where that individual's actions fall within the domain of that society's rules and canons.

Ethics helps us not only in distinguishing between right and wrong but also in knowing why and on what grounds our judgment of human actions is justified. Ethics, therefore, is a field of inquiry whose subject is human actions, collectively called human conduct, which are performed consciously, willfully, and for which one can be held responsible. According to Fr. Fagothey [1], such acts must have knowledge that signifies the presence of a motive, voluntariness to signify that it is willed, and freedom to signify the presence of free choice to act or not to act.

The purpose of ethics is to interpret human conduct, acknowledging and distinguishing between right and wrong. The interpretation is based on a system. This system, according to Fr. Fagothey, uses a process of argumentation consisting of a mixture of inductions and deductions. In most cases, these arguments are based on historical schools of thought called ethical theories. There are different kinds of ethical theories, and within each theory there may be different versions of that theory.

2.2 Ethical Theories

For centuries, in different societies, human actions have been judged good or bad, right or wrong, based on theories or systems of justice developed, tested, revised, and debated by philosophers and/or elders in that society. Such theories are commonly known as ethical theories. Codes of ethics have then been drawn up based on these ethical theories. The processes of reasoning, explanation, and justification used in ethics are based on these theories. There are many ethical theories, but we consider only a few that are most widely discussed and used, namely, consequentialism, deontology, human nature, relativism, hedonism, and emotivism.

2.2.1 Consequentialism

In consequentialism ethical theory, human actions are judged good or bad, right or wrong, depending on the results of such actions—a desirable result denotes a good action and vice versa. There are three commonly discussed types of consequentialism theory:

1. *Egoism*: This theory puts an individual's interests and happiness above everything else. With egoism, any action is good so long as it maximizes an individual's overall happiness. There are two kinds of egoism: ethical egoism, which states how people ought to behave as they pursue their own interests, and psychological egoism, which describes how people actually behave. For example, if

a family wanted to be happier, an ethical egoism theorist would prescribe to each family member how he or she ought to behave to achieve individual happiness first before considering the happiness of the family. A psychological egoism theorist, however, would describe how each individual family member should actually behave to achieve his or her happiness and hence the happiness of the family as a whole.

2. *Utilitarianism*: In contrast to egoism, this theory puts a group's interest and happiness above those of an individual, for the good of many. Thus, an action is good if it benefits the maximum number of people. Among the forms of utilitarianism are the following:
   - Act Utilitarianism: Tells one to consider seriously the consequences of all actions before choosing the one with the best overall advantage, happiness in this case, for the maximum number of people [4].
   - Rule Utilitarianism: Tells one to obey those rules that bring the maximum happiness to the greatest number of people. Rule utilitarianism maintains that a behavioral code or rule is good if the consequences of adopting that rule are favorable to the greatest number of people [4]

3. *Altruism*: In altruism, an action is right if the consequences of that action are favorable to all except the actor.

2.2.2 Deontology

The theory of deontological reasoning does not concern itself with the consequences of the action but rather with the will of the action. An action is good or bad depending on the will inherent in it. According to deontological theory, an act is considered good if the individual committing it had a good reason to do so. This theory has a duty attached to it. In fact, the word "deontology" comes from two Greek words, *deon*, meaning duty, and *logos*, meaning science [3]. For example, we know that killing is bad, but if an armed intruder enters your house and you kill him or her, your action is good, according to deontologists. You did it because you had a duty to protect your family and property.

2.2.3 Human Nature

This theory considers human beings as endowed with all faculties and capabilities to live in happiness. We are supposed to discover and then develop those capabilities. In turn, those capabilities become a benchmark for our actions, and our actions are then gauged and judged on how much they measure up to those capabilities. According to the famous Greek philosopher Aristotle, an individual committing an evil action is lacking in some capabilities.

2.2.4 Relativism

This theory is negatively formulated, denying the existence of universal moral norms. It takes right and wrong to be relative to society, culture, or the individual. Relativism also states that moral norms are not fixed in time.

2.2.5 Hedonism

Hedonism is one of the oldest ethical theories. It claims that pleasure is the only good thing in human life, the end of life as the highest good. A hedonist acts only for maximum pleasure, and whatever he or she does, it is done to maximize pleasure or minimize pain. There are two types of hedonism: psychological hedonism, which claims that in fact what people seek in their everyday actions is pleasure, and ethical hedonism, which claims that people ought to seek pleasure, and that pleasure is the moral good. Modern hedonists use the word pleasure to mean happiness.

2.2.6 Emotivism

This theory maintains that ethical statements are neither true nor false and cannot be proven; they are really only statements about how someone feels [4]. Philosophers use these theories as engines to help them to understand and justify human actions. Although over the years and in different places changing values have been attached to human actions, these ethical theories have remained relatively unchanged; this means that although ethics as a discipline is evolving, ethical reasoning has relatively remained the same. In other words, Aristotle and Plato's reasoning to explain and justify human actions is still valid, although the premises surrounding human actions are changing with time and with every new technology.

The process of ethical reasoning takes several steps, which we refer to as layers of reasoning, before one can justify to someone else the goodness or badness, rightness or wrongness, of one's action. For example, if someone wants to convince you to own a concealed gun, he or she needs to explain to you and justify why it is good to have a concealed gun. In such an exercise, the person may start by explaining to you that we are living in difficult times and that no one is safe. You may then ask why no one is safe, to which the person might reply that there are many bad people out there in possession of high-powered guns waiting to fire them for various and very often unbelievable reasons. So owning a gun will level the playing field. Then you may ask why owning a gun levels the playing field, to which the answer would be that because if the bad guys suspect that you own one just like theirs, they will think twice before they attack you. You may further ask why this is so; the answer may be that if they attack you, they themselves can get killed in the action. Therefore, because of this fear you are not likely to be attacked. Hence, owning a gun may save your life and enable you to continue pursuing the ultimate concept of the good life: happiness.

On the other hand, to convince somebody not to own a concealed gun again needs a plausible explanation and several layers of reasoning to demonstrate why owning a gun is bad. Why is it a bad thing, you would ask, and the answer would be because bad guys will always get guns. And if they do, the possibility of everyone having a concealed gun may make those bad guys trigger-happy to get you before you get them. It also evokes the image of the Wild West filled with gun-toting people daring everyone to get a kick out of what may be a boring life. You would then ask why is this situation dangerous if no one fires? The reply might be because it creates a potential situation in which innocent people may get hurt and therefore an unhappy situation is created, denying people happiness and the good life. The explanation and reasoning process can go on and on for several more layers before one is convinced that owning a gun is good or bad. The act of owning a gun is a human act that can be judged as either good or bad, right or wrong, depending on the moral and ethical principles used.

The spectrum of human actions on which ethical judgments can be based is wide ranging, from simple traditional and easy-to-understand actions, such as killing and stealing, to complex and abstract ones, such as hacking, cellular telephone scanning, and subliminal human brain alterations. On one side of this spectrum, the inputs have straight output value judgments of right and wrong or good and evil. The other end of the spectrum, however, has inputs that cannot be easily mapped into the same output value judgments of good and bad or right and evil. It is at this side of the input spectrum that most new human actions created as a result of computer technology are found. It is at this end, therefore, that we need an updated definition of ethics—a functional definition.

2.3 Functional Definition of Ethics

Let $A = \{a_1, a_2, a_3, \ldots, a_n\}$ be a collection of identifiable objects, ai, $i = 1, 2, \ldots, n$. We call this collection a set. A function f defined on set A is a rule that takes elements of A and assigns them values into another set R, called the range of the function. The set A is the domain of f. We represent the function f as $f{:}A \rightarrow R$. A function defined on two sets A and B takes pairs (a, b) of elements $a \in A$ and $b \in B$ and assigns to each pair a value r in the range set R. For example, let $A = \{a1, a2, a3\}$ and $B = \{b1, b2\}$. Then $f(A, B) \rightarrow C$ is a mapping $f(ai,bj) = rk$ for all $ai \in A$, $bj \in B$, and $rk \in C$ where $rk = aj*bj$ for some operation * defined on elements of A and B.

An example of a function such as f would be the mixing of two colors. Suppose A is a can of blue paint and B is a can of yellow paint. Let f be the process of mixing these two colors from both cans. After mixing the contents or some of the contents of can A with those of can B, the resulting mixture is the green color put in can C.

Let us use this model to construct a functional definition of ethics. Let the set A be the set of all possible human actions on which it is possible to pass a value judgment. For example, if you think of an artwork, the human actions on it could be an array of things such as lifting it, hiding it, and stealing it. So define $A = \{a_1, a_2, a_3, \ldots\}$.

Let the second set B consist of many ethical or moral theories such as the ones we have discussed in the previous sections. So B could contain theories like egoism, act utilitarianism, and others. Define $B = \{b_1, b_2, b_3, \ldots\}$. Finally, let R, the third set, be the set of all possible value judgments on the human actions in A based on the ethical theories in B. The function f maps each pair (a, b) of elements, with $a \in A$ and $b \in B$ to a binary value in R. The first set is the set of input parameters. The inputs are human actions on which it is possible to pass a judgment. The second set consists of the ethical theories discussed earlier, like consequentialism, deontology, and human nature. The third set $R = \{RIGHT$ or $WRONG, GOOD$ or $BAD\}$, the range of the function f on the two sets A and B, is the value set. Now define a function f on a pair of elements (a, b) with $a \in A$ and $b \in B$ to produce an element $r \in R$ as $f: (a, b) \to r$. We call this function the ethics decision function. Recalling our earlier discussion of ethics, function f represents a sequence of explanations and reasoning on the elements of sets A and B. The elements of R have two values: 1 for GOOD or RIGHT and 0 for WRONG or BAD.

Because the power of reasoning associates to each pair of elements (a, b), with a in A and b in B, a binary value equivalent to good, bad, right, or wrong using the set B of ethical theories, we represent this function as follows:

$$f(a,b) \to \left\{ \frac{1\{"right," "or" "good"\}}{0\{"bad," "or" "wrong"\}} \right.$$

for all $a \in A$ and $b \in B$

What is the relationship between this function, f, and the human mind? If you reflect on it you will see that the human mind seems to employ a similar function in making ethical and moral judgments. Notice that the human mind associates an integer value 0 or 1 to all human actions it perceives through sight, smell, touch, and hearing. Let us use an example to explain this. Suppose you see somebody breaking into a church. Chances are you are going to like or dislike that action. If you like it, you associate the "like" value to an integer 1 and if you dislike it, you again associate this "dislike" value to an integer value 0. We tend to associate these two integer values to everything our mind perceives.

In making your decision whether you liked the action of the person who broke into the church, you probably based your "judgment" of this action on how that action registers in one of the moral and ethical theories. If it does, and it will always fall in at least one of the theories, then you will associate a weight depending on the hierarchy of reasoning you go through to justify right or wrong. Let us use this new functional model of ethics to get a glimpse into the prospects of ethics in the future. Advances in computer technology can greatly influence this model. An explanation is in order. The presence of computer technology creates multitudes of possibilities for every human action and greatly enhances and expands the input set A. The expansion of set A is likely to bring fuzziness to our traditional definition of ethics. Thus, there is a need to expand our definitions of ethics to meet the constantly changing technology-driven landscape of human actions.

2.4   Ethical Reasoning and Decision Making

Both reasoning and logic are important elements in daily human interactions. Reasoning is a human cognitive process of looking for ways to generate or affirm a proposition. Cognitive processes are mental functions or activities that are grouped based on *experience, interpretation, foreseeing, ordering, analyzing, valuing, and making connections.* Logic on the other hand, based on the Greek meaning, is the tool for distinguishing between truth and falseness. Human beings, on a daily basis, engage in reasoning and logic to achieve the desire results from a problem or an issue. Both reasoning and logic are important in decision making.

Each day we make hundreds of decisions, from what we will wear to what side of the bed to sleep on. When making these everyday decisions, many people tend to rely on a variety of biases and heuristics as they do their reasoning. This kind of reasoning based on intuition unfortunately leads to wrong and ethical decisions. Ethical reasoning is integrating ethical principles in the reasoning process. Each day we are faced with a variety of ethical or moral decisions, ranging from simple ones such as lying about a spouse's choice of clothing to hard ones such as contributing to an abortion campaign.

Ethical decision making is the process of making a decision that results in a least number of conflicts. Such a process requires the decision maker to do the following [5]:

- Recognize the inherent ethical conflicts through comprehension, appreciation, and evaluation of all ethical dimensions of the problem
- Know the parties involved
- Be aware of alternatives
- Demonstrate knowledge of ethical practices
- Understand how the decision will be implemented and who will be affected
- Understand and comprehend the impact of the decision of the parties involved

2.4.1   A Framework for Ethical Decision Making

Different elements make a good framework for an ethical decision.
    The most common elements that must be in a good framework are these:

- Recognizing inherent ethical conflicts through comprehension, appreciation, and evaluation of all ethical dimensions of problem
- Understanding the problem and the facts of the problem
- Knowing the parties involved
- Being aware of alternatives
- Demonstrating knowledge of ethical practices

- Understanding how the decision will be implemented and who will be affected
- Understanding the impact the decision will have on the parties affected
- Understanding and comprehending the impact of the decision of the parties involved

Taking these elements of the framework into consideration when making a decision lessens the number of conflicts and the severity of the impact resulting from the decision.

2.4.2   Making and Evaluating Ethical Arguments

In real life, especially in professional life, or in whatever we do, we are going to be faced with an ethical problem for which we need to seek solutions. Many real-life problems have systematic structures on which the search for a solution is based. For example, mathematical problems have rules called algorithms to follow. Many other real-life problems can be modeled in such a way that an algorithm can always be found, or in such cases where no mathematical formula can be used, empirical models can be used. Ethical problems are not like problems in a structured environment, where there are rules to follow. The main question is how to find solutions to ethical problems. We find solutions to ethical problems through a process, or series of steps, which often leads to an ethically justified resolution of the problem. Ethical reasoning either brings a resolution to an ethical problem or, at worst, helps to deepen our understanding of the ethical problem, which may eventually lead to the resolution of the problem at a future date. As we pointed out earlier, the process of ethical reasoning involves a set of layers of reasoning.

The process of ethical reasoning and ethical problem resolution can be likened to the process of software engineering. As in software engineering, the process goes through a number of stages with specific facts and responsibilities before a genuine solution to the problem is found. Before a resolution is embarked on, there must be a clear understanding of the problem. A clear picture of the relevant facts or specifications must be developed. A good description of these facts is then written down and guided by these facts; a set of layers of reasoning is entered into. Although the initial description of the problem is crucial, it should not be the last. As the reasoning process develops, the initial description could be revised and expanded, which may bring more understanding of the problem and may lead to the revision of our reasoning layers as further steps in the reasoning process are added or removed as additional information appears.

The process of ethical reasoning must avail the decision maker with a safe or valid alternative from a multitude of alternatives presented by the ethical problems. This safe alternative is the way out of the ethical muddles presented by the ethical problem. As the process of reasoning progresses, the following information will start to emerge [7]:

(i) Information to confirm whether the problem is really an ethical problem
(ii) Information on whether further description of the facts can add anything to the resolution process of the problem
(iii) Information to identify the key ethical theories, principles, and values that fit the safe alternatives being pursued
(iv) Information on the strength and validity of the ethical theory chosen and whether there are possible conflicts in the ethical theories, principles, and values with the reasoning processes and facts

When a final decision has been made, an evaluation of that decision is needed.

The goal of evaluating an ethical argument is to make sure that each of the alternatives being considered is "weighted" against all others using the facts at hand developed earlier, and, in some cases, based on anticipated outcomes to our decisions. In so doing, we determine which alternative is best based on sound reasoning. Two outcomes are possible: one, we pick the best alternative, in which case our reasoning showed more validity of the facts of the problem than all other alternatives, or two, we may find that we are unable to determine a winning alternative. In this case, it means that there is no convincing reasoning in any one of the two or more deadlocking alternatives. This quandary may require any one of the following: the addition of more layers of reasoning, addition of new facts, or replacement of ethical theories and principles in the argument. In either of the two cases, however, justification of the choice of alternatives is based on examining all the reasons given for all the alternatives. A thorough examination of our reasoning is based on the criticism of the ethical reasoning used for each alternative. There are several critical strategies used to achieve a good examination of the reasoning process, including whether the reasoning used was [7]:

(i) Based on factual assumptions that are actually false or unsupported by good evidence. If assumptions are false or unsupported by any evidence, the reasons that make use of them are suspect and carry little weight, if any, or
(ii) Valid. A reasoning is valid if its premises are true. Then the conclusion is also very probably true.

2.5 Codes of Ethics

The main domains in which ethics is defined are governed by a particular and definitive regiment of rules called "codes of ethics." These rules, guidelines, canons, advisories, or whatever you want to call them, are usually followed by members of the respective domains. Depending on the domain, ethical codes can take any of the following forms:

(i) Principles, which may act as guidelines, references, or bases for some document
(ii) Public policies, which may include aspects of acceptable behavior, norms, and practices of a society or group
(iii) Codes of conduct, which may include ethical principles
(iv) Legal instruments, which enforce good conduct through courts

Although the use of codes of ethics is still limited to professions and high-visibility institutions and businesses, there is a growing movement toward widespread use. The wording, content, and target of many codes differ greatly. Some codes are written purposely for the public; others are targeting employees, and yet others are for professionals only. Reproduced here is the ACM Code of Professional Conduct.[1]

Association of Computing Machinery (ACM) Code of Ethics and Professional Conduct

On October 16, 1992, ACM's Executive Council voted to adopt a revised Code of Ethics. The following imperatives and explanatory guidelines were proposed to supplement the Code as contained in the new ACM Bylaw 17.

Preamble

Commitment to ethical professional conduct is expected of every member (voting members, associate members, and student members) of the Association for Computing Machinery (ACM). This code, consisting of 24 imperatives formulated as statements of personal responsibility, identifies the elements of such a commitment. It contains many, but not all, issues that professionals are likely to face. Section 2.1 outlines fundamental ethical considerations; Sect. 2.2 addresses additional, more specific considerations of professional conduct. Statements in Sect. 2.2 pertain more specifically to individuals who have a leadership role, whether in the workplace or in a volunteer capacity, for example, with organizations such as ACM. Principles involving compliance with this Code are given in Sect. 2.4.

The Code is supplemented by a set of Guidelines, which provide explanation to assist members in handling the various issues contained in the Code. It is expected that the guidelines will be changed more frequently than the Code. The Code and its supplemented Guidelines are intended to serve as a basis for ethical decision making in the conduct of professional work. Second, they may serve as a basis for judging the merit of a formal complaint pertaining to violation of professional ethical standards.

It should be noted that although computing is not mentioned in the moral imperatives section, the Code is connected with how these fundamental imperatives apply to one's conduct as a computing professional. These imperatives are expressed in a general form to emphasize that ethical principles that apply to computer ethics are derived from more general ethical principles. It is understood that some words and phrases in a code of ethics are subject to varying interpretations, and that any ethical principle may conflict with other ethical principles in specific situations. Questions related to ethical conflicts can best be answered by thoughtful consideration of fundamental principles, rather than reliance on detailed regulations.

1. GENERAL MORAL IMPERATIVES
   As an ACM member I will...
   1.1 Contribute to society and human well-being.
   1.2 Avoid harm to others.

---

[1] © 1993 Association of Computing Machinery, Inc.

1.3   Be honest and trustworthy.
1.4   Be fair and take action not to discriminate.
1.5   Honor property rights including copyrights and patents.
1.6   Give proper credit for intellectual property.
1.7   Respect the privacy of others.
1.8   Honor confidentiality.

2. MORE SPECIFIC PROFESSIONAL RESPONSIBILITIES
    As an ACM computing professional I will…
    2.1   *Strive to achieve the highest quality, effectiveness, and dignity in both the process and products of professional work.*
    2.2   *Acquire and maintain professional competence.*
    2.3   *Know and respect existing laws pertaining to professional work.*
    2.4   *Accept and provide appropriate professional review.*
    2.5   *Give comprehensive and thorough evaluations of computer systems and their impacts including analysis of possible risks.*
    2.6   Honor contracts, agreements, and assigned responsibilities.
    2.7   Improve public understanding of computing and its consequences.
    2.8   Access computing and communication resources only when authorized to do so.

3. ORGANIZATIONAL LEADERSHIP IMPERATIVES
    As an ACM member and an organizational leader, I will…
    3.1   Articulate social responsibilities of members of an organizational unit and encourage full acceptance of those responsibilities.
    3.2   Manage personnel and resources to design and build information systems that enhance the quality of working life.
    3.3   Acknowledge and support proper and authorized uses of an organization's computing and communications resources.
    3.4   *Ensure that users and those who will be affected by a system have their needs clearly articulated during the assessment and design of requirements; later the system must be validated to meet requirements.*
    3.5   Articulate and support policies that protect the dignity of users and others affected by a computing system.
    3.6   Create opportunities for members of the organization to learn the principles and limitations of computer systems.

4. COMPLIANCE WITH THE CODE
    As an ACM member, I will…
    4.1   *Uphold and promote the principles of this code.*
    4.2   *Treat violations of this code as inconsistent with membership in the ACM. GUIDELINES*

1. GENERAL MORAL IMPERATIVES
    As an ACM member I will…
    1.1   *Contribute to society and human well-being.*
          This principle concerning the quality of life of all people affirms an obligation to protect fundamental human rights and to respect the diversity of all cultures. An essential aim of computing professionals is to minimize negative consequences of computing systems, including threats to health and safety. When designing or implementing systems, computing professionals must attempt to ensure that the products of their efforts will be used in socially responsible ways, will meet social needs, and will avoid harmful effects to health and welfare.
          In addition to a safe social environment, human well-being includes a safe natural environment. Therefore, computing professionals who design

and develop systems must be alert to, and make others aware of, any potential damage to the local or global environment.

1.2   *Avoid harm to others.*

"Harm" means injury or negative consequences, such as undesirable loss of information, loss of property, property damage, or unwanted environmental impacts. This principle prohibits use of computing technology in ways that result in harm to any of the following: users, the general public, employees, and employers. Harmful actions include intentional destruction or modification of files and programs leading to serious loss of resources or unnecessary expenditure of human resources such as the time and effort required to purge systems of computer viruses.

Well-intended actions, including those that accomplish assigned duties, may lead to harm unexpectedly. In such an event the responsible person or persons are obligated to undo or mitigate the negative consequences as much as possible. One way to avoid unintentional harm is to carefully consider potential impacts on all those affected by decisions made during design and implementation. To minimize the possibility of indirectly harming others, computing professionals must minimize malfunctions by following generally accepted standards for system design and testing. Furthermore, it is often necessary to assess the social consequences of systems to project the likelihood of any serious harm to others. If system features are misrepresented to users, coworkers, or supervisors, the individual computing professional is responsible for any resulting injury.

In the work environment, the computing professional has the additional obligation to report any signs of system dangers that might result in serious personal or social damage. If one's superiors do not act to curtail or mitigate such dangers, it may be necessary to "blow the whistle" to help correct the problem or reduce the risk. However, capricious or misguided reporting of violations can, itself, be harmful. Before reporting violations, all relevant aspects of the incident must be thoroughly assessed. In particular, the assessment of risk and responsibility must be credible. It is suggested that advice be sought from other computing professionals. (See principle 2.5 regarding thorough evaluations.)

1.3   *Be honest and trustworthy.*

Honesty is an essential component of trust. Without trust an organization cannot function effectively. The honest computing professional will not make deliberately false or deceptive claims about a system or system design, but will instead provide full disclosure of all pertinent system limitations and problems. A computer professional has a duty to be honest about his or her own qualifications, and about any circumstances that might lead to conflicts of interest. Membership in volunteer organizations such as ACM may at times place individuals in situations where their statements or actions could be interpreted as carrying the weight of a larger group of professionals. An ACM member will exercise care to not misrepresent ACM or positions and policies of ACM or any ACM units.

1.4   *Be fair and take action not to discriminate.*

The values of equality, tolerance, respect for others, and the principles of equal justice govern this imperative. Discrimination on the basis of race, sex, religion, age, disability, national origin, or other such factors is an explicit violation of ACM policy and will not be tolerated. Inequities between different groups of people may result from the use or misuse of information and technology. In a fair society, all individuals would have equal opportunity to participate in, or benefit from, the use of computer resources regardless of race, sex, religion, age, disability, national origin, or other such similar factors.

However, these ideals do not justify unauthorized use of computer resources, nor do they provide an adequate basis for violation of any other ethical imperatives of this code.

1.5 *Honor property rights including copyrights and patents.*

Violation of copyrights, patents, trade secrets, and the terms of license agreements is prohibited by law in most circumstances. Even when software is not so protected, such violations are contrary to professional behavior. Copies of software should be made only with proper authorization. Unauthorized duplication of materials must not be condoned.

1.6 *Give proper credit for intellectual property.*

Computing professionals are obligated to protect the integrity of intellectual property. Specifically, one must not take credit for others' ideas or work, even in cases where the work has not been explicitly protected, by copyright or patent, for example.

1.7 *Respect the privacy of others.*

Computing and communication technology enables the collection and exchange of personal information on a scale unprecedented in the history of civilization. Thus, there is increased potential for violating the privacy of individuals and groups. It is the responsibility of professionals to maintain the privacy and integrity of data describing individuals; this includes taking precautions to ensure the accuracy of data, as well as protecting it from unauthorized access or accidental disclosure to inappropriate individuals. Furthermore, procedures must be established to allow individuals to review their records and correct inaccuracies. This imperative implies that only the necessary amount of personal information be collected in a system, that retention and disposal periods for that information be clearly defined and enforced, and that personal information gathered for a specific purpose not be used for other purposes without consent of the individual(s). These principles apply to electronic communications, including electronic mail, and prohibit procedures that capture or monitor electronic user data, including messages, without the permission of users or bona fide authorization related to system operation and maintenance. User data observed during the normal duties of system operation and maintenance must be treated with strictest confidentiality, except in cases where it is evidence for the violation of law, organizational regulations, or this Code. In these cases, the nature or contents of that information must be disclosed only to proper authorities. (See 1.9.).

1.8 *Honor confidentiality.*

The principle of honesty extends to 'issues of confidentiality of information whenever one has made an explicit promise to honor confidentiality or, implicitly, when private information not directly related to the performance of one's duties becomes available. The ethical concern is to respect all obligations of confidentiality to employers, clients, and users unless discharged from such obligations by requirements of the law or other principles of this Code.

2. MORE SPECIFIC PROFESSIONAL RESPONSIBILITIES
As an ACM computing professional I will…

2.1 *Strive to achieve* the highest quality, effectiveness, and dignity in both the process and products of professional work.

Excellence is perhaps the most important obligation of a professional. The computing professional must strive to achieve quality and to be cognizant of the serious negative consequences that may result from poor quality in a system.

2.2 *Acquire and maintain* professional competence.

Excellence depends on individuals who take responsibility for acquiring and maintaining professional competence. A professional must participate in setting standards for appropriate levels of competence, and strive to achieve those standards. Upgrading technical knowledge and competence can be achieved in several ways—doing independent study, attending seminars, conferences, or courses—and being involved in professional organizations.

2.3 *Know and respect existing laws pertaining to professional work.*

ACM members must obey existing local, state, provincial, national, and international laws unless there is a compelling ethical basis not to do so. Policies and procedures of the organizations in which one participates must also be obeyed. But compliance must be balanced with the recognition that sometimes existing laws and rules may be immoral or inappropriate and, therefore, must be challenged. Violation of a law or regulation may be ethical when that law or rule has inadequate moral basis or when it conflicts with another law judged to be more important. If one decides to violate a law or rule because it is viewed as unethical, or for any other reason, one must fully accept responsibility for one's actions and for the consequences.

2.4 *Accept and provide appropriate professional review.*

Quality professional work, especially in the computing profession, depends on professional reviewing and critiquing. Whenever appropriate, individual members should seek and utilize peer review as well as provide critical review of the work of others.

2.5 *Give comprehensive and thorough evaluations of computer systems and their impacts including analysis of possible risks.*

Computer professionals must strive to be perceptive, thorough, and objective when evaluating, recommending, and presenting system descriptions and alternatives. Computer professionals are in a position of special trust, and therefore have a special responsibility to provide objective, credible evaluations to employers, clients, users, and the public. When providing evaluations the professional must also identify any relevant conflicts of interest, as stated in imperative 1.3. As noted in the discussion of principle 1.2 on avoiding harm, any signs of danger from systems must be reported to those who have opportunity or responsibility to resolve them. See the guidelines for imperative 1.2 for more details concerning harm, including the reporting of professional violations.

2.6 *Honor contracts, agreements, and assigned responsibilities.*

Honoring one's commitments is a matter of integrity and honesty. For the computer professional, this includes ensuring that system elements perform as intended. Also, when one contracts for work with another party, one has an obligation to keep that party properly informed about progress toward completing that work. A computing professional has a responsibility to request a change in any assignment that he or she feels cannot be completed as defined. Only after serious consideration, and with full disclosure of risks and concerns to the employer or client, should one accept the assignment. The major underlying principle here is the obligation to accept personal accountability for professional work. On some occasions other ethical principles may take greater priority. A judgment that a specific assignment should not be performed may not be accepted. Having clearly identified one's concerns and reasons for that judgment, but failing to pro-

cure a change in that assignment, one may yet be obligated, by contract or by
law, to proceed as directed. The computing professional's ethical judgment
should be the final guide in deciding whether or not to proceed. Regardless
of the decision, one must accept the responsibility for the consequences.
However, performing assignments against one's own judgment does not
relieve the professional of responsibility for any negative consequences.

2.7 *Improve public understanding of computing and its consequences.*

Computing professionals have a responsibility to share technical knowledge with the public by encouraging understanding of computing, including
the impacts of computer systems and their limitations. This imperative
implies an obligation to counter any false views related to computing.

2.8 *Access computing and communication resources only when authorized to
do so.* Theft or destruction of tangible and electronic property is prohibited
by imperative 1.2: "Avoid harm to others." Trespassing and unauthorized
use of a computer or communication system is addressed by this imperative. Trespassing includes accessing communication networks and computer systems, or accounts and/or files associated with those systems,
without explicit authorization to do so. Individuals and organizations have
the right to restrict access to their systems so long as they do not violate the
discrimination principle (see 1.4). No one should enter or use another's
computing system, software, or data files without permission. One must
always have appropriate approval before using system resources, including
communication ports, file space, other system peripherals, and computer
time.

3. ORGANIZATIONAL LEADERSHIP IMPERATIVES
As an ACM member and an organizational leader, I will...

3.1 *Articulate social responsibilities of members of an organizational unit and
encourage full acceptance of those responsibilities.*

Because organizations of all kinds have impacts on the public, they must
accept responsibilities to society. Organizational procedures and attitudes
oriented toward quality and the welfare of society will reduce harm to members of the public, thereby serving public interest and fulfilling social
responsibility. Therefore, organizational leaders must encourage full participation in meeting social responsibilities as well as quality performance.

3.2 *Manage personnel and resources to design and build information systems
that enhance the quality of working life.*

Organizational leaders are responsible for ensuring that computer
systems enhance, not degrade, the quality of working life. When implementing a computer system, organizations must consider the personal and
professional development, physical safety, and human dignity of all workers. Appropriate human–computer ergonomic standards should be considered in system design and in the workplace.

3.3 *Acknowledge and support proper and authorized uses of an organization's
computing and communications resources.*

Because computer systems can become tools to harm as well as to benefit an organization, the leadership has the responsibility to clearly define
appropriate and inappropriate uses of organizational computing resources.
Although the number and scope of such rules should be minimal, they
should be fully enforced when established.

3.4 *Ensure that users and those who will be affected by a system have their
needs clearly articulated during the assessment and design of requirements; later the system must be validated to meet requirements.*

Later the system must be validated to meet requirements. Current system users, potential users, and other persons whose lives may be affected by

a system must have their needs assessed and incorporated in the statement of requirements. System validation should ensure compliance with those requirements.

3.5   *Articulate and support policies that protect the dignity of users and others affected by a computing system.*

Designing or implementing systems that deliberately or inadvertently demean individuals or groups is ethically unacceptable. Computer professionals who are in decision-making positions should verify that systems are designed and implemented to protect personal privacy and enhance personal dignity.

3.6   *Create opportunities for members of the organization to learn the principles and limitations of computer systems.*

This point complements the imperative on public understanding (2.7). Educational opportunities are essential to facilitate optimal participation of all organizational members. Opportunities must be available to all members to help them improve their knowledge and skills in computing, including courses that familiarize them with the consequences and limitations of particular types of systems. In particular, professionals must be made aware of the dangers of building systems around oversimplified models, the improbability of anticipating and designing for every possible operating condition, and other issues related to the complexity of this profession.

4.   COMPLIANCE WITH THE CODEACM
As an ACM member, I will...

4.1   *Uphold and promote the principles of this Code.*

The future of the computing profession depends on both technical and ethical excellence. Not only is it important for ACM computing professionals to adhere to the principles expressed in this Code, each member should encourage and support adherence by other members.

4.2   *Treat violations of this code as inconsistent with membership in the ACM.*

Adherence of professionals to a code of ethics is largely a voluntary matter. However, if a member does not follow this code by engaging in gross misconduct, ACM may be terminated. This Code and the supplemental Guidelines were developed by the Task Force for the Revision of the ACM Code of Ethics and Professional Conduct: Ronald E. Anderson, Chair, Gerald Engel, Donald Gotterbarn, Grace C. Hertlein, Alex Hoffman, Bruce Jawer, Deborah G. Johnson, Doris K. Lidtke, Joyce Currie Little, Dianne Martin, Donn B. Parker, Judith A. Perrolle, and Richard S. Rosenberg. The Task Force was organized by ACMISIGCAS and funding was provided by the ACM SIG Discretionary Fund. This Code and the supplemental Guidelines were adopted by the ACM Council on October 16, 1992.

2.5.1   Objectives of Codes of Ethics

Different domains and groups of people formulate different codes of ethics, but they all have among them the following objectives:

1. Disciplinary: By instilling discipline, the group or profession ensures professionalism and integrity of its members
2. Advisory: The codes are usually a good source of tips to members and offer advice and guidance in areas where there are fuzzy moral issues.

3. Educational: Ethical codes are good educational tools for members of the domain, especially the new ones who have to learn the do's and don'ts of the new profession. These codes are also a good source of renewal for the older members needing to refresh and polish their possibly waning morals.
4. Inspirational: Besides being disciplinary, advisory, and educational, the codes should also carry subliminal messages to those using them to inspire them to be "good."
5. Publicity: One way for professions to create a good clientele is to show that they have a strong code of ethics and, therefore, their members are committed to basic values and are responsible.

2.6   Reflections on Computer Ethics

2.6.1   New Wine in an Old Bottle

We have so far defined computer ethics as a subset of set A in the functional definition of ethics. We next elaborate on this by pointing out some likely differences between set A in the traditional definition and set A in the functional definition, which now includes computer ethics. Although the overall picture remains the same, there are differences in the overall implementation of the models because of the changes in set A of the functional definition. These differences are manifested in several places, as discussed in the following sections.

2.6.1.1 Changing Premises
Although it is true that the outcome of the ethics value function remains the same, the domain set itself has changed and will keep changing. The number of input possibilities for every human action keeps on growing with new advances in computer technology. For example, take the act of forgery, which traditionally involves taking somebody's document, making changes to it, and getting a benefit as a result. Suppose the document is a check. Let us also assume, all other acts notwithstanding, that you have the document in your hand, in this case the check. Traditionally, your inputs were limited to making changes to the signature and probably changing the date, and cashing it meant literally walking to the financial institution either to deposit it or asking the teller to cash it after producing identification. Although these acts are still possible and readily accepted, new and cleverer ways have emerged as computer technology has advanced. First, now the inputs to set A of an act like this are numerous, no longer limited to the original two. They range from scanning the check to electronically reproducing almost an original check, to cashing it or depositing it without ever stepping in any financial institution, even in the late hours of the night. All these offerings were of course unheard of just a few years back, but they are giving thieves more ways to do their job and making it very difficult for financial institutions and law enforcement agents to do theirs.

2.6.1.2 Different Temptations

In traditional ethics, there were few temptations prompting unethical actions. But according to Richard Rubin [6], computer technology has generated many more temptations for each input action. He outlines seven of these new temptations:

1. *Speed*: The speed of gathering information has greatly increased, causing unethical actions to be carried out in shorter times, thus decreasing the chances of detection. When the chances of being caught are slim, many perpetuators think that they can get away with it.
2. *Privacy and anonymity*: The great availability of computers and computer-related technology in less visible places such as people's homes; high, cheap, and fast communication equipment; and software that can guarantee anonymity are creating a highly tempting environment for unethical acts.
3. *Nature of medium*: The ability to copy digital data without erasing or altering the original in any way causes little or no suspicion and hence encourages unethical activities.
4. *Aesthetic attraction*: Technology, especially when it is new, seems to offer challenges to those who try to use it. Thus, there is a sigh of relief and a sign of great achievement if one overcomes a technological obstacle. In the same way, if an intruder tries to break into a computer system, the sign of success and the euphoria thereafter overshadows the incivility of the act itself.
5. *Increased availability of potential victims*: With the widespread use of computers and the ever-widening reach of computer networks, an individual can now reach an unprecedented audience. This scope in itself creates an urge to attempt things that one would otherwise not have done.
6. *International scope*: The boundary-less nature of many computer networks, including the Internet, has created a temptation of its own. Now the entire world is well within reach by a touch of a button. This accessibility can tempt many intruders, many trying to circumvent their country's laws, and others thinking that an illegal act done in another country cannot be prosecuted in their own country. There are many temptations here.
7. *The power to destroy*: Computers seem to give this enormous invisible power to those who have them. This seemingly omniscient power may be a temptation to some. Although some of these temptations can still be found in the set of the old temptations, most of them are new.

2.6.1.3 Different Means of Delivery

What used to be the traditional means of carrying out an act such as stealing has changed. With the expanded set of outcome possibilities come expanded delivery systems for the crime. For example, let us go back to the check. The traditional way of cashing a check was to go to the bank. With computers facilitating new ways of banking, you can get your check cashed without ever visiting the bank, even in the middle of the night.

2.6.1.4 Complacent Society

A majority of computer-related actions are either deliberately ignored by society for fear of publicity or they are hailed as novel science: either members of society are still caught in the spell of the new wonder machine or that they have gotten so comfortable with the new wonder machine that they let their moral and ethical standards slide. Whatever it is, society is too complacent about computers, and until this attitude changes, computer ethics is likely to remain different from traditional ethics.

2.6.1.5 Ethical Muddles

With the possibility of numerous inputs from events, new difficulties of choice and justification cause ethical dilemmas, creating conflicting arguments and counterarguments on an input possibility of an event. This situation occurs because computers produce new situations that sometimes fall within our existing laws, rules, and moral principles, and sometimes fall outside these guidelines.

2.7   Technology and Values

Every now and then, a new technology is introduced in our midst, intended to make our lives easier. Some of these technologies do not last for more than a month; others take hold and become revolutionary in magnitude. Those which become successful most often influence society by creating new possibilities that may raise new moral and ethical concerns and consequently create vacuums and new dilemmas in that society's basic sets of moral values. Computer technology has been one of these successful technologies. In its very short duration, it has had such a strong impact and influence on society, and if it continues the present trend unchecked, it is likely to become one of the greatest revolutions in the history of humankind, far greater than the agricultural and industrial revolutions. Society as a whole seems to be engulfed in this revolution and no cultural and/or society norm will, in the end if there is an end, be left unaffected.

Successful technological revolutions tend to create tempting situations that often result in a loosening of individual moral values, and the computer revolution tops that list. Worldwide cultural, political, and social underpinnings and values are undergoing a silent, but tremendous, change as new computer products come on the market and the revolution gathers momentum. It is moving so fast that it is stripping us of our ability to cope. Although we are constantly in need of new moral principles and new ethical values to fit the changing landscape, we cannot formulate, debate, and put in place such principles and values fast enough before they are outdated. More important still, even if we were able to come up with new values and moral principles, we would still lack the conceptual models within which such values and principles can be applied.

Many new situations resulting from the computer revolution are outdating our basic sets of values. Take, for example, the processes of handling forgeries in monitory currencies. There are laws on the books in almost every country against forgeries of any kind, let alone forgeries of currencies. These laws are further reinforced with individual moral values. One can, for example, reproduce and print millions of almost identical notes of a country's currency. Suppose even further that one produces a software program that reproduces the bank notes and enriches oneself. One's conscience of course tells the person that what one is doing is wrong, but the new technological advances are so tempting and making it so easy and so available that one can start rationalizing one's acts: I created or bought the program with my own money, I did all the work by myself, and after all it is highly unlikely that I can be caught because people cannot even tell the difference. All one is doing is creating a vacuum in one's basic set of values, and society needs to find a way to fill that moral vacuum so as to prevent individuals from taking moral vacations! As computer and telecommunication revolutions pick up speed, creating new avenues of use and access such as the Internet and the World Wide Web, thus giving users room and reasons to take moral vacations, there is an urgent need to do the following:

1. Formulate new laws to strengthen our basic sets of values, which are being rendered irrelevant by computer technology.
2. Construct a conceptual model in which the new laws can be applied successfully.
3. Launch a massive education campaign to make society aware of the changing environment and the impact such an environment is having on our basic values.

The first two objectives are beyond the scope of this book, which mainly focuses on the third objective, educating the public concerning ethical issues raised by the computer revolution.

Issues for Discussion   "Thou shalt not kill." What does this mean? When can you kill and it is OK? What can you kill and it OK?

Exercises

1. How would you define ethics to the following audiences?
   - Seventh-graders
   - College students
   - Members of the clergy
2. Why are acts such as abortion legal in some societies and not in others?
3. Does technology bring relevant changes in ethics?
4. Use the traditional model of ethics to explain the effects of technology on ethics to seventh-graders.
5. What are the merits of computer ethics education?
6. Why should we study computer ethics?
7. There are two views on teaching computer ethics. State these views. What view do you agree with and why?
8. Why do we need ethical theories?

9. According to the human nature theory, you are supposed to develop your capabilities, and your actions are based on those capabilities. If individuals have few developed capabilities (because of circumstances beyond their control, for example), should they be responsible for their actions?
10. Discuss the existence of universal moral norms.
11. Discuss the effects of time on moral norms.
12. Using graphics, demonstrate the working of the functional definition of ethics.
13. Professional organizations usually use professional codes of ethics to enforce discipline in their members. Do codes always work?
14. Suggest an alternative to the professional codes of ethics and demonstrate that your alternative can work.
15. How does technology affect ethics? morality?

References

1. Fr. Fagothey A (1959) Right and reason, 2nd edn. Tan Books and Publishers, Rockford
2. Solomon R (2004) Morality and the good life: an introduction to ethics through classical sources, 4th edn. McGraw-Hill, New York
3. Johnson DJ (2009) Computer ethics, 4th edn. Pearson Education, Upper Saddle River
4. Encyclopedia of philosophy. http://www.utm.edu/research/lep/ni/
5. Velasquez M, Moberg D, Meyer MJ, Shanks T, McLean MR, DeCosse D, André C, Hanson KO. A framework for thinking ethically. Markkula Center for Applied Ethics at Santa Clara University. http://www.scu.edu/ethics/practicing/decision/framework.html
6. Rubin R (1996) Moral distancing and the use of information technology: the seven temptations. In: Kizza JM (ed) Social and ethical effects of the computer revolution. McFarland, Jefferson
7. Tomlinson T (1993) Nursing ethics. Western Schools. https://www.msu.edu/~tomlins4/Vita.pdf

Further Reading

Edel A, Flower E, O'Connor FW (1989) Morality, philosophy, and practice: historical and contemporary readings and studies, 3rd edn. Random House, New York

Ethics and the Professions

Learning Objectives

After reading this chapter, the reader should be able to

1. Identify ethical issues that arise in professional decision making and determine how to address them.
2. Analyze global computing issues that influence professional decision making.
3. Describe the mechanisms that typically exist for day-to-day ethical decision making.
4. Identify progressive stages in a whistle-blowing incident.
5. Specify the strengths and weaknesses of relevant professional codes as expressions of professionalism and guides to decision making.

Real-Life Experiences: The Kansas City Pharmacist

In August 2001, Robert Courtney, a Kansas City pharmacist was indicted on 20 felony counts of product tampering, drug adulteration, and drug misbranding. Courtney illegally diluted Gemzar and other expensive chemotherapy drugs to make money.

What was more alarming was the fact that he had hundreds of cancer patients most of them relying on chemotherapy treatments for survival. According to the FBI, at least one patient who received the diluted drugs died.

Courtney was caught when a representative of Eli Lilly and Co., the pharmaceutical company that manufactures Gemzar, became suspicious from records that indicated that a Kansas City doctor was receiving much more Gemzar from Courtney's pharmacy than the actual amount of Gemzar the pharmacy was purchasing from the manufacturer.

(continued)

© Springer International Publishing Switzerland 2016
J.M. Kizza, *Ethics in Computing*, Undergraduate Topics in Computer Science,
DOI 10.1007/978-3-319-29106-2_3

Real-Life Experiences: (continued)
  After the doctor was notified and the drug was tested, U.S. federal agents were then informed. It was found that Courtney was selling up to three times the amount of drugs he was purchasing from the drug manufacturer [1].

Discussion Questions
  1. What crime did Robert Courtney commit?
  2. Was it proper to arrest Robert Courtney? Why or why not?
  3. Do you think Robert Courtney was responsible for the assumed death?

3.1 Introduction

What is a profession? It is a trade, a business, or an occupation of which one professes to have extensive knowledge acquired through long years of experience and formal education and the autonomy of and responsibility to make independent decisions in carrying out the duties of the profession. To profess is to make a public declaration, a claim of something. In the case of a professional, that something is knowledge in the knowledge domain of that which makes up that occupation or trade. Webster's dictionary similarly defines *profession* as "a: a calling requiring specialized knowledge and often long and intensive academic preparation; b: a principal calling, vocation, or employment; c: the whole body of persons engaged in a calling." [2]. Well-known professions are law, medicine, and engineering.

In our study of professions and the people who profess the deep knowledge of the profession, we focus on four themes: (1) evolution of professions, (2) the making of an ethical professional, (3) the professional decision-making process, and (4) professionalism and ethical responsibilities. These four themes cover all the activities of a professional life. First, we look at the beginnings of professions, describe the characteristics of professionals, and discuss how these characteristics are supported by commitment, integrity, responsibility, and accountability. We then describe the ways professionals are made: through both formal education and informal unstructured in-service. When professionals enter the workforce, their duties involve decision making. We therefore look at the process of decision making, the problems involved, and the guilt felt about what are perceived as wrong decisions and how to avoid them. Professionals in their working environment encounter problems every day that require them to check in with their moral code. We focus on professionalism and ethical responsibilities as one of those areas that requires continual consultation with individual morality and discuss how these affect professions.

3.2   Evolution of Professions

3.2.1   Origins of Professions

The concept of a profession is actually not new; however, the word *profession* today carries a far different connotation than it did during the Middle Ages. According to Bolivar A. Senior [3], the word *profession* referred to a commitment formally *professed* by a person to become a member of a religious order, and a *professional* was the person who has *professed* the commitment. Senior writes, because early universities drew most of their faculty from religious orders, these teachers eventually were called *professors* . Richard Sizer [4] states that professions started in medieval times with the craftsmen's guilds and in inns. These guilds were responsible for apprenticeship standards, competence, and performance of their members. Little distinction was made between manual labor and intellectual groups. But as small intellectual groups developed, such as those of clerics, the first requirements of achievements and maintenance of professional criteria started to emerge. The emphasis on intellectual capabilities for membership in a group became increasingly important as time passed. Sizer states that professions in eighteenth-century England were regarded as "occupations for the 'gentlemen,' offering a safe social niche but not large material rewards." The Industrial Revolution is credited with establishing professions in engineering, accounting, and banking [4]. Over the years, however, material rewards have increased and a set of requirements has evolved.

Over the years, the term profession and its requirements for membership evolved into two categories: the *learned* professions, which required individuals with a deep knowledge of the profession acquired through years of formal education; and *common* professions, which required the individuals to be noblemen who in theory did not really need to work for a living: they were *liberated* from the need to work, but should learn the profession anyway. The first liberal profession was the military career [3]. When the life of the nobility became less influential, especially after the French Revolution, the *common* distinction of professions came to be known as *trades,* probably as we know them today. However, *trades*, as today, still required one to hold a higher ethical standard.

3.2.2   Requirements of a Professional

There are three basic professional requirements, and over the years as the professions evolved, these three elements have taken different forms.

1. *A set of highly developed skills and deep knowledge of the domain.* Although professional skills are developed through long years of experience, such skills must be backed up by a very well developed knowledge base acquired through long years of formal schooling. Acquiring a sophisticated level of knowledge is crucial because skills based on shallow knowledge of the domain could be

damaging to the profession in cases involving decisions that require understanding, analysis, and adoption of concepts to suit the environment or the problem. This requirement alone is enough to differentiate between professionals and skilled laborers who acquire considerable skills from long years of working in the same domain, such as auto mechanics and landscape designers.

2. *Autonomy.* Because professionals provide either products or services, there is always a relationship between the provider of the service and the receiver of the service or the provider of the product and the receiver of the product. In this relationship we are concerned with the power balance. In the case of a professional, the power is in favor of the professional. Take the relationship between a lawyer and a client or a physician and a patient, for example. In either case, there is a power play in favor of the provider of the service. If we consider the example of an auto mechanic, however, there is also a power play in the equation, but this time the power is in favor of the customer, not the provider of the service. There are also marked differences in the way the service is provided by professionals and nonprofessionals. In the case of a professional, there is more room to vary the way a service or a product is provided without consulting the receiver of the service or the product, meaning that professionals have autonomy to vary the way the service is provided without asking the receiver for confirmation or consent. However, in the case of nonprofessionals, the provider of the service cannot vary the way the service is to be delivered without checking with the customer. For example, when you take a car for repair, the mechanic cannot vary from what you agreed on without formally asking you.

3. *Observance of a code of conduct* . A working professional usually observes these four types of codes [5]:
   - *The professional code*: a set of guidelines provided to the professional by the profession spelling out what a professional ought to do and not do. A professional code protects both the image of the profession and that of the individual members. Thus, it is a requirement for the profession that members adhere to the code.
   - *A personal code*: a set of individual moral guidelines on which professionals operate. In many ways these guidelines are acquired by professionals from the cultural environment in which they grow up or live in and the religious beliefs they may practice. Whatever the case, a personal code supplements the professional code significantly.
   - *The institutional code*: a code imposed by the institution for which the professional is working. This code is meant to build and maintain the public's confidence in the institution and its employees.
   - *The community code*: a community standard code developed over a period of time based on either the religion or culture of the indigenous people in the area. It may be imposed by civil law or the culture of the community in which the professional works.

Fig. 3.1 Codes governing
human actions

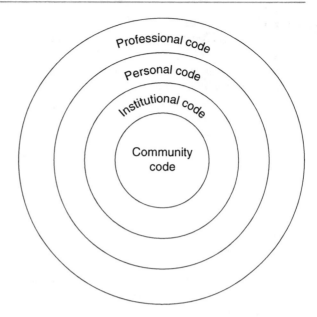

The interaction among the four codes can be explained as follows: consider each code as a circle inside another circle with the community code at the center of these concentric circles. Outside the community code is the institutional code enclosed by the personal code, which is enclosed by the professional code (see Fig. 3.1).

Any action performed by a professional working at a local institution is contained in the outermost circle. Therefore, for such action to be ethical, moral, and legal, it must be in conformity with all the codes and intersect all codes.

Let us consider an example. Suppose a physician is working in a community hospital where the hospital and the community do not support euthanasia. If the doctor is asked by his or her patients to assist them in taking their own life, the doctor must examine all four codes before coming to a decision. First, the professional code may not support euthanasia whether the doctor's individual moral code does or does not. So, because the institutional, community, and the professional codes do not support euthanasia, the doctor may not find it in his or her best interest to grant the patients their wishes even if he or she agrees with the patient. As we discuss later, the requirement that any action taken by a professional must fall within the intersection of the four sets of codes may present moral dilemmas for the professional in the decision-making process and consequently tarnish the professionalism of the individual.

3.2.3   Pillars of Professionalism

Professionalism is supported by four pillars: commitment, integrity, responsibility, and accountability.

3.2.3.1 Commitment
Commitment, according to Humphreys, has these six characteristics [6]:

1. *The person making the commitment must do so willingly without duress.* The person executing the commitment must like what he or she is doing. If commitments are in the form of assignments with little autonomy, it is more likely the commitment may not be present.
2. *The person responsible must try to meet the commitment, even if help is needed.* Because commitments are not assignments, the person who has made the commitment is assumed to have the know-how, the autonomy to vary steps, and the skills to do the job. Professionals possess these characteristics, plus they have the ability to seek the necessary skills from others to circumvent obstacles that may arise, so more commitment is expected of them.
3. *There must be agreement on what is to be done, by whom, and when.* Professionals entering into a commitment must have advance knowledge of what is to be done and who is likely to do what part. Entering into a commitment without adequate advance knowledge is highly unprofessional. When the work is divided among other professionals, they themselves must make the same commitment for their respective parts and, in this case, commitment for those smaller parts is as important as the commitment for the whole job. If the smaller parts are assigned to nonprofessionals, they are considered assignments, and the commitment must lie with the professional assigning the parts. Such commitment is carried out through supervision of the nonprofessional members of the team.
4. *The commitment must be openly and publicly stated.* Open commitments are transparent and easily correctable if there are problems. Professional commitments must fall within the allocated resources of time, material, and money. If a commitment is public, there are more chances that most of the sourcing, acquisition, distribution, and use of resources will be transparent, and thus the job is likely to be done more smoothly.
5. *The commitment must not be made easily.* Before entering into a commitment, professionals should do research to make sure that what they are entering into is not a Trojan horse (something or someone intended to defeat or subvert from within).
6. *Before the committed date, if it is clear it cannot be met, advance notice must be given and a new commitment negotiated.* It is a sign of responsibility and commitment to have the courage to tell others of shortfalls in parts of the agreement, so if there is anything to be done to meet the deadlines, it is done without acrimony.

3.2.3.2 Integrity
Integrity means a state of undivided loyalty to self-belief. It is honesty, uncompromising self-value, and incorruptible. The word "integrity" comes from the Latin word *integratas*, which means entire, undivided, or whole. To stay undivided in

one's beliefs professionally requires three maxims of integrity: namely, vision, love of what one is doing, and commitment to what one has to do.

- *Vision.* Having vision is the capacity to anticipate and make a plan of action that will circumvent obstacles and maximize benefits. Vision is a sign of good leadership, and professionals who have the initiative, the autonomy, and the authority in the provider–client relationship exemplify leadership.
- *Love.* Numerous studies have shown that people who love what they do do it better than those who do it because they have to. In school, children who have a love for a subject perform far better than those who do it because it is a requirement. When people choose professions, they should do so because they have a love for the work. The amount of love put in helps maintain morality in one's actions because what is being done is no longer a chore but a creation, and as we know, people love their own creations.
- *Commitment.* The vision and love applied to the work bonds the individual to whatever he or she is doing until it is done: this is commitment as we defined it earlier.

3.2.3.3 Responsibility

Responsibility concerns roles, tasks, and actions and their ensuing consequences. For example, as parents we have an obligation and a duty to bring up our offspring.

That is parental responsibility. But responsibility also depends on a person's value system, which is based on his or her environment and culture. There are various types of responsibilities, including personal, communal, parental, and professional, and these responsibilities vary depending on the age of the individual and his or her position in society. For example, the responsibilities of a 5-year-old are far different from those of a 40-year-old. Clearly the responsibilities of a country's chief executive are different from those of a janitor. When individuals choose a lifestyle implied in a career or a vocation, they choose and must accept the package of responsibilities that go with that lifestyle.

Responsibilities of a Professional as a Provider A professional in either a provider–client or a provider–customer relationship represents the provider of either a service or a product. This relationship, as we pointed out earlier, is a contract between the two parties. The relationship consists of three major types of responsibilities: service, product, and consequential.

Service Responsibilities
For a professional to provide a service to a client, there must be a contract binding the professional and the client. In this contract, as in any other contract, the professional has specific responsibilities regarding the time of delivery of the service, the quality of the service, and the consequences after the service has been rendered. For example, in the time-constraint responsibility, the service must be rendered within

an agreed timeframe; if not, a new time must be negotiated. In the quality of service responsibility, the service must meet its desired goal so far as the client is concerned, and it must have the expected value. The consequence responsibility involves the safety of the client from harm, both physical and financial, after receiving the service. The provider must take all these responsibilities seriously.

Product Responsibilities If the contract between the provider and the client involves a product, the provider has the responsibility to deliver the product agreed upon on time, in good shape and of quality, and to provide documentation for the safe use of the product. The provider of the product is responsible for all liabilities that might arise as a result of use of the product. In liability cases, the provider responsibility depends on the contract and the degree of harm. We say more about liabilities in Chaps. 6 and 8.

Consequential Responsibilities In a television medical drama episode I watched, an operating room scene showed a female doctor dancing to a reggae tune while operating on a patient and unknowingly sewing the patient up with a surgical metal clip still in the patient's chest. In the next scene the patient has died and the autopsy shows the metal clip is still in his chest. Before the results of the autopsy, the doctor remembers her error and naturally becomes remorseful, not knowing whether to tell the family right away or wait until the medical report is issued. She knows full well that whatever the case, the family is going to sue her and the hospital, and probably her job at that hospital and her medical career are over. There is remorse on the part of the doctor and anger on the part of the patient's family, all because one person did not fulfill her responsibilities.

Remorse and anger are aftereffects of an action gone wrong, in this case a professional service. Whether a professional has provided a service or a product, there are always aftereffects of that action. Oftentimes one is praised for a service well done and the best product ever provided, but there are also times when one is remorseful because a service did not produce what it was intended to or a product did not live up to expectations. In the worst case scenario the service or product may cause physical or financial harm to the client. In such cases, one expects liabilities for the service or product, and the professional must accept those consequential responsibilities. In the case of the doctor, the service she provided fell short of what was expected, and she had to face the consequential responsibilities of her actions, which at times not only include the parties involved but may also involve innocent bystanders.

3.2.3.4 Accountability

One way we can define accountability is the obligation to answer for the execution of one's assigned responsibilities. This process involves the "cycle of setting measurable goals, planning what needs to be done to meet those goals, reporting progress towards goals, evaluating the reports, and using that feedback to make improvements" [7]. Accountability involves these three key elements [8]:

1. *A set of outcome measures that reliably and objectively evaluate performance*: In every profession there is a minimum set of measures that every individual in that profession must meet. This set must be carefully selected, and those measures must be attainable. However, these measures vary according to the profession and the individual activity to be performed by the professional. For example, in the teaching profession, one of the measures might be the success rate of students when they take standardized examinations.
2. *A set of performance standards defined in terms of these outcome measures*: Similar to outcome measures, performance standards must be carefully chosen and attainable. These standards are also very dependent on the profession, but each profession must have a set of common performance standards for all its members for every type of service or product provided by that profession. For the teaching profession, the standard of output measures might be the passing of standardized examinations at a certain predetermined level. In the law profession, it might be the ability of a judgment to stand on subsequent appeals. Whatever standard measure is chosen, it must be plausible and measurable.
3. *A set of incentives for meeting the standards and/or penalties for failing to meet them*: The incentives chosen must be good enough so as not to create undesirable motives. For example, if the incentives are too good, they may force professionals to put the interest of their customers and clients below the interest of attaining the measures. If the incentives are monetary, they may force professionals to put the interest of making money ahead of the services they are supposed to offer. Similarly, the penalties prescribed must not be so harsh that they drive away those who intend to enter the profession. Harsh penalties also tend to make people who are in the wrong hide their actions and dig in deeper for fear of being discovered.

3.3   The Making of an Ethical Professional: Education and Licensing

In our discussion of the evolution of the professions, we have noticed the never-ending requirements of an individual seeking membership in the chosen profession or trade to either have a deep knowledge of the profession acquired through formal education or to be intrinsically of a "gentleman's calling," willing to hold a higher ethical standard. To continue to uphold these essential requirements in both professions and trades, let us now discuss three items that encourage, maintain, and improve that higher ethical standard: these are formal education, licensing, and professional codes of conduct. Professionals must follow a specific process to meet and maintain those professional requirements.

3.3.1   Formal Education

For formal education to be effective in teaching and enforcing the pillars of professionalism, it must be targeted and incremental. Let us walk through the making of
an information technology professional as an example. In elementary school, as
students are introduced to information technology, they should be told not to use
machines to destroy other people's property or to hurt others. But these cautions
should be explained in an age-appropriate way. For example, children should be
taught responsible ways of using computers and the Internet.

They should be told not to visit certain Web pages, to avoid getting involved in
relationships online, to not give personal and family information online, and not to
arrange for a rendezvous online or offline. In addition, they should be told to respect
others' work and property, whether they are online or off. Cases have already been
reported of children as young as 14 years old breaking into computer systems and
destroying records. In fact, many of the computer network attacks, and a good number of the headline-making incidents, have been perpetuated by young people,
sometimes as young as 10 years of age. For example, in a certain county in
Tennessee, several ninth-graders broke into their school computer system and
infected it with a virus that wiped out most of the school records. It is believed the
students got the virus off the Internet [9]. The content of what is taught must be
relevant and sensitive to different age groups and professionals.

As students go through high school, content should become progressively more
sophisticated. The message about responsible use of computers should be stressed
more. The teen years are years of curiosity and discovery, and many young people
find themselves spending long hours on computers and other online devices. Those
long hours should be spent responsibly. Although a significant portion of the message should come from parents, schools should also be part of this partnership by
offering courses in responsible use of computers. The teaching could focus on ethics: students should be given reasons why they cannot create and distribute viruses,
download copyrighted materials off the Internet, and use the Internet to send bad
messages to others. These ethical reasons go beyond the "do it and you will be
expelled from school" type of threats.

In college, of course, the message is more direct. There are several approaches
that bring the message across to students:

 (i) Students take formal courses in professional ethics in a number of professional
     programs in their respective colleges.
(ii) Without taking formal courses as part of their curriculum, students are taught
     substantial amounts of information ethics sprinkled throughout their courses in
     both general education and their major.
(iii) A capstone course is used in the general education requirements, and informa-
     tion ethics content is added to that course. Many colleges now require com-
     puter literacy as a graduation requirement. Use that course to add ethics
     content.
(iv) At exit, a 1-h information ethics course is required, which can be taken online.

Once they join the workplace environment, these professionals should be required to attend informal refresher sessions, seminars, and in-service workshops periodically.

3.3.2   Licensing Authorities

Licensing grants individuals formal or legal permission to practice their profession, which tips the balance of power in the giver–receiver equation in favor of the giver. Before a license is issued, certain formalities must be accomplished; for example, testing the competence of the aspirant for the specific knowledge and skills required. If such a test is not passed, the licensing authority may deny issuing the license. Beside testing for competence, the licensing authority also provides the licensee with a set of rules required to keep the license. If the rules are violated, the authority may have the prerogative of either sanctioning the licensee or recalling the license. Clearly, a license is a privilege, not a right, and if licensees want to maintain that right, they must follow the prescribed code. Licenses can be (and have been) used as both control and educating instruments to enforce rules, laws, and certain group or society norms.

Many professions license members, and most of these professions require the potential licensee to take and pass examinations that sometimes test both knowledge and skills. Many professions, to keep members updated and compliant with their codes, limit the validity of their licenses to specific time periods so members must renew their licenses. They then tie license renewal to passing of continuing examinations, which helps ensure that members stay knowledgeable in the profession. Professions also use periodic licensing examinations to check on member compliance with codes. If members have in the past violated a code and been reported, such members may not have their licenses renewed even if they pass all examinations.

It is quite evident that in those professions with no licensing requirements, discipline has been and continues to be a problem, whereas in those maintaining vigorous licensing requirements, relatively few disciplinary problems have emerged. Because every profession strives for a good image, many legitimate professions require licensing for membership. Licensing enables professions to enforce their rules by law. For example, physicians can lose their license to practice if they do anything unlawful or unethical. Once such a license is withdrawn, a physician cannot practice medicine. Although there are many professions with licensing requirements but with no enforcement mechanism, an increasing number of professions are opting to require enforceable licensing to keep their image untainted.

3.3.3   Professional Codes of Conduct

The primary purpose of professional codes of conduct is to promote the public image of the profession by specifying and enforcing the ethical behavior expected from its members. Accordingly, and in most cases, professional codes consist of standards, canons, and rules of conduct that address the following areas [10]:

- Moral and legal standards
- Professional–client relationship
- Client advocacy
- Professional–public relationships
- Sanction mechanics
- Confidentiality
- Assessment
- Compliance
- Competence
- Certified professional credentials for those professions that use certification [9]

For professional codes of conduct to be effective, a profession must institute a system of enforcement, reporting, hearing procedures, sanctions, and appeals. Codes without such systems in place are completely ineffective.

3.3.3.1 Enforcement

Experience and studies have shown that professions with enforceable codes have fewer discipline problems among their members than those with no codes or those with codes but without enforcement mechanisms. Those professions with fewer disciplinary problems naturally have better images. Because the purpose of codes for any profession is to create and maintain a good image, those professions without codes should come up not only with codes, canons, and guidelines, but also with enforcement mechanisms, and those with codes but with no enforcement system should add the enforcement. It is common knowledge that laws, codes, canons, or guidelines are not obeyed until and unless some type of enforcement machinery is in place. There are various techniques of enforcement, most of which have no civil authority. The most widely used are professional ethics boards, standing committees, or review boards charged with the following actions:

- Drawing up the codes of ethics for the profession if none exist
- Revising codes if and when necessary
- Conducting education campaigns at the membership level
- Distributing copies of the codes to every member
- Developing disciplinary procedures
- Receiving complaints, conducting hearings, counseling members, and sanctioning members found guilty
- Promoting the image of the profession [11]

3.3.3.2 Reporting of Grievances

There are two main reporting procedures. The first is the typical organizational route in which a complaint is reported first to the local chapters if it exists. The complaint then makes its way to the top, usually to the national ethics committee.

The second is the short-circuit procedure in which reporting can be done at any level and then from there a complaint is forwarded all the way to the top. Professions may vary these two types of reporting, mainly in the area of who is supposed to report a professional in violation. In some professions, the reporting must be done by a member of the profession in good standing and nobody else. In this case, concerned members of the public must report their complaint to a member of the profession, who then forwards the complaints to the committee. In other professions, any member of the public can initiate a complaint with the local professional board. Whichever way a complaint is reported, there should be a way to inform members of the profession and the public on the procedures of reporting and who can and cannot file a complaint, and there must be established channels of communication.

3.3.3.3 Hearing Procedures
Generalization of hearing proceedings is because of the many factors involved: for example, the nature, the financial standing, and the structure of the profession; the kind of enforcement procedures being used; and the penalty to be imposed. If there is no enforcement procedure or if the penalty is not significant, the accused member may not even appear for the scheduled hearing. Professions should consider all these factors when formulating the hearing procedures. For example, hearings should be held at the profession's nearest field office to save members from traveling long distances. If there is no field office, arrangements should be made to find a location convenient to both the accused and the hearing committee members, and the hearing process itself should be as short as possible.

3.3.3.4 Sanctions
If a hearing committee decides that a member is guilty of the offenses charged, then the committee must propose sanctions to fit the violations committed by the member. The committee may decide to recommend any one or a combination of the following: probation, revocation of certification, request for resignation, and suspension from the profession at the member's expense. If a probation option is taken, the committee must clearly specify the nature, duration, and conditions of the probation. Also, there must be a person to whom the professional is to report for all requirements of the probation, including supervision. After the sanctioned member fulfills the requirements of the penalty, a recommendation can be made to reinstate the member in good standing.

3.3.3.5 Appeals
A profession must have an appeals process on the books for the sanctioned professional who is not satisfied with either the ruling of the committee or the penalty imposed. Such guidelines should state clearly the procedure for appeals, how the appeal instrument is to be handled, who attends to the appeals, and the maximum amount of time an individual has between the time he or she receives a judgment and the filing of the appeal. The time allotted for a judgment on the appeal should also be stipulated. The profession must also state whether an appealing member should continue executing his or her duties or be prohibited from doing so until the

appeal is complete. In certain professions, appealing members are either put on administrative leave, suspended, or allowed to carry on with their duties pending the decision of the appeal.

Here is an example of a professional code of conduct for

The Institute of Electrical and Electronics Engineers, Inc.

CODE OF ETHICS 2
We, the members of the IEEE, in recognition of the importance of our technologies affecting the quality of life throughout the world, and in accepting a personal obligation to our profession, its members and the communities we serve, do hereby commit ourselves to the highest ethical and professional conduct and agree:
1. To accept responsibility in making engineering decisions consistent with the safety, health, and welfare of the public and to disclose promptly factors that might endanger the public or the environment
2. To avoid real or perceived conflicts of interest whenever possible and to disclose them to affected parties when they do exist
3. To be honest and realistic in stating claims or estimates based on available data
4. To reject bribery in all its forms
5. To improve the understanding of technology, its appropriate application, and potential consequences
6. To maintain and improve our technical competence and to undertake technological tasks for others only if qualified by training or experience, or after full disclosure of pertinent limitations
7. To seek, accept, and offer honest criticism of technical work, to acknowledge and correct errors, and to credit properly the contributions of others
8. To treat fairly all persons regardless of such factors as race, religion, gender, disability, age, or national origin
9. To avoid injuring others, their property, reputation, or employment by false or malicious action
10. To assist colleagues and coworkers in their professional development and to support them in following this code of ethics

3.4   Professional Decision Making and Ethics

Now we come to our third theme on professionalism and ethics: the process of professional decision making. Here we focus on professional dilemmas and guilt associated with decision making.

3.4.1   Professional Dilemmas in Decision Making

Dilemmas in decision making are quite common in the everyday activities of a professional. The process of decision making resembles mapping with input parameters and an output decision. The input parameters in the decision-making process are premises. To each premise a value is attached. The mapping uses these values along with the premises to create an output, which is the decision. For example, if I have to make the decision whether to walk to church or take the car, the set of premises might include, among others, time, parking, safety, and gas. The values attached to these premises are that if I go by car, I save time, I need a parking space, walking is good exercise, I need money to buy gas. If I decide to walk, my decision might be based on a set of premises including health and money to which I may attach the following values: walking to church 1 day a month is good exercise and it saves me money for gas. The mapping function takes these premises together with the values and outputs a "logical" decision. This mapping function is similar to the one we used in the ethics definition in Chap. 3. Dilemmas in decision making are caused by questioning the values attached to one's premises as inputs to the decision being made. One's input values may be clouded by conflicting codes of conduct, advances in technology, or incomplete or misleading information.

3.4.1.1 Conflicting Codes of Conduct

In Fig. 3.1 of Sect. 3.2.2, we showed that every decision made by a professional must take into account the interrelationships of professional, personal, institutional, and local codes. The decision must be made in such a way that all four codes agree.

Decisions outside the core intersection must be weighted carefully because they always result in controversy. Take the case of the famous Michigan pathologist Dr. Kevorkian, the so-called Doctor Death. Dr. Kevorkian became a hero to some who believed in assisted suicide and Doctor Death to others who did not. He managed to force a debate over assisted suicide on the entire nation by repeatedly helping people to kill themselves using his "death machine," for a total of at least 47 people. In the 7 years in which he accelerated his killing and before he was eventually charged and put in prison, Dr. Kevorkian actually scoffed at the law, scorned elected and religious leaders, and won over juries. Dr. Jack Kevorkian became more known for his stand on assisted suicide than on his long years of professional service. The controversy was generated by the conflict in the codes, namely, the medical professional code of conduct, which includes the Hippocratic oath, and the local code, that is, the code of the town, county, and the state of Michigan (the institutional code does not apply because he was retired).

3.4.1.2 Advances in Technology

Dilemmas in decision making may also be caused by advances in technology. Computer technology in particular has created more muddles in the decision-making process than any other technology. Advances in computer technology create a multitude of possibilities that never existed before. Such possibilities present professionals with myriad temptations (see Sect. 3.5.1.2).

3.4.1.3 Incomplete or Misleading Information

Not having all the information one needs before making a decision can be problematic. Consider the famous prisoners' dilemma. Two people are caught committing a crime, and they are taken to different interrogation rooms before they have a chance to coordinate their stories. During the interrogation each prisoner is told that the other prisoner has agreed to plead guilty on all charges. Authorities inform the prisoner that agreeing to plead guilty on the charges as the other prisoner has done will bring him or her a reduced sentence. But rejecting the plea will of course mean that the accused is not cooperating with the investigation, which may result in him or her receiving the maximum punishment allowable. Each prisoner has four recourses:

- Plead guilty without the friend pleading guilty, which would mean deserting a friend
- Refuse to plead guilty and the friend pleads guilty, which would mean betrayal and probably a maximum sentence
- Plead guilty and the friend pleads guilty, which means light sentences for both of them
- Both refusing to plead guilty and probably both receiving a light sentence or a maximum sentence

Whatever option the prisoners take is risky because they do not have enough information to enable them to make a wise decision. There are similar situations in professional life when a decision has to be made without enough information available and within time constraints. In such a situation the professional must take extra care to weigh all possibilities in the input set of premises and their corresponding values.

Taking all these into account and using the ethical framework we developed in the previous chapter can help the professional in making decisions that are just, fair, and plainly ethical.

3.4.2   Guilt and Making Ethical Decisions

In an ethical decision-making process, decisions are made based on, and reflect, consequences, individual liberties, and justice. To achieve this, individuals can use any other ethical theories to frame or make ethical choices that reflect the selected criteria. However, whatever theory used, the outcome falls into one of the following three criteria:

- *Utilitarian criterion:* in which decisions are made solely on the basis of their intended outcomes or consequences
- *Rights criterion:* in which decisions are made based on the set of liberties the society enforces, such as the Magna Carta and the Bill of Rights
- *Justice criterion:* which reflects justice; decisions are made so that they are fair, impartial, and equitable to all

As we saw in Chap. 2 (Sect. 2.2.5), guilt is our natural internal judgment system, punishing ourselves based on our moral standards or the group's standards. Guilt therefore plays a crucial part in ethical decision making. In the decision-making process, guilt normally sets in right after the decision or a choice is made. And because guilt stays with the individual over a period of time, sometimes becoming cumulative, as we pointed out earlier, it may affect that individual's future decisions. Its effects on future decision-making processes center round new values being attached to the premises of the input set to the decision function. A guilty person reexamines his or her value set attached to all premises that come into play in the decision-making process. Sometimes guilt produces doubts about the present values attached to the premises without producing new and better values. Guilt causes decision makers to agonize over decisions. As we noted in Chap. 2, an excess of guilt could cause an individual to withdraw from society, which could be more dangerous because a withdrawn person may start to challenge the values attached to the premises as he or she tries to justify the guilt, resulting in bad decisions being made.

Although decisions are based on the outcome of an individual's deliberations, considering all input parameters and attaching values to these premises calls for a thorough examination of each premise by the individual. This process is aided by the individual reflecting on these basic steps:

- Examining the ethically relevant issues, principles, standards, and practices
- Determining the different parties (and their special interests) who will be affected by the decision
- Deciding on an alternative course of action if and when the outcome of the decision is not what is expected
- Considering the probable consequences (short and long term) of each alternative on each of the different parties involved
- Thinking of consulting with a trusted colleague if the situation is complex, risky, or there is undue personal involvement
- Determining how personal values, biases, beliefs, or self-interests influenced the decision (either positively or negatively) and whether the consequences of the decision have been evaluated
- Being prepared to (1) assume responsibility for the consequences of the action, including correction of negative consequences, if any; (2) reengage in the decision-making process if the ethical issue is not resolved; and (3) evaluate the system(s) within which the issue arose, to identify and remove the circumstances that might facilitate and reward unethical practices

3.5 Professionalism and Ethical Responsibilities

This is the last of our four themes in professionalism and ethics. We focus here on professionalism and ethical responsibilities that include whistle-blowing, harassment, and discrimination.

3.5.1 Whistle-Blowing

The term whistle-blowing gives the impression of an act of seeking public attention. This behavior is what we see in a sports event whenever a foul is committed. The referee blows a whistle to call public attention, including that of the athlete, to the unsportsmanlike act committed. In some countries, law enforcement personnel use whistles to draw public attention to what they deem unlawful acts and to seek help.

The purpose of whistle-blowing in the workplace and the goal of a whistle-blower are the same as in the sports arena: calling to public attention, including and especially to that of a higher authority such as a government, what is considered an illegal or mismanaged act. Whistle-blowing can be internal, in which case the attention is sought internally and remains within organizational channels, or it can be public, in which case it alerts everyone.

Every day people, especially employees, witness wrongdoing on the job. What they witness usually can jeopardize not only their health, safety, or lives but the well-being of others. Quite often many witness such illegal acts but choose to remain silent in the face of such misconduct because they think it is not their responsibility or they believe it will not make a difference. Yet others fear to cause problems on the job. A few brave it out to save lives. However, quite often, instead of receiving praise for their brave actions and high integrity, they are often targeted for retaliatory acts such as investigations, ridicule, blacklisting (especially in their trade), harassment, intimidation, demotion, and sometimes outright dismissal.

So, in light of these threats, the most important aspect of whistle-blowing is to remain anonymous. Revealing the identity of a whistle-blower could be dangerous. Besides the obvious risks of potential job loss and poor or inadequate legal protection, there is also a psychological and sometime emotional price to pay for whistle-blowing. Personal friends and family may turn against you. At work you may be labeled a troublemaker, leading people with whom you work to treat you as an outcast. Thus, care must be taken before whistle-blowing to ensure anonymity. The most difficult decision may involve finding a good medium that will ensure that confidentiality and anonymity. It is difficult and almost impossible to expect total anonymity for a whistle-blower, however, because the need for sufficient information to support allegations may result in revealing one's identifying details.

Different whistle-blowing methods have been used for years, ranging from traditional ones to more modern computer-aided means.

3.5.1.1 Computer-Aided Methods

Most common methods are anonymous, including anonymous remailers who use a software program to strip the header and all other identifying data from an original e-mail before forwarding it to its destination. Because the remailer does not include any return address on the e-mail, it attaches a pseudonymous address in case you need a reply. Before using anonymous remailers, however, exercise caution because the authorities can force the server administrator to reveal the owner of the pseudonymous name and address in cases of emergencies and other coercion.

3.5.1.2 Traditional Methods

A cross section of traditional methods is used in whistle-blowing. Historically, whistle-blowing has used spy-like methods to pass on information to either the public or a higher authority. All methods that ensure anonymity can be used: the most common include face-to-face communication with a public person who will ensure your anonymity; talking with the news media, which can keep your identity a secret; hotlines that alert the caller identity; and writing letters.

Whistle-blowing has been praised by many as courageous actions taken by a few good people with a moral conscience who risk everything to call public attention to illegitimate business practices and illegal and immoral actions. Others have condemned whistle-blowing as acts of vendetta, revenge, and greed that should not be encouraged. In fact, most whistle-blowers are either fired employees or unhappy ones. The following situations can complicate whistle-blowing.

- *Fear of reprisals*: Many illegal and immoral acts go unreported because would-be whistle-blowers fear reprisals such as physical harm, job loss, reassignment to less desirable, sometimes demeaning jobs, suspension from work, and denial of promotions or training. In one survey, John Keenan and Charles Krueger report that this fear is real in potential whistle-blowers. Their survey indicated that not many organizations were willing to protect the whistle-blower. In fact, only one-half of the managers surveyed indicated a willingness to protect a whistle-blower [12].
- *Suspicion surrounding whistle-blowing*: Not every whistle-blower should be taken seriously because not all of them are sincere. Some whistle-blowers are driven by greed, vendettas, anger, or revenge. In fact, many known cases of whistle-blowing were provoked when management and the employee disagreed. In other cases, whistle-blowing is caused by booty promises, especially by governments, to reward anybody with a certain percentage of the proceeds from whistle-blowing. In the United States, for example, private employees can sue any company on behalf of the government under the 1986 amendment to the False Claims Act (see Appendix B available to download from this book's Springer webpage) commonly known as a qui tam action, if that company has any dealings with the federal government. Under this law, a person who discovers fraud against the government can file a civil suit if the government does not take the case. As an incentive to whistle-blowing, any money recovered is shared between the government and the plaintiff, who can receive as much as 30 % of the amount involved in the fraud.
- *Membership in organizational channels*: Sometimes a whistle-blower act may be ignored because the whistle-blower is a member of the company or business organizational channel. Vivian Weil cites two whistle-blowers who are not considered as such because they called public attention to a serious ethical and moral problem but remained within the lines of command and, therefore, were not taken seriously. Both Roger Boisjoly and colleague Allan MacDonald of Morton Thiokol in Utah are known to have opposed the launch of the fated "Challenger" but were overwhelmed by management, and they then blew the whistle in the hearings of the Presidential Commission set by President Ronald Reagan.

Because whistle-blowing can save lives and reduce waste, the U.S. government encourages people who witness illegal acts and government waste to whistle blow. Besides enacting laws such as the False Claims Act that seek to expose fraud in federal contracts, the government also suggests that the would-be whistle-blower observe the following steps [13]:

1. Before taking any irreversible steps, talk to family and close friends about your decision to blow the whistle.
2. Be alert and discreetly attempt to learn of any other witnesses who are upset about the wrongdoing.
3. Before formally breaking ranks, consider whether there is any reasonable way to work within the system by going to the first level of authority. If this is not possible, think carefully about whether you want to "go public" with your concerns or remain an anonymous source. Each strategy has implications: the decision depends on the quantity and quality of your evidence, your ability to camouflage your knowledge of key facts, the risks you are willing to assume, and your willingness to endure intense public scrutiny.
4. Develop a plan, such as the strategically timed release of information to government agencies, so that your employer is reacting to you, instead of vice versa.
5. Maintain good relationships with administration and support staff.
6. Before and after you blow the whistle, keep a careful record of events as they unfold. Try to construct a straightforward, factual log of the relevant activities and events on the job, keeping in mind that your employer will have access to your diary if there is a lawsuit.
7. Identify and copy all necessary supporting records before drawing any suspicion.
8. Break the cycle of isolation, research, and identify and seek a support network of potential allies, such as elected officials, journalists, and activists. The solidarity of key constituencies can be more powerful than the bureaucracy you are challenging.
9. Invest the funds to obtain a legal opinion from a competent lawyer.
10. Always be on guard not to embellish your charges.
11. Engage in whistle-blowing initiatives without using employer resources.
12. Do not wear your cynicism on your sleeve when working with the authorities.

3.5.2 Harassment and Discrimination

Harassment is to verbally or physically create an environment that is hostile, intimidating, offensive, severe, pervasive, or abusive based on a number of parameters including one's race, religion, sex, sexual orientation, national origin, age, disability, political affiliation, marital status, citizenship, or physical appearance. Discrimination, on the other hand, is a process of making decisions that negatively affect an individual, such as denial of a service, based wholly, or partly, upon the real or perceived facts of one's race, religion, sex, sexual orientation, national origin, age, disability, political affiliation, marital status, or physical appearance.

Harassment and discrimination are serious breaches of human rights. In fact, harassment is a form of discrimination. If not attended to, harassment not only affects just a few individuals but eventually grows to affect everyone in the organization. The following steps are needed in fight against harassment and discrimination:

(i) *Awareness*. There are no clear signs of harassment, but in most cases harassment is manifested in the following signs: unhappiness, anxiety, discomfort, stress, and lifestyle changes. If some or all of these signs start to appear in the environment of an individual, then there is harassment. Discrimination is even harder to detect than harassment. However, there is discrimination if the decisions made are based upon the discriminatory factors previously listed.

(ii) *Prevention*. The main tool for the prevention of harassment and discrimination is that an organization has a clear and simply written policy framework setting out the procedures that must be utilized if harassment and discrimination occur. The procedures must include awareness/education, the complaint process, sanctions, and redress.

3.5.3 Ethical and Moral Implications

The act of whistle-blowing is meant to alert and call the public to be witnesses to illegal acts that may be hazardous to their health and well-being or that may waste public resources. Of course, as we pointed out earlier, there are many other reasons for whistle-blowing. Are whistle-blowers living saints who fight evil to bring serious problems to light, thus contributing to the protection of the public's welfare? Does this explain the small numbers of whistle-blowers, although it is known that there are organizations in which a high potential for catastrophe can develop and somehow remain unexposed despite many people being aware of the problems?

Even people with high moral standards can be prevented from doing what is morally right because of the privileges, rights, and freedoms they stand to lose within the organization if they become known. People who feel accused and those allied to them tend to hit back to deflect attention from the accused. Retaliation is very damaging. So a would-be whistle-blower either decides to stay in line and live with a moral dilemma, but survive, or resign and live with a clear conscience. For a professional, a decision such as this presents a complex moral conundrum because if he or she stays within the organization, retaliation is almost predictable. Staying with the organization also presents other problems to both whistle-blower and colleagues. For example, collegial relationships and networks are disrupted. However, whistle-blowing is morally justifiable when the activities involved pose serious danger and harm to human life. The moral concept of whistle-blowing is good; it helps those who dare not speak out and all others who are affected.

Harassment and discrimination are both evil acts that not only challenge the conscience of an individual doing the acts but also create a situation that brings discomfort and inferiority to the targeted individual. It is, however, unfortunate that most individuals perpetuating the acts of discrimination and harassment lack the moral conviction and conscience.

Exercises

1. Define professionalism and list three elements of professionalism.
2. Why are the following concepts important for professionalism? Justify your answers.
   - Commitment
   - Integrity
   - Responsibility
   - Accountability
3. Discuss the merits of licensing software professionals.
4. Give an example of a decision that involves the examination of all four categories of codes.
5. Why is whistle-blowing so controversial? What are its pros and cons?
6. Why are harassment and discrimination so difficult to detect?
7. Is computer technology negatively or positively affecting harassment and discrimination?
8. Discuss the effects of whistle-blowing on a whistle-blower.
9. Study and discuss the False Claims Act.
10. Has the False Claims Act been successful?
11. Why is ethical decision making like software engineering?
12. Are whistle-blowers saints or blackmailers?
13. Why is it so difficult to make an ethical decision in today's technologically driven society?
14. What role does guilt play in professional decision making? Why it is so important?
15. Does every valid ethical argument involve a set of layers of arguments?
16. Suggest a more fitting role for licensing authorities.

References

1. Government Accountability Project's handbook for whistleblowers, the whistleblower's survival guide: courage without martyrdom. http://www.whistleblower.org/www/Tips.htm
2. Gillam C. Eli Lilly Sued in Missouri cancer drug case. YahooNews. Reuters. http://dailynews.yahoo.com/h/nm/20010827/sc/crime_cancer_dc_2.html
3. Webster's dictionary
4. Sizer R (1996) A brief history of professionalism and its relevance to IFIP. In: Berleur J, Brunnstein K (eds) Ethics of computing: codes, spaces for discussion and law. Chapman & Hall, London
5. Kizza JM (1996) Professionalism, ethical responsibility, and accountability. In: Kizza JM (ed) Social and ethical effects of the computer revolution. McFarland, Jefferson
6. Humphreys WS (1987) Managing for innovation: leading technical people. Prentice Hall, Englewood Cliffs
7. The minister answers questions on accountability framework. http://ednet.edc.gov.ab.ca/level1/news/in-focus/accountability.html
8. References: California Community Colleges (6870) http://www.lao.ca.gov/chf6870.html

9. McMahan M (1997) Hearing set for school computer hackers. Chattanooga Free Press, 22 March 1997, sect. C1
10. References: for codes of ethics. http://rehab.educ.ucalgary.ca/lowser/edps581/references.html
11. Kizza JM (1996) The role of professional organizations in promoting computer ethics. In: Kizza JM (ed) Social and ethical effects of the computer revolution. McFarland, Jefferson
12. The Canadian Code of Ethics for Psychologists (1991) http://www.cycor.ca/Psych/pub.html; http://www.cycor.ca/Psych/ethics.html
13. Weil V. Whistle-blowing: what have we learned since the Challenger? http://www.nspe.org/eh1.html

Further Reading

Johansson C, Ohlsson L. An attempt to teach professionalism in Engineering education. http://www.hk-r.se/bib/rapport/2–93.html
Thomas JW. Integrity as professionalism: ethics and leadership in practice. http://www.fs.fed.us/intro/speech/jwt_saf.htm

Anonymity, Security, Privacy, and Civil Liberties

4

Learning Objectives

After reading this chapter, the reader should be able to

1. Summarize the legal bases for the right to privacy and freedom of expression.
2. Analyze stated security procedures for "weak points" that an attacker could exploit and explain how they could (or will) fail.
3. Propose appropriate security measures for different situations.
4. Describe current computer-based threats to privacy.
5. Explain how the Internet may change the historical balance in protecting freedom of expression.
6. Describe trends in privacy protection as exemplified in technology.

Scenario 3: Did You Say Privacy? What Privacy?

Surveillance technology has progressed to the point that it is possible to identify individuals walking city streets from satellites in orbit. Telephone, fax, and e-mail communications can routinely be monitored. Personal information files are maintained on citizens from cradle to grave. There is nowhere to run … nowhere to hide. Personal privacy is dead.

24/7 OF THE (UN)KNOWN CITIZEN

W.H. Auden (1907–1973) notes in his poem "The Unknown Citizen" that his unknown citizen was a "modern man" for "he was fully insured, and his Health-card shows he was once in hospital but he left cured. Both Producers Research and High-Grade Living declare he was fully sensible

(continued)

© Springer International Publishing Switzerland 2016
J.M. Kizza, *Ethics in Computing*, Undergraduate Topics in Computer Science,
DOI 10.1007/978-3-319-29106-2_4

Scenario 3: (continued)

to the advantages of the installment plan, and he had everything necessary to the Modern Man, A phonograph, a radio, a car, and a Frigidaire" [1]. *Our citizen is definitely a modern man, more so than the archaic Auden's, for he owns all modern life's amenities, plus a company car, a cellular phone, and a reserved parking spot. He is computer savvy, with a computer in his office and at home. The normal day of our citizen starts at 6 a.m. when he is awakened by soft music from a radio. The radio reports that futures are up, indicating higher stock price opening. He jumps out of bed and switches on his computer to put in a "buy" order for a stock he has been meaning to buy.*

Snapshot #1: *Tempest*

Several yards outside his private home, someone with a Tempest (a criminal, government agent, private investigator) is recording all that our citizen is doing. The information our man has used on the computer has been recorded by the Tempest.

HEADLINER # 1: "PRIVACY LOST: THE DEMISE OF PRIVACY IN AMERICA" [2]

As our citizen pulls out of the garage, he notices that he is low on gas, so he pulls up at the nearest Conoco gas station. Being a modern man as he is, he decides to pay at the pump.

Snapshot #2: *The transaction record is entered into a Conoco database and, of course, Visa database.*

Without worry he pulls away, speeding to work.

HEADLINER #2: "SPYING ON EMPLOYEES: BIG BROTHER HAS HIS EYE ON YOU … SNOOPING SISTER IS SUPERVISING YOU" [3]

Snapshot #3: *"Wherenet Tracking Knows Where You Are at Every Moment"*

Just before 8 a.m., he arrives at his workplace, pulling into his reserved parking spot. He enters the lot with an electronic key.

Snapshot #4: *Company network and surveillance cameras start their full day of recording his activities. At 8:02 a.m. he settles into his office. He starts the day's activities with several e-mails to read and a few calls to return.*

HEADLINER # 3: "SNOOPING BILL TO BECOME LAW BY NOVEMBER" [4]

Snapshot #5: *Echelon*

At 12:01 p.m. he receives a call from the company representative in Greece to discuss the new company marketing strategy he proposed last month.

(continued)

Scenario 3: (continued)

At 3:15 p.m. he heads to his doctor's appointment. He has been complaining of knee pains. His doctor orders for a few tests. They are done quickly, the labs taking as much detail from him as possible and his doctor updating his medical record. His insurance will pay for part of the visit. So the insurance is billed and his other medical record is updated. He pays by check. His other financial record is updated.

As he leaves his doctor's office at 4:30 p.m., he decides to call it a day and head home. He calls his office to inform his secretary that he is heading home!

Snapshot #6. *"Big Brother in the Flesh: New Technology Could Make Us All a Part of the Collective, Permanently Supervised from Above"* [5] *On the way home, he remembers that he needs a few groceries. So he heads to Kroger's. At the grocery store, he picks up a few things and he is picked up.*

Snapshot #7: *Kroger's Surveillance Cameras. At the checkout counter, he gives in a dollar coupon for the chicken soup and he also hands in a Kroger's card to save 75 cents off chili on the week's special for Kroger's most valuable customers.*

Snapshot #8: *Kroger's database records the day's transaction. To receive the card, the citizen provided Kroger with his home address, income, family size, and age.*

Snapshot #9: *Celeria*

At 5 p.m. he leaves Kroger's and heads home. But on the way home, he receives a call from his girlfriend on his private cellular phone inviting him for dinner at her place.

At 5:30 p.m. he turns into his private driveway only to notice spilt garbage. He wonders whether the city garbage collectors did it. He puts the car in the garage and comes back to clean the driveway. The neighbor informs him that he noticed two guys going through his garbage, and they later drove away.

HEADLINER #4: "FORGET THE FIREWALL: GUARD YOUR GARBAGE AGAINST 'DUMPSTER-DIVING' HACKERS" [6]

After cleaning the driveway, he checks his snail mail. He notices that they are all bills!

HEADLINER #5: "WHO IS READING YOUR BILLS" [7]

At 6 p.m. before he leaves for his girlfriend's house, the citizen decides to check his e-mail and complete some correspondence.

(continued)

Scenario 3: (continued)
Snapshot #10: *Carnivore*
At 7 p.m. he leaves for his girlfriend's house. He might spend the night there!
The girlfriend is also modern and lives in a "Digital Home."

HEADLINER # 6: "LATEST SURVEILLANCE LEAVES NOTHING
TO CHANCE: EXPLORING THE DARK SIDE OF THE DIGITAL
HOME" [8]
Next morning, he will drive the company car to work! What else do we need
to know? Is he happy? That is absurd. As Auden would put it: Had he been
unhappy, we would have known!

Discussion Questions

1. Where do we go from here?
    *   *Legislation*
    *   *Regulation*
    *   *Self-help*
2. *Do they work?*
3. *Do you believe we still have individual privacy?*
4. *What do you think is the best way to safeguard privacy?*
5. *How much interference by government in your life can you tolerate to feel*
    secure?
6. *How much privacy are you willing to give up to feel secure?*

4.1   Introduction

Social, economic, and technological advances have dramatically increased the
amount of information any individual possesses. Increasing demand for information
and easier access to it have also created challenges. We have come to learn that
information is a treasure in itself: the more you have, the better. Having valuable
intellectual, economic, and social information creates enormous opportunities and
advantages for an individual because information has become a vital resource in this
information age.

Even though information is a treasure, it can also be a liability; for example, we
are constantly seeking ways to acquire, keep, and dispose of it. We want to make
sure that what is seen and heard privately does not become public without our
consent.

In our technologically advanced society, a number of factors have contributed to
the high demand for information and the subsequent need for anonymity, security,

privacy, and the safeguard of our civil liberties. Among the main contributing factors are the following:

- High digitalization of information and increasing bandwidth
- Declining costs of digital communication
- Increased miniaturization of mobile computing devices and other communications equipment
- Greater public awareness by the news media of the potential abuse of digital communication, especially the Internet

4.2 Anonymity

The Greeks used the word $\alpha\nu\omega\nu\nu\mu\acute{\iota}\alpha$ to describe the state of being nameless. Anonymity is being nameless, having no identity. Because it is extremely difficult for anybody to live a meaningful life while being totally anonymous, people usually use some type of anonymity. Consider these several types:

- *Pseudo-identity*: An individual is identified by a certain pseudonym, code, or number (compare with a writer's pen name): this is referred to as pseudo-anonymity. It is used frequently in the "Witness Protection" program. This is the most common variant of anonymity.
- *Untraceable identity*: One is not known by any name including pseudo-names.
- *Anonymity with a pseudo-address to receive and send correspondence with others*: This technique is popular with people using anonymous remailers, user groups, and news groups [1]

4.2.1 Anonymity and the Internet

The nature of the Internet, with its lack of political, cultural, religious, and judicial boundaries, has created a fertile ground for all faceless people to come out in the open. In particular, the Internet provides two channels through which anonymous acts can be carried out.

1. *Anonymous servers*: With advances in software and hardware, anonymity on the Internet has grown through anonymous servers. There are two types of anonymity servers:
   (a) Full anonymity servers, where no identifying information is forwarded in packet headers.
   (b) Pseudonymous servers, which put pseudonym in forwarded packet headers, keeping the real identity behind a pseudonym, but being able to receive and forward all packets sent to the pseudonym to the real server.

Anonymity servers are able to accomplish this through the use of encryption. We are not going to discuss further how this encryption is done.

2. *Anonymous users*: Another Internet channel to assure anonymity is for users to assume pseudonyms and use Internet services such as bulletin boards, chat rooms, and social online networks anonymously. Sensitive and sometimes highly personal or classified information has been posted to popular user groups, news groups, and chat rooms. Anonymity of postings is also assured through the use of data transmission protocols such as Simple Mail Transfer Protocol (SMTP) and Network News Transfer Protocol (NNTP), which accept messages to servers with arbitrary field information [1].

As we discuss anonymity on the Internet, we need to point out that neither anonymity or pseudonymity is 100 % anonymous. As anybody with a rudimentary knowledge of computing networking would know, there is always a possibility to find those who misuse the Internet this way.

4.2.2   Advantages and Disadvantages of Anonymity

There are several advantages and disadvantages to anonymity. We consider some of these here, starting with advantages.

- Anonymity is good when a whistle-blower uses it to check unhealthy activities within the organization. Although whistle-blowers are controversial, they are good in a number of cases, especially when there is abuse of the office and resources. We discussed whistle-blowing in Chap. 3.
- Anonymity is good in case of national security so that underground spies can gather information that is good for national defense.
- Where there is intimidation and fear of reprisals, anonymity is good because useful information may be revealed.
- Anonymity is good for some relationships and the security of some people.

   There are also disadvantages to anonymity.

- Criminals and embezzlers can use it to their advantage, especially in online social networks.
- Many disputes could be solved if information from individuals who are party to these disputes can reveal the necessary information.

4.2.3   Legal View of Anonymity

As we have pointed out in the last section, anonymity has its good and bad sides. More important, society may not be safe if many criminals use anonymity to hide their criminal activities. Anonymity can also bring suffering in social relationships in society. So, in a number of cases, it is necessary for either a local authority or national legislatures to pass laws that regulate when and who can use anonymity legally. In the current environment of the Internet, there are serious debates on the freedoms of individuals on the Internet and how these freedoms can be protected in the onslaught of people under anonymity in cyberspace.

> **Discussion Issues**
>
> 1. List and discuss roles in society that require one to be anonymous and if this is beneficial to society.
> 2. Discuss the major disadvantages of anonymity, especially in cyberspace.

4.3 Security

In general, security can be considered a means to prevent unauthorized access, use, alteration, and theft or physical damage to property. Security involves these three elements:

1. *Confidentiality*: To prevent unauthorized disclosure of information to third parties. This is important in a number of areas including the disclosure of personal information such as medical, financial, academic, and criminal records.
2. *Integrity*: To prevent unauthorized modification of files and maintain the status quo. It includes system, information, and personnel integrity. The alteration of information may be caused by a desire for personal gain or a need for revenge.
3. *Availability*: To prevent unauthorized withholding of information from those who need it when they need it. We discuss two types of security: physical security, which involves the prevention of access to physical facilitates such as computer systems, and information security, which involves prevention of access to information by encryption, authentication, and other means.

4.3.1 Physical Security

A facility is physically secure if it is surrounded by a barrier such as a fence, has secure areas both inside and outside the facility, and can resist penetration by intruders. Physical security can be guaranteed if the following four mechanisms are in place: deterrence, prevention, detection, and response [2].

1. *Deterrence* is used to defend systems against intruders who may try to gain access. It works by creating an atmosphere intended to scare intruders.
2. *Prevention* is used in mechanisms that work by trying to stop intruders from gaining access.

3. *Detection* should be the third line of defense. This mechanism assumes the intruder has succeeded or is in the process of gaining access to the system, so it tries to "see" that intruder who has gained or who is trying to gain access.
4. *Response* is an aftereffect mechanism that tries to respond to the failure of the first three mechanisms. It works by trying to stop or prevent damage or access to a facility.

4.3.2 Physical Access Controls

To ensure physical security, a regimen of access controls must be put in place. In physical access control, we create both physical barriers and electronic protocols that will authenticate the user of the resource whose security we are safeguarding.

4.3.2.1 Physical Security Barriers

The physical barrier can be a fence made of barbed wire, brick walls, natural trees, mounted noise or vibration sensors, security lighting, closed-circuit television (CCTV), buried seismic sensors, or different photoelectric and microwave systems [2]. The area surrounding the facility can be secured using locks and keys, window breakage detectors, infrared and ultrasonic detectors, interior microwave systems, animal such as dogs, and human barriers such as security guards.

4.3.2.2 Electronic Access Controls

With advances in technology, we are moving away, although not totally, from the physical barriers to more invasive electronic controls that include card access control systems, firewalls, and the third, and probably the most important area, the inside, may be secured using electronic barriers such as firewalls and passwords.

Passwords

A password is a string of usually six or more characters to verify a user to an information system facility, usually digital systems. Password security greatly depends on the password owner observing all these four "never" cardinal rules:

1. Never publicize a password.
2. Never write a password down anywhere.
3. Never choose a password that is easy to guess.
4. Never keep the same password for an extended period of time.

Password security is not only important to individuals whose files are stored on a system, it is also vital to the system as a whole, because once an intruder gains access to one password, he or she has gained access to the whole system, making all its files vulnerable. Thus, system security is the responsibility of every individual user of the system.

Firewalls

A firewall is hardware or software used to isolate the sensitive portions of an information system facility from the outside world and limit the potential damage that can be done by a malicious intruder. Although there is no standardization in the structure of firewalls, the choice of firewalls depends on the system manager's anticipated threat to the system. Most firewalls are variations of the following three models [3]:

- *Packet filters:* Packet-level filters contain gates that allow packets to pass through if they satisfy a minimum set of conditions, and choke or prevent those packets that do not meet the entry conditions. The minimum conditions may include packets to have permissible origin or destination addresses, as determined by the network administrator. The filter firewalls can also configure and block packets with specific TCP or UDP packet port numbers, or filter based on IP protocol types. As we see later, packet filters have a weakness in that they cannot stop or filter a packet with malicious intent if the packet contains the permissible attributes.
- *Proxy servers:* These servers work on the protected portions of the network that usually provide information to outside users requesting access to those portions. That is, the firewall protects client computers from direct access to the Internet. Clients direct their requests for an Internet connection through the proxy server. If individual client requests conform to the preset conditions, then the firewall will act on the request; otherwise, it is dropped. These firewalls require specialized client and server configurations depending on the application.
- *Stateful inspection:* These firewalls combine both the filter and proxy functions. Because of this, it is considered complex and more advanced. The conditions for a stateful inspection are, as the filter, based on a set of rules. In contrast to filters, these rules are not based on TCP or UDP but on applications as are proxy servers. They filter packets by comparing their data with archived friendly packets.

4.3.3 Information Security Controls

Information security includes the integrity, confidentiality, and availability of information at the servers, including information in files and databases and in transition between servers, and between clients and servers. The security of information can be ensured in a number of ways. The most common are cryptography for information transmission and authentication and audit trails at the information source and information destination servers. Cryptography, the science of writing and reading coded messages, forms the basis for all secure transmission, through three functions: symmetrical and asymmetrical encryption, and hash functions.

4.3.3.1 Encryption

Encryption is a method that protects the communications channel from sniffers, programs written for and installed on the communication channels to eavesdrop on network traffic, examining all traffic on selected network segments. Sniffers are easy to write and install and difficult to detect. Cryptography uses an encryption algorithm and key to transform data at the source, called plaintext, turn it into an encrypted form called ciphertext, usually an unintelligible form, and finally recover it at the sink. The encryption algorithm can either be symmetrical or asymmetrical.

Symmetrical encryption, or secret key encryption as it is usually called, uses a common key and the same cryptographic algorithm to scramble and unscramble the message as shown in Fig. 4.1. The security of the transmitted data depends on the fact that eavesdroppers with no knowledge of the key are unable to read the message. One problem with symmetrical encryption is the security of the keys, which must be passed from the sender to the receiver.

Asymmetrical encryption, commonly known as public key encryption, uses two different keys, a public key known by all and a private key known by only the sender and the receiver. The sender and the receiver each has a pair of these keys, one public and one private. To encrypt a message from sender A to receiver B (Fig. 4.2), both A and B must create their own pairs of keys. Then A and B exchange their public keys: anybody can acquire them. When A is to send a message M to B, A uses B's public key to encrypt M. On receipt of M, B then uses his or her private key to decrypt the message M.

A *hash function* takes an input message M and creates a code from it. The code commonly referred to as a *hash* or a *message digest*, is discussed more in the next section. A one-way hash function is used to create a digital signature of the message, just like a human fingerprint. The hash function is therefore used to provide the message's integrity and authenticity.

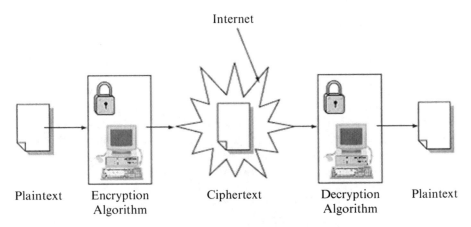

Plaintext	Encryption Algorithm	Ciphertext	Decryption Algorithm	Plaintext

Fig. 4.1 Symmetrical encryption

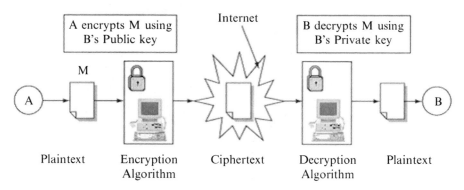

Fig. 4.2 Asymmetric encryption

4.3.3.2 Authentication

Usually it is difficult for a system to verify the identity of a user, especially a remote user. Thus, authentication is a process whereby the system gathers and builds up information about the user to assure that the user is genuine. In data communication, authentication is also used to ensure the digital message recipient of the identity of the sender and the integrity of the message. In computer systems, authentication protocols based on cryptography use either secret-key or public-key schemes to create an encrypted message digest that is appended to a document as a digital signature.

The digital signature is similar to a handwritten signature in printed documents. Similar to handwritten signatures, digital signatures ensure that the person whose signature the system is authenticating is indeed the true person, but digital signatures provide a greater degree of security than handwritten signatures. Also, digital signatures once submitted can never be disowned by the signer of a document claiming the signature was forged: this is called non-repudiation. A secure digital signature system consists of two parts: (1) a method of signing a document, and (2) authentication that the signature was actually generated by whomever it represents.

The process of signing the document, that is, creating a digital signature, involves a sender A passing the original message M into a hash function H to produce a message digest. Then, A encrypts M together with the message digest using either symmetrical or asymmetrical encryption, and then sends the combination to B. Upon receipt of the package, B separates the digital signature from the encrypted message. The message M is put into a one-way hash to produce a message digest, and B compares the output of the hash function with the message digest A sent. If they match, then the integrity of the message M together with the signature of the sender are both valid (see Fig. 4.3).

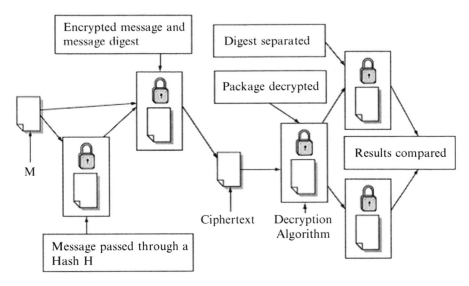

Fig. 4.3 Digital signature and authentication

Physical Authentication Methods. Authentication of users or user surrogates is usually based on checking one or more of the following user items [4]:

- *User name* (sometimes *screen name*).
- *Password.*
- *Retinal images*: The user looks into an electronic device that maps his or her retinal image: the system then compares this map with a similar map stored on the system.
- *Fingerprints*: The user presses on or sometimes inserts a particular finger into a device that makes a copy of the user fingerprint and then compares it with a similar image on the system user file.
- *Physical location*: The physical location of the system initiating an entry request is checked to ensure that a request is actually originating from a known and authorized client machine. To check the authenticity of such a client, the network or Internet Protocol (IP) address of the client machine is compared with the one on the system user file. This method is used mostly in addition to other security measures because it alone cannot guarantee security: if used alone, it provides access to the requested system to anybody who has access to the client machine.
- *Identity cards*: Increasingly, cards are being used as authenticating documents. Whoever is the carrier of the card gains access to the requested system. As is the case with physical location authentication, card authentication is usually used as a second-level authentication tool because whoever has access to the card automatically can gain access to the requested system.

4.3.4   Operational Security

Operation security involves policies and guidelines that organizations, including all employees, must use to safeguard the assets of the organization, including its workers. These policy guidelines are spelt out in a document we call a security policy. It also includes guidelines for security recovery and response in case of a security incident.

4.4   Privacy

4.4.1   Definition

According to Jerry Durlak [5], privacy is a human value consisting of four elements he calls rights. We put these rights into two categories. The first category includes three rights that an individual can use to fence off personal information seekers; the second category contains those rights an individual can use to control the amount and value of personal information given out.

1. Control of external influences:
   * *Solitude*: The right to be alone without disturbances
   * *Anonymity*: The right to have no public personal identity
   * *Intimacy*: The right not to be monitored
2. Control of personal information:
   * *Reserve*: The right to control one's personal information including the methods of dissemination of that information.

The notion of privacy is difficult to accurately define because the definition of privacy depends on matters such as culture, geographic location, political systems, and religious beliefs.

4.4.2   Types of Privacy

Although there are varied definitions of privacy, the several types of privacy we discuss here are not influenced by the factors we have outlined in the previous section.

4.4.2.1 Personal Privacy
This type of privacy involves the privacy of personal attributes. The right to privacy of all personal attributes would mean the prevention of anyone or anything that would intrude or violate that personal space where those attributes are: this would include all types of intrusions including physical searches, video recording, and surveillance of any type. In a number of countries, there are statutes and acts similar

to the U.S. Fourth Amendment, which guarantees the right of the people to be secure in their persons, houses, papers, and effects, against unreasonable searches and seizures.

> **Discussion issue**
>
> Discuss a few of these statutes and acts.

4.4.2.2 Informational Privacy

In the previous section, we discussed the privacy of an individual meaning that we want to ensure the privacy of an individual by preventing any intrusions through physical and electronic access to that individual's attributes. Informational privacy, in contrast to personal privacy, concerns the protection of unauthorized access to information itself. Of course, there are different strands of information that we have to protect, including the following:

- *Personal information*: Most personal information of value includes information on personal lifestyles such as religion, sexual orientation, political affiliations, or personal activities.
- *Financial information*: Financial information is important not only to individuals but also to organizations. Financial information is a very valued asset because it gives the organization the autonomy it needs to compete in the marketplace.
- *Medical information*: Medical information is very personal and very important to all of us. For personal, employment, and insurance purposes, many people want their medical information to be private.
- *Internet*: In this new age, the Internet keeps track of all our activities online. With an increasing number of people spending an increasing number of time online in social networks and the digital convergence becoming a reality with every passing day, not only will our social life be online but soon all our lives will be also. We want those activities and habits private.

4.4.2.3 Institutional Privacy

Institutions and organizations want their data private not only for business advantages but also for the life of the business. The research data, the sales and product data, the marketing strategies, and the activities of the organization all need to be private.

4.4.3 Value of Privacy

Privacy has traditionally been perceived as valuable and has even gained more importance in the information age because it guards an individual's personal identity, preserves individual autonomy, and makes social relationships possible.

However, these days in the information age, the value of privacy has been eroded. We can no longer guarantee our privacy. It has left many wondering whether there is such a thing as privacy any more. As the scenario at the start of this chapter demonstrates, no one has guaranteed privacy any more unless such an individual is no longer part of the society. From the telephone calls you make that identify you through caller ID, to every transaction you pay for either by credit card or by check, and to the multitude of forms you fill out from getting your pet groomed to having a prescription filled, you are identifiable and you have nowhere to hide. The most abused number, the Social Security number, is used as a personal ID by many companies, including health insurance companies, that use it as a customer ID in spite of the repeated warning from the federal government not to do so. In its effort to help stop the erosion of individual privacy, the U.S. Congress passed the Gramm–Leach–Bliley Financial Services Modernization Act of 1999, but put in reverse conditions, the so-called opt-out discussed in Sect. 4.4.3.1, that make the Act useless.

We consider three attributes of privacy: personal identity, autonomy, and social relationships.

4.4.3.1 Personal Identity

As information becomes more precious, it becomes more important for individuals to safeguard personal identity. Personal identity is valuable because it enshrines personal privacy. Unfortunately, with rapid advances in technology, especially computer technology, it has become increasingly difficult to protect personal identity.

4.4.3.2 Autonomy

Humans need to feel that they are in control of their own destiny. They need their autonomy. The less personal information other people have about an individual, the more autonomous that individual can be, especially in decision making. However, other people will challenge one's autonomy depending on the quantity, quality, and value of information they have about that individual. People usually tend to establish relationships and associations with individuals and groups that will respect their personal autonomy, especially in decision making.

4.4.3.3 Social Relationships

In some societies where marriages are arranged, parents on both sides try to collect as much information about each other as possible before they commit their offspring in marriage. In societies where there are no arranged marriages, the parties involved usually spend a period of time dating. The dating time is spent collecting as much information as possible about each other. The couple then uses this information to make a decision about marrying. However, each party may try to conceal some information because some seemingly valuable information may not be worthwhile and may even lead to the breakup of the relationship.

4.4.4   Privacy Implications of the Database System

4.4.4.1 Information Gathering

Have you paid enough attention to the number of junk mails, telephone calls during dinner, and junk e-mails you have been getting? If so, you may have thought about who has your name on a list and what they are doing with it. In recent years, tele-marketers have been having a field day as technological advances have replaced the door-to-door salesman. Many companies you have done business with may have sold or shared your personal information to other companies, and tracing the source may be difficult. In many cases, we do not preserve our privacy as we defined privacy earlier. We have helped information seekers, such as companies, in gathering and databasing information from us. We do this every time we apply for discount cards from grocery stores, gas stations, and merchandise stores, and every time we fill out information on little cards to enter contests, and every time we give out our Social Security number and telephone numbers to store clerks in department stores. The information they collect from us is put into databases and is later sold to the highest bidder, usually a marketer.

Information gathering is a very serious business that is increasingly involving a growing number of players which traditionally were governments gathering mostly defensive information on weapon systems. However, with globalization and the Internet, the doors to the information-gathering field have been thrown open. Now individuals, companies and organizations, and of course governments, are all competing, sometimes for the same information.

The tools of the trade have also improved tremendously, becoming more stealthy, much smaller, and of course more accurate. With the modern tools of gathering information, no one is safe anymore. Because of our habits online, Internet crawlers are in action visiting our machines stealthily and gathering a wealth of information. There is no longer the need to get your information from the cards you fill out at shopping malls and grocery stores. There are better and faster ways now. There are tremendous legal and privacy issues that we have to confront. First, most of the information collected from us, that we come to know about, which is a fraction of what they take, is collected without our consent.

Although the problem is skyrocketing, there is minimum effort to curtail the practice. This is a result of a number of reasons, the most important of which is that the rate at which technology is developing is continuously outstripping our legal systems and our ability to legislate, late alone enforce, the new laws. Several attempts have been made, including the Gramm–Leach–Bliley Financial Services Modernization Act, aimed at restricting financial institutions such as banks and brokerages from sharing customers' personal information with third parties.

Although the Financial Services Modernization Act has given financial institutions an information bonanza, the Act also tries in some ways to protect the customer through three requirements that the institutions must disclose to us:

(i) *Privacy Policy*: Through this, the institution is bound to tell us the types of information the institution collects and has about us and how it uses that information

(ii) *Right to Opt-Out*: Through this, the institution is bound to explain our recourse to prevent the transfer of our data to third-party beneficiaries
(iii) *Safeguards*: Through such, the institution must put in place policies to prevent fraudulent access to confidential financial information

However, this same law, as many of its kind, has allowed these same U.S. financial institutions to merge and form what have been called financial supermarkets. This one Act has opened a door for these companies to merge and consolidate customer data from several sources.

4.4.5 Privacy Violations and Legal Implications

Privacy, as we have defined it, is a basic human value that is at the core of human dignity and autonomy. Because of this recognition, many major and historical documents such as the Fourth Amendment to the U.S. Constitution, the UN Universal Declaration of Human Rights, the Council of Europe, and many national and multinational treaties contain enshrined clauses of the individual's right to privacy. It is believed that privacy forms the foundation of a free and democratic society.

However, this fundamental right is violated every day in many ways. Although individual privacy rights have been violated for years, the advent of the Internet has accelerated the rate and scale of violations. There are numerous contributing factors or causes of violations. Let us look at some here:

(i) Consumers willingly give up information about themselves when they register at websites, at shopping malls to win prizes, and in mailing solicitations.
(ii) Consumers lack the knowledge of how what they consider a little bit of information can turn into a big invasion of privacy.
(iii) Inadequate privacy policies.
(iv) Failure of companies and institutions to follow their own privacy policies.
(v) Internet temptation, as discussed in Sect. 3.5.1.2, that enables businesses to reach individuals in a very short time in the 'privacy' of their homes and offices.

Because of the Internet's ability to reach many people with ease, major privacy violators have been online companies such as DoubleClick, an Internet advertising company. DoubleClick used its dominant position on the Internet to reach as many people as possible. With this opportunity, DoubleClick quietly abandoned its original policy of providing only anonymous data collected from its Internet users to marketers and started combining its online user profiles with information from direct mailers and others. The combined information could easily be used to identify the Internet users as DoubleClick's tracking could now reveal names, addresses, and purchasing habits.

After massive user protests, the threat of lawsuits, and notices from the U.S. Federal Trade Commission (FTC), DoubleClick gave up on their intended plan, putting the proposal on hold and claiming that they would seek user permission before launching the matching data plan [6]. Yahoo!, Inc, another Internet company, was sued by Universal Image, Inc., a company that makes educational videos. Universal sued Yahoo! for not living up to a contract to provide data, including customer e-mail information that Universal had signed with Broadcast.com, Inc., before Yahoo acquired it [10].

Because of the anticipated growth of the Internet, there is widespread agreement that privacy rights are under serious attack and that something has to be done. The measures that are needed to protect both the user and consumer need to be varied to include legislation like the U.S. Consumer Protection Act, enforcement, and self-help.

Other privacy violations include intrusion, misuse of information, interception of information, and information matching.

4.4.5.1 Intrusion

Intrusion is an invasion of privacy by wrongful entry, seizing, or acquiring possession of the property of others. For example, hackers are intruders because they wrongfully break into computer systems whether they cause damage or not. With computer network globalization, intrusion is only second to viruses among computer crimes, and it is growing fast.

4.4.5.2 Misuse of Information

Human beings continually give out information in exchange for services. Businesses and governments collect this information from us honestly to provide services effectively. The information collected, as discussed in Sect. 5.4.3, is not just collected only to be stored. This information is digital gold to these companies. They mine the gold from us and sell it to the highest bidder. There is nothing wrong with collecting personal information when it is going to be used for a legitimate reason, for the purpose for which it was intended. However, the problem arises when this information is used for unauthorized purposes; collecting this information then becomes an invasion of privacy.

4.4.5.3 Interception of Information

Interception of information is unauthorized access to private information via eavesdropping, which occurs when a third party gains unauthorized access to a private communication between two or more parties. Information can be gathered by eavesdropping in the following areas:

- At the source and sink of information, where either client or server intrusion software can listen in, collect information, and send it back to the sender
- Between communication channels by tapping into the communication channels and then listening in

4.4.5.4 Information Matching

The threat of information matching can best be highlighted by an old story recounted by Richard O. Mason [7], who says it has been retold so many times that its accuracy is probably in doubt; however, its message remains the same.

Here is the story:

A couple of programmers at the City of Chicago's computer center began matching tape files from many of the city's different data processing applications on name and I.D. They discovered, for example, that several high-paid city employers had unpaid parking fines. Bolstered by this revelation they pressed on. Soon they uncovered the names of several employees who were still listed on the register but who had not paid a variety of fees, a few of whom appeared in the files of the alcoholic and drug abuse program. When this finding was leaked to the public, the city employees, of course, were furious. They demanded to know who had authorized the investigation. The answer was that no one knew. Later, city officials established rules for the computer center to prevent this form of invasion of privacy from happening again [7].

The danger with information matching is that there is no limit to what one can do with the collected information, and no one knows what the profiles built from the matched information will be used for and by whom. Hundreds, maybe thousands, of databases with individual records are gathered from an individual over a lifetime. Can you recall how many forms you have filled in since you were a child? They may be in the thousands. Each one of these forms contains a set of questions asking for specific information about you. Each time an individual gives a certain answer to any one of these questions, the answer is used to establish a link with hundreds of other databases [7]. Hundreds, perhaps thousands, of databases have personal Social Security numbers. Such databases include driver's records, vital statistics, Social Security administration, medical records, schools, work, and public local, county, state, and federal databases. With the Social Security number as the search key, all these databases can very easily be linked together. In addition to these two links, many other keys can be used as links between databases.

The threat to information matching does not originate only from linking individual records in different databases: it also can come from erroneous or outdated (stale) information. Errors can enter information in basically three areas: (i) at the source, where it occurs mainly through incorrect input such as typing the letter "l" of the alphabet instead of the numeral "1" (one); (ii) during transmission because of transmission interference; and (iii) at the sink, mainly as a result of poor reception. Information becomes stale when it becomes outdated. Unfortunately, erroneous and stale information is frequently used. For example, in the U.S. alone, according to Mason, more than 60,000 local and state agencies by 1986 had routinely provided data to the National Crime Information Center, where on a daily basis close to 400,000 requests were made to the center from law enforcement agents across the country. However, studies showed that the data were in error 4–6% of the time [7]. Thus, an equal number of requests from law enforcement agents were filled with false information, probably placing many innocent individuals in awkward situations. Another example, which may not involve crime information, would be erroneous information collected by a credit reporting agency and used in approving such services as loans, mortgages, and credit cards. If stale information is used, there is a danger that an individual could be denied credit unfairly, and it is widely known how difficult it is to remove that stale information from an individual's credit record.

4.4.6 Privacy Protection and Civil Liberties

Perhaps there is no one agreed-upon set of civil liberties. Many rights scholars have different sets of rights that they put under the umbrella of civil liberties. But the most accepted set of civil liberties are grouped into the following four categories: (i) criminal justice, that includes police powers, personal liberty, and the right to a fair trial; (ii) basic freedoms of speech, assembly, association, movement, and no discrimination; (iii) freedom of information; and (iv) communications and privacy.

Rapid advances in computer technology, and in particular the advent of the Internet, have all created an environment where detailed information on individuals and products can very easily and cheaply be moved, merged, compared, and shared. With the help of sophisticated network scanning and spying software such as STARR, FreeWhacker, Stealth Keyboard Logger, Snapshotspy, Surf Spy, Net Spy, and NPC Activity Monitor, no personal information on any computer on any network is safe.

Although this is good for law enforcement agencies such as the local police and FBI to track down criminals, and for banks to prevent fraud, and businesses to move data and process customer orders quickly and efficiently, the accessing and sharing of personal data by companies, associations, government agencies, and consumers without an individual's knowledge is a serious threat to the security and well-being of the individual. So, there must be ways to take precautions to protect against the misuse of personal information without consent. We have already indicated that personal privacy is a basic civil liberty that must be protected as is any other civil liberty such as the right to free speech. In many countries, there are guidelines and structures that safeguard and protected privacy rights. These structures and guidelines, on the average, fall under the following categories:

1. *Technical*: Through the use of software and other technically based safeguards, and also by education of users and consumers to carry out self-regulation. For example, the Electronic Frontier Foundation has the following guidelines for online safeguards [7]:
   (a) Do not reveal personal information inadvertently.
   (b) Turn on cookie notices in your Web browser, and/or use cookie management software or infomediaries.
   (c) Keep a "clean" e-mail address.
   (d) Do not reveal personal details to strangers or just-met "friends."
   (e) Realize you may be monitored at work. Avoid sending highly personal e-mails to mailing lists, and keep sensitive files on your home computer.
   (f) Beware of sites that offer some sort of reward or prize in exchange for your contact or other information.
   (g) Do not reply to spammers, for any reason.
   (h) Be conscious of Web security.
   (i) Be conscious of home computer security.
   (j) Examine privacy policies and seals.

(k) Remember that you alone decide what information about yourself to reveal—when, why, and to whom.

(l) Use encryption!

2. *Contractual*: through determination of which information such as electronic publication, and how such information is disseminated, are given contractual and technological protection against unauthorized reproduction or distribution. Contractual protection of information, mostly special information like publications, is good only if actions are taken to assure contract enforceability

3. *Legal*: through the enactment of laws by national legislatures and enforcement of such laws by the law enforcement agencies. For example, in the United States the following acts are such legal protection instruments [9, 10]:

(a) Children's Online Privacy Protection Act.

(b) Consumer Protection Act.

(c) Freedom of Information Act (1968) as amended (5 USC 552).

(d) Fair Credit Reporting Act (1970).

(e) Privacy Act (1974): regulates federal government agency record keeping and disclosure practices. The act allows most individuals to seek access to federal agency records about themselves and also requires that personal information in agency files be accurate, complete, relevant, and timely.

(f) Family Educational Right and Privacy Act (1974): requires schools and colleges to grant students or their parents access to student records and limits disclosure to third parties.

(g) Tax Reform Act (1976): restricts disclosure of tax information for nontax purposes.

(h) Right to Financial Privacy Act (1978): provides bank customers the privacy of financial records held by banks and other financial institutions.

(i) Electronic Funds Transfer Act (1978): requires institutions providing EFT to notify its customers about third-party access to customer accounts.

(j) Privacy Protection Act (1980): prevents unannounced searches by authority of press offices and files if no one in the office is suspected of committing a crime.

(k) Federal Managers Financial Integrity Act (1982).

(l) Cable Communications Policy Act (1984).

(m) Electronic Communication Act (1986): broadens the protection of the 1968 Omnibus Crime Control and Safe Streets Act to include all types of electronic communications.

(n) Computer Matching and Privacy Protection Act (1986): sets standards for the U.S. government computer matching programs, excluding matches done for statistical, law enforcement, tax, and certain other causes.

(o) Computer Security Act (1987).

(p) Video Privacy Protection Act (1988): prohibits video rental stores from disclosing which films a customer rents or buys.

(q) Driver's Privacy Protection Act (1994): prohibits the release and use of certain personal information from state motor vehicle records.

(r) Telecommunication Act (1996): deregulates the cable and telephone companies to enable each company to become involved in the business of the other.

(s) Medical Records Privacy Protection Act (1996):
   (i) Recognizes that individuals possess a right of privacy with respect to personally identifiable health information
   (ii) Provides that this right of privacy may not be waived in the absence of meaningful and informed consent, and
   (iii) Provides that, in the absence of an express waiver, the right to privacy may not be eliminated or limited except as expressly provided in this act.

(t) Digital Millennium Copyright Act (2000).

(u) The Gramm–Leach–Bliley Financial Services Modernization Act (2000).

4.5   Ethical and Legal Framework for Information

4.5.1   Ethics and Privacy

The issues involving ethics and privacy are many and cover wide areas including morality and law. The rapid advances in computer technology and cyberspace have resulted in rapid changes in these issues and the creation of others. For example, before the Internet, the best way to correspond with a colleague was to either write or type a note, mail it, and, of course, trust a postal carrier. Your worry was not that the carrier would snoop and read its contents, but whether the carrier would deliver it in a timely fashion. Many people never worried because they knew that tampering with mail was a federal offense.

Now, however, with the advent of the Internet and electronic messages, confidentiality is a great concern. Computer technology has raised more privacy questions than it can answer. Is there any confidentiality in electronic communication? Is anything that goes in the clear over public communication channels secure anymore? Are current encryption protocols secure enough? What laws need to be in place to secure any one of us online? Who should legislate them? Who will enforce them? We need a first an ethical framework resembling the one we developed in Chap. 2. But in addition to this, we also need a legal framework. Both these frameworks would probably help. The questions are who will develop these frameworks? and who will enforce them?

Discussion Issues

Attempt to draft an ethical framework discussed here. What do you need to include?

   What should be in the legal framework? Who should enact the laws in the framework?

4.5.2   Ethical and Legal Basis for Privacy Protection

The explosion of interest in the Internet, with growing numbers of people obtaining access to it, has also increased the potential for Internet-related crime. The arrest of Kevin D. Mitnick, one of the Federal Bureau of Investigation's (FBI) most wanted computer criminals in 1995, ignited anew the debate on the issue of ethics and security. Mitnick was arrested by the FBI after several years on the agency's most wanted computer criminals list. His arrest was a result of months of work by Tsutomu Shimomura, a renowned cybersleuth.

Mitnick's acts, and many after his, highlight how vulnerable the Internet is and how vulnerable we are whenever we use it. Security and ethical issues do not and should not come into play only when a crime is committed. These issues are also raised when individuals and companies act in ways that are considered harmful or have the potential of being harmful to a sector of society. Consider online postings, for example. As the Internet grows, companies and individuals are flocking to the Internet to post and advertise their wares. Until recently, the focus of Internet security and ethics was on pornographic images accessible to children. But of late a multitude of concerns have sprung up as new Internet technologies and services have sprung up, for example, online social networks.

What is the way forward? How can we ethically and legally encounter the new Internet technologies and services without interfering in people's loves and businesses as they use these new services?

Exercises

1. Define security and privacy. Why are both important in the information age?
2. What is anonymity? Discuss two forms of anonymity.
3. Discuss the importance of anonymity on the Internet.
4. Is total anonymity possible? Is it useful?
5. Develop two scenarios: one concerned with ethical issues involving security, and the other considering ethical issues involving privacy.
6. Is personal privacy dead? Discuss.
7. List and discuss the major threats to individual privacy.
8. Identity theft is the fastest growing crime. Why?
9. Why is it so easy to steal a person's identity?
10. Suggest steps necessary to protect personal identity.
11. Governments are partners in the demise of personal privacy. Discuss.
12. Anonymity is a double-edged sword. Discuss.
13. Are the steps given in Sect. 4.4.5 sufficient to prevent identity theft? Can you add more?
14. What role do special relationships play in identity theft?
15. Modern-day information mining is as good as gold! Why or why not?
16. How do consumers unknowingly contribute to their own privacy violations?
17. How has the Financial Services Modernization Act helped companies in gathering personal information?

References

1. Detweiler L. Identity, privacy, and anonymity on the Internet. http://www.fwn.rug.nl/fennema/ marko/archive/privacy.txt
2. Seven G. Lex Luthor and the legion of doom/hackers presents: identifying, attacking, defeating, and bypassing physical security and intrusion detection systems. Lod/H Tech J. http:// underground.org/publications/lod/lod-1.3.html
3. Lowe DV. Security overview: introduction. http://www.compclass.com/~vincent/fin4/fin4. html
4. Scherphier A. CS596 Client–server programming security. http://www.sdsu.edu/~turtle/cs596/ security.html
5. Durlak J. Privacy and security. Commun Tomorrow. http://renda.colunato.yorku.ca/com-4tom/1296.html
6. Rodger W (2000) Sites targeted for privacy violations. *USA Today*, June 13, 2000
7. Mason R (1991) Four ethical issues of the information age. In: Dejoie R, Fowler G, Paradice D (eds) Ethical issues in information systems. Boyd & Fraser, Boston
8. Johnson DJ (2009) Computer ethics, 4th edn. Pearson Education, Upper Saddle River
9. Landon K (1996) Markets and piracy. Commun ACM 39(9):92–95
10. Second amended verified original petition and application for TRO and temporary injunction. *Universal Image, Inc.* v. *Yahoo, Inc.* http://www.tomwbell.com/netlaw/universal/yahoo.html

Further Reading

Privacy lost: the demise of privacy in America. http://dorothyseeseonline.tripod.com/newsline/id3. html

Spying on employees: big brother has his eye on you … snooping sister is supervising you. http:// www.successunlimited.co.uk/related/snoop.htm

Tactics of a high-tech detective. *New York Times*. http://www.takedown.com/coverage/tactics.html

Auden WH (1995) The unknown citizen. In: Kennedy XJ, Gioia D (eds) Literature: an introduction to fiction, poetry, and drama, 6th edn. Harper Collins, New York, pp 611–612

Eisenberg D. Who is reading your bills? A court ruling on privacy riles the FCC. http://www.cnn. com/ALLPOLITICS/time/1999/08/30/privacy.html

Garrison T (1999) Latest surveillance leaves nothing to chance: exploring the dark side of the digital home. *Realty Times*. February 10, 1999. http://realtytimes.com/rtnews/rtipages/19990210 digitalhomes.htm

Lynch I (2000) Snooping bill to become law by November [27-07-2000]. http://www.vnunet.com

McClure S, Scambray J (2000) Forget the firewall: guard your garbage against 'Dumpster Diving' hackers. LISTSERV@SecurityFocus.com. Friday, 7 July, 2000

Mieszkowski K (2000) Big brother in the flesh: new technology could make us all a part of the collective, permanently supervised from above, September 21, 2000 Edition. http://www.lasvegasweekly.com

Rachels J (1991) Why privacy is important. In: Dejoice R, Flower G, Radice PA (eds) Ethical issues in information systems. Boyd & Fraser, Boston

Schiesel S (1997) On the web, new threats to young are seen. *New York Times*, March 7, 1997

Intellectual Property Rights and Computer Technology

5

Learning Objectives

After reading this chapter, the reader should be able to

1. Distinguish among patent, copyright, and trade secret protection.
2. Discuss the legal background of copyright in national and international law.
3. Explain how patent and copyright laws may vary internationally.
4. Outline the historical development of software patents.
5. Discuss the consequences of software piracy on software developers and the role of relevant enforcement organizations.

Scenario 4: Cybersquatting: Is It Entrepreneurship or Intellectual Theft?

Just before the 2000 New York senatorial campaign, Chris Hayden paid $70 each for the exclusive 2-year rights to the following Internet addresses: www. hillary2000.com, www.hillaryclinton2000.com, and www.clinton2000.com. A few weeks later, Mrs. Hillary Clinton, the then U.S. first lady, declared her candidacy for the state of New York senatorial race. The Clinton campaign team wanted her presence on the web, but they could not use any of the three names, though they rightly belonged to Mrs. Clinton. Deciding not to challenge Mr. Hayden in the middle of an election campaign, the team opted to buy the rights for www. hillary2000.com from Mr. Hayden. However, Mr. Hayden decided to engage a broker to demand $15,000 for the use of the name [1].

(continued)

© Springer International Publishing Switzerland 2016
J.M. Kizza, *Ethics in Computing*, Undergraduate Topics in Computer Science,
DOI 10.1007/978-3-319-29106-2_5

Scenario 4: (continued)
Cybersquatting, as the practice of grabbing somebody's name and registering it with an Internet registration company in anticipation of reaping huge rewards, is becoming widespread.

Discussion Questions

1. *Is Mr. Hayden violating Mrs. Clinton's intellectual rights?*
2. *Can Mr. Hayden claim free speech protection for the use of the names?*
3. *Should there be laws to make the practice illegal?*

5.1   Definitions

Intellectual property (IP) broadly describes tangible things such as ideas, inventions, technologies, artworks, music, and literature to which one can claim ownership. Ownership of IP for any of these things may result in economic gain as rewards to personal initial investments before they acquire value. It is a set of legal rights that result from intellectual activity in the industrial, scientific, literary, and artistic fields [2]. Intellectual property rights (IPR) are legal rights bestowed on an individual or a group that created, designed, or invented the activities or processes which led to the intellectual property in domains such as science and technology, business, industry, and the arts. These legal rights, most commonly in the form of patents, trademarks, and copyright, protect the moral and economic rights of the creators, in addition to the creativity and dissemination of their work [2].

5.2   Computer Products and Services

Computer products consist of those parts of the computer you can see and touch (e.g., the keyboard, CPU, printer, and monitor). These parts are considered products because they have tangible form and intrinsic value. A service is an act carried out on behalf of someone, usually a customer. If the service is to be paid for, the provider must strive to please the customer; it is crucial. If the service is not to be paid for, the act must then be performed to the liking of the provider.

Services have intrinsic value to the customer or recipient but have no tangible form. For example, a patient going to a doctor for treatment receives a service that has an intrinsic value, especially if the patient gets better, but it has no tangible form. A computer service can take the form of repairing a computer product and/or configuring and installing a computer network, neither of which has a tangible form but does offer considerable intrinsic value to the owner. Computer products can be defined easily because they have tangible form and intrinsic value. Services can also

Fig. 5.1 Flowchart

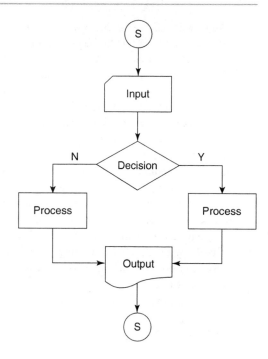

be defined easily because they have intrinsic value to the customer or the recipient, and in most cases to the provider, although they have no tangible form. Computer software, however, cannot be so easily classified as either a product or a service. Since it entered the marketplace, therefore, legal protection of computer software has been very problematic.

Computer software is a set of logical instructions to perform a desired task. This logical sequence follows an algorithm. The development of this sequence of instructions goes through the following phases:

1. *Logic map*: The plan of the idea, process, or an algorithm to accomplish the task. A plan is a flowchart of logic control with four major stations, namely, the input, output, processing, and decision box connected by arrows indicating the direction of flow of logic (see the flowchart in Fig. 5.1). Within the flowchart itself, there may be loops that express repetition of certain parts of the logic of that flowchart. Effective implementation of the flowchart achieves the desired effects of the program for the designated task.
2. *The source code*: A result of the implementation of the flowchart, turning the flowchart into a set of instructions using a programming language of choice.
3. *The object code*: The second stage of the implementation of a flowchart in which the source code, with the help of either a compiler or an assembler, is turned into strings of zeros and ones. In this form, the program is referred to as an object code. This step is not yet fully an operational form of the program because at this stage the program lacks variable addresses that have yet to be reconciled. It is also missing library routines that are added in the next stage.

4. *Memory-based executable code*: After the object code is finished, it is passed to the linker, another one of the system programs, whose job is to look for all missing variable addresses and library and personal routines and include them in the object code to produce a load module. The load module is now ready to be loaded if execution is needed. The job of loading the module is done by another system program called a loader. Most programs bought from vendors and software producers are in this executable form. The program at this stage has intrinsic value to the software producer and probably to the buyer, but it has no tangible form if you do not consider the medium it is on.

5. *Microcode*: Another form of executable code, but differing from the type of code we have just described, this code is not loaded in physical memory. It is coded and loaded on ROM (the read-only memory of the computer, which cannot be written on by the user) or burned into the computer hardware at the time of manufacture. If this code is loaded in ROM it can only be erased electronically or by using ultraviolet light. If, however, it is incorporated into the hardware, it is not easily changed and it cannot be erased. In this form the program is referred to as microcode. For a program in hardware, execution is normally achieved through the logical flow in the assemblies of hardware components.

In support of either hardware-based or memory-based programs, programmers, usually the creators of these programs, write documentation and technical manuals to accompany the program and help the user of the software. Our references to computer programs here, therefore, include memory-based and hardware-based programs together with the technical manuals and all related documentation.

In our definition of computer software, whether hardware based or memory based, including technical writings, note that computer software, if it is considered at the execution stage without the technical documentation, has an intrinsic value both to the developer and to the buyer, but it may not have a tangible form unless you consider the medium it is on (e.g., the disk). For example, during tax filing season when you buy a tax program to help you with taxes, you either download the program or get a couple of CDs with the program on them and a number of manuals and flyers. You can ignore the flyers in your package because they are usually for commercial purposes, but the purpose of the manuals is to help you learn how to use the program. You can touch the manuals, the CDs, and so on, but you cannot touch the program itself. That is, the manuals and CDs all have a tangible form and probably some intrinsic value, but the program itself does not have a tangible form, although it has the most intrinsic value. In this case, we can classify such software as a service.

Not having a tangible form, however, does not by itself rule out software as a product. According to Deborah Johnson [3], the courts do not equate products with what is tangible. Courts have defined things such as energy and leases as products, although none has a tangible form. So there are cases when we can consider software as a product.

In his article "Negligence for Defective Software," Jim Prince [4] puts software into three categories. The first category includes off-the-shelf software such as Windows and others that one can buy ready to use with no alterations allowed by the producer. This category he calls the "canned" software. The customer gets it as is. The second category is the software specifically ordered by the customer from the software house or producer to fit the customer's very specific needs, similar to going to your physician for a specific illness. The third category is software the customer buys off the shelf, but with changes allowed, or the customer adds certain parts to the software to meet some specific needs. According to Prince, category 1 software is considered to be a product, whether it has a tangible form or not; category 2 software is considered to be a service; and category 3 software is a new class he calls "mixed case."

5.3   Foundations of Intellectual Property

Gaining the skills to provide computer technology products, services, and software requires a considerable investment in both time and money. Thus, the individuals who do this work should reap financial rewards for their efforts. Such rewards create an atmosphere of creativity and competitiveness, which in turn creates jobs that drive the economy. This creativity must therefore be protected, for if it falters because of lack of protection, then the economy of the country falters along with it.

Computer technology in particular was born of this individual creativity and the adventurism of young entrepreneurs. To encourage these innovators, society must protect their efforts and resources. To do this, a specific set of rights, collectively known as intellectual property rights, has been recognized, and laws have protecting intellectual rights been enacted and extended to cover software by different countries and groups of countries to protect those rights.

Intellectual property rights form a wide scope of mechanisms that include copyrights, patents, trademarks, protection of trade secrets, and, increasingly, personal identity rights. Each of these instruments of protection is regulated by a body of laws and statutes we discuss throughout this chapter. Unfortunately, some of these laws are not universal; they only apply in one country. And even within the United States, the same laws may not apply in all states. In particular, we look at intellectual property rights as they apply to computer products, services, and software.

5.3.1   Copyrights

Internationally, copyright is a right, enforceable by law, accorded to an inventor or creator of an expression. Such expressions may include creative works (literary, dramatic, musical, pictorial, graphic, artistic) together with audiovisual and architectural works and sound recordings. In general, every original work that has a tangible form and is fixed in a medium is protectable under the copyright law. The history of copyright laws can be traced back to eighteenth-century England with the so-called statute of Queen Anne around 1710 setting a pattern for formal copyright statutes. England was followed by the United States in 1790 when the first U.S. copyright law was enacted by Congress, and by France in 1793 [5].

Since then, copyright laws have spread worldwide. Examples of international copyright bodies include the Berne Convention in 1886, of which the United States was not a signatory until 1989, the 1952 Universal Copyright Convention (UCC), and the Berne and Paris conventions in 1971. To ensure that conventions stay current and signatory countries observe them, a number of world bodies have been created mainly to administer the conventions. The World Intellectual Property Organization (WIPO) created in 1967 was the first to be charged with such a task. Later, the UN Educational Scientific and Cultural Organization (UNESCO) together with WIPO were assigned to administer the UCC, and finally the World Trade Organization (WTO) is now charged with administrating the Trade-Related Aspects of Intellectual Property Rights (TRIPPS) agreement concluded under the Uruguay round of the General Agreement on Tariffs and Trade (GATT). Besides these large and more comprehensive organizations, there are also numerous small regional organizations such as the North American Free Trade Agreement (NAFTA) [5].

These organizations, together with national legislatures, keep these conventions and national copyright acts current through amendments. For example, in the United States the 1790 copyright law was amended in 1831 and then again in 1870. In 1909, Congress enacted the Copyright Act, which underwent two amendments, and in 1976 Congress enacted the current Copyright Act, which came into effect in 1978. This act has already undergone several amendments, mainly because of advances in computer technology.

Each country has its own requirements for the issuance of a copyright. In the United States, for example, there are three requirements for copyright protection of a work under the 1978 U.S. Copyright Act: originality, fixation, and expression; in Canada, it is originality and fixation. The U.S. copyright laws cover all original works fixed in tangible forms regardless of medium, and such works must be expressions, not ideas [4]. The scope of works or creations meeting these criteria is wide: it includes artistic, pictorial, graphic, and sculptural works; musical and sound recordings; audiovisual works including television and motion pictures; and literary works and other printed materials such as books, greeting cards, journals, flyers, and leaflets; the list goes on.

However, a number of creative fixable works are excluded from this extensive list because they are considered either trivial or utilitarian. The list for these is also a long one: it includes such items as calendars, schedules of events, scorecards, ideas, facts, names, common language phrases, titles, and blank forms. Although some of these may not be protected by the copyright laws, they may be protected somewhere else, for example, by trademark or patent laws.

5.3.1.1 Works in the Public Domain

When the copyright on a work expires, that work goes into the public domain. Other works in the public domain include those owned by governments, non-copyrightable items we listed earlier such as ideas and facts, works intentionally put in the public domain by the owner of the copyright, and works that lost copyrights for various reasons before the copyrights expired.

Works in the public domain are not protected by the copyright law and can be used by any member of the public without prior permission from the owner of the work. Examples of such works in the United States include works published before 1978 whose copyright has not been renewed and, therefore, have no valid copyright notice. A copyright notice consists of a copyright symbol denoted by ©, the word "copyright," the year the copyright was granted, and the name of the copyright owner. For example: copyright © 1995 John Mukasa.

5.3.1.2 Application for a Copyright

For authors and creators of works who need this kind of protection, the process begins with an application to the copyright office. Each country's copyright office has different requirements. The U.S. Copyright Office requires an applicant to include with the application a copy of the work for which a copyright is sought and to file for copyright within 3 months of the first distribution of the work.

Upon receipt of the application by the Copyright Office, it is reviewed to ensure it meets the three criteria of originality, fixation, and expression for the issuing of a copyright.

Fixation, a remnant of the Gutenberg era, and now the most controversial element in the current debate about intellectual property rights in the digital age, refers to the tangible form in which the creation is perceived by others. For example, computer programs arc fixed in binary code. For performing arts such as drama, the script is the fixation. In the fine arts, the painting or the sculpture is the fixation. It is important in creative work to have fixation because it clearly demonstrates and defines the tangible form of the creation and the domain and parameters of such a creation.

Similar to fixation, the protection of a creation requires proof of originality. The originality requirements differentiate among facts, ideas, and expressions as creations. Facts are considered common property for all humanity; no one has a right to an unknown or known fact because it is not considered an invention; the same principle applies to theories, mathematical, scientific, and others. Ideas, as are facts, are also considered common property and therefore are not copyrightable. Thus, originality is only possible through expressions. Such expressions may include ideas, theories, and other inventions. The packaging must be original if protection is sought. Packaging includes remakes of protected works. This type of packaging is what scholars of copyrights call derived works. For an interesting discussion of this, refer to *The Copyright Book* by William E. Strong [6]. The review process is very extensive and thorough and takes some time before it is complete. Upon approval, the recipient must place a notice of copyright ownership in all parts and copies of the work.

5.3.1.3 Duration of a Copyright

In the United States the duration of copyright protection falls into two periods: those copyrights granted before the 1978 Copyright Act and those granted after that date. If a copyright was received for a published work before 1978, that copyright lasts for 75 years after the date of issuance. For unpublished works, the copyrights will expire on December 31, 2002 regardless of when they were issued. If the copyright was received after 1978, the work remains protected by copyright laws for the lifetime of the author plus 50 years. In the case of more than one author of the work, the protection lasts for the lifetime of the longest living author plus 50 years. For all works made for hire, that is, works made as part of contracted employment, the coverage lasts 75 years from the date of the first publication or 100 years from the date of creation [5].

5.3.2 Patents

In contrast to the copyright, which protects expressions, patents protect inventions or discoveries. In the United States, patent rights are protected just like copyright rights.

In many countries, patent protection rights, as are those of copyrights, are provided for by the constitution. The U.S. Constitution, for example, states it this way: "to promote the progress of science and useful arts, by securing for limited times to authors and inventors the exclusive right to their respective writing and discoveries." In accordance with this, Congress has enacted and continually revised patent laws to suit the times. These laws give inventors or discoverers living within U.S. borders and territories the exclusive rights to make, use, or sell their invention or discovery for a specific period of time, so long as there was full disclosure of the invention or discovery at the time the patent application was filed.

Because of the disclosure requirement that every patent applicant must meet, the patent is more of a contract between the inventor or discoverer and the government. For this contract to be binding, each party to the contract must keep its part: the government's part to protect the exclusive rights of the inventor or discoverer while such a person recovers his or her investments for a period of time, that of the inventor or discoverer to make a full disclosure to the government of the invention or discovery. With this disclosure the government makes sure the public benefits from the discovery or the invention while it is still under patent protection and more after.

5.3.2.1 What Is Patentable?

In the United States, an invention or discovery is patentable if it meets two basic requirements. The first requirement is that the invention or discovery for which the patent is sought is new and useful, or is a new and useful improvement of any of the following: process, manufacture (covering all products that are not machines), and machine (covering all mechanisms and mechanical products and composition of matter, which includes all factory-manufactured life forms).

The second requirement is that the invention or discovery must satisfy the following four conditions, and all must apply:

1. *Utility*: An invention or discovery serves a basic and minimum useful purpose to the general public or to a large percentage of the public without being a danger to the public, illegal, or immoral.

2. *Novelty*: The invention or discovery for which a patent is sought must be new, not used, known, or published somewhere before.
3. *Nonobviousness*: The invention or discovery for which patent protection is sought must not have been obvious to anyone with ordinary skills to produce or invent in its disclosed form.
4. *Disclosure*: There must be adequate disclosure of the product for which a patent is sought. Such a disclosure is often used by the Patent Office in its review to seek and prove or disprove the claims on the application form and also to enable the public to use the invention or discovery safely and gainfully after the period of protection.

5.3.2.2 Application for a Patent
In many countries, the process of obtaining a patent begins with the filing of an application with the patent office. As we already discussed, the application must give a clear and detailed disclosure of the invention or discovery including its workings, experiments made, data used, results obtained, safety record, and effectiveness if used properly. Its weaknesses, if observed, and all pertinent information that may be required if the Patent Office is to carry out a similar experiment must also be submitted.

5.3.2.3 Duration of a Patent
After the review process is completed—and this may take some time depending on the disclosure provided and the type of invention or discovery—the patent is then issued to the applicant for the invention, and only for that invention, not including its variations and derivatives. The protection must last for a number of years, 17 years in the United States. During this time period, the patent law protects the inventor or discoverer from competition from others in the manufacture, use, and sale of the invention or discovery.

5.3.2.4 Public Domain
The patent law does not protect ideas, but only the process of carrying out an idea. Competitors may take the same idea and use a different process to arrive at their own inventions or discoveries, which can then be patented as novel. When the patent protection expires, the patent together with all disclosures go into the public domain for anyone to use.

5.3.3 Trade Secrets

A trade secret is information that gives a company or business a competitive advantage over others in the field. It may be a formula, a design process, a device, or trade figures. Thus, there is no one acceptable description or definition of trade secrets. The generic definition is that it is a collection of information in a given static format with strategic importance. The format may be a design expressing the information, a formula representing the collection of information, a pattern, a symbol, or an insignia representing the information. Whatever the format the collected information takes, it must have given or offered an advantage to the owner which places that owner a degree above the competition.

In the United States, in contrast to the other intellectual properties we have described so far, trade secrets have no federal protection. All trade secret laws are state laws.

However, trade secret owners are further protected by express or implied contract laws and laws of unfair competition, which are backed by federal statutes.

5.3.3.1 Characteristics of Trade Secrets

Because it is difficult to define a trade secret, it is important that we characterize what makes a trade secret. According to Neitzke [7], a trade secret is characterized by the following:

1. The extent to which the information is known outside the business. If many people outside the company or business know or have access to the collection of information that constitutes the trade secret, then it is no longer a trade secret.
2. The extent of measures taken by individuals possessing the trade secret to guard the secrecy of the information. If the information is to remain known by as few people as possible, there must be a detailed plan to safeguard that information and prevent it from leaking.
3. The value of the information to the owner and to the competitor. If the collection of information forming the trade secret has little or no value to the competitor, then it can no longer be a trade secret because it offers no definite advantage to the owner over the competitor. It does not matter whether the owner values the information; so long as it is not valued in the same way by the competitor, it is not regarded as a trade secret.
4. The amount of effort or money spent by the owner to develop or gather the information. The logic here is usually the more money the developer puts in a project, the more value is placed on the outcome. Because there are some information or project outcomes that do not require substantial initial investments, the effort is what counts here.
5. The ease or difficulty with which the information could be properly acquired or duplicated by others. If it will take much effort and money to duplicate the product or the information, then its value and therefore advantage to the competitor diminishes.

The conditions that characterize a trade secret are in direct conflict with the requirements of a patent. Remember the main requirement for obtaining a patent is the full disclosure of all the information surrounding the product and its workings; this directly conflicts with the need for secrecy in trade secrets. So, the patent applicant cannot claim a patent and at the same time claim protection using the trade secret laws.

5.3.3.2 Duration of Trade Secrets

Trade secrets have an indefinite life of protection so long as the secrets are not revealed.

5.3.4   Trademarks

A trademark is a label identifying a product or service. It is a mark that attempts to distinguish a service or a product in the minds of the consumers. The label may be any word, name, picture, or symbol. It is very well known that consumers tend to choose between products through association with the product's brand name. For example, the Golden Arch is a trademark for McDonald's restaurants. There are many other fast-food restaurants (e.g., Burger King), but none of them can use the Golden Arch as their trademark. The Golden Arch differentiates McDonald's from all other fast-food restaurants and may give it an advantage over its competitors in the industry. Because trademarks are used by consumers to choose among competing products, they are vigorously protected by their owners.

Differing from patents and copyrights, however, trademarks are not so protected and enshrined in constitutions. For example, in the United States, trademark laws, as are trade secrets, are based on state statutes. At the federal government level the trademark laws can be found in the Lenham Act and the new Trademark Cyberpiracy Prevention Act 1999 [8].

Although the patent gives owners the exclusive right to use, sell, and make use of the invention or discovery, and the copyright law gives owners the exclusive rights to copying their works, the trademark gives its owner the right to prevent others, mostly competitors, from using the same or similar symbol to market their products.

5.3.4.1 Categories of Trademarks

Trademark is a general term that includes a service mark, a certification mark, and a collective mark. A service mark is usually used in the sale or advertising of a service. It is supposed to uniquely identify that service. A circle with checked lines distinguishes AT&T telecommunication services from those of BTT, MCI, and many others. A certification mark is used as a verifier or to authenticate the characteristics of a product, a service, or group of people who offer a certain service. For example, colleges attach seals to diplomas as marks to certify the educational attainment of the holders. A collective mark is mainly used by a group of people to indicate membership in an organization or association. For example, people who take and pass certain specialty examinations can use a mark such as CPA, PhD, or MD to indicate they belong to those groups.

5.3.4.2 Characteristics of Trademarks

It is said that a picture is worth a thousand words. So, it is assumed by trademark owners that a symbol is worth 1000 words and, therefore, their marks are always saying something to the customers, at least in theory. A variety of marks are used by product and service companies to enhance the commercial value of their products or services in the eyes of the public by association. General wisdom is that the more recognizable is the mark, the more valuable will be the product or service.

In addition to categorizing trademarks by what they cover, as we did in the last section, let us also group them according to what they say. Trademarks as symbols of sales to the consumer are generally supposed to tell the consumer about the services or the products they are intended to boost. The impression the mark gives to a consumer, the likelihood of the existence of such a mark, and the ease of obtaining registry put it in one of the following characteristic groups:

- *Arbitrary marks*: Trademark symbols that say nothing about the product or service are usually used arbitrarily with a product or service, but over time they become associated with that product or service. Most arbitrary marks are one or more words or a collection of letters already in linguistic use but with no associated meaning. Many established trademarks start as arbitrary marks, and consumers eventually come to associate them with the product or service. For example, McDonald's Golden Arch may have had no meaning at the beginning and still may have no meaning to "outsiders" unless they know of the association.
- *Suggestive marks*: Symbols or writings that are usually in the public domain may be twisted by people to say something about their products or services. These marks may suggest to the customer the features, qualities, and other characteristics of the product or service. A good example here would be a mark such as "GolfRight" as a trademark for a company manufacturing a new brand of golf balls. The two words "golf" and "right" were taken out of the public domain and combined to describe the product with the creation of a new word, "GolfRight."
- *Descriptive marks*: These usually contain a description of the intended purpose of the mark but say nothing about the product or service. For example, if you create a program that you think simplifies the tax-preparing process, you may use a trademark called "Easy-Tax."
- *General marks*: New marks are unrelated and with no suggestive features, qualities, and characteristics of the products or services they are said to represent. In contrast to the arbitrary marks, general marks are not linguistically bound. A general mark could be any symbol. General marks are desirable because they are easy to register, because the likelihood of the existence of a similar mark is minimal. An example is the use of a graphic symbol such as an arrow for a product or service.

5.3.4.3 Registration of a Trademark

An application for a trademark must contain and present all relevant information. It must also describe the product or service for which the trademark is being sought, the class of goods and services, and the date of first issue of the mark. Marks are registered only if they meet certain criteria. The core requirement is that the mark must not cause confusion with similar marks used by others. In the United States a mark is registered as a trademark only if it meets the following criteria:

1. It must be in good "taste" for the public: not immoral, deceptive, or illegal.
2. It must not have suggestive connotations to its origin.
3. It must not be a symbol of any recognized country.
4. It must not use people's likenesses, either after death or if living, without prior consent.

5.3.4.4 Duration of a Trademark

In the United States, a valid trademark is protected for 10 years. If an extension is needed it can be granted for another 10 years.

5.3.5   Personal Identity

Identity theft is a crime committed when one misrepresents oneself, with or without success, as another person to get the victim's information so that the perpetrator can receive goods and services in the name of the fraud victim. Identity theft is now one of the fastest growing crimes in the United States and in a number of other countries as well. Although it is still not considered to be a crime in some countries, national legislatures are in full gear enacting laws to criminalize it. When it happens, it takes probably an instant, but it can take a long period of time before it is discovered. By then, the information misuse, financial loss, and psychological damage can be devastating, but this is nothing compared to the agony one goes through trying to control, manage, and recover from the damage caused. Doing this can sometimes take years and be very costly.

Techniques to steal personal identity include the following [9]:

(i)   Advertising in newspapers and mostly on the Internet. The most common technique now, pretext calling, is where people misrepresent themselves as law enforcement agents, social workers, and potential employers to obtain the private data of others from banks and other financial institutions.

(ii) From readily available how-to books and discussion groups, perpetrators get foolproof methods of wangling financial information from bank employees.

(iii) Use of telemarketing scams to trick consumers into revealing personal data.

(iv) Abundant authentic-looking fake IDs, including Social Security cards, birth certificates, and driver's licenses, are on sale online.

(v)   Going through one's trash for personal information.

(vi) Using the post office to redirect one's mail to a perpetrator's box number.

(vii) Criminals are increasingly using radio scanners to eavesdrop on personal calls.

5.3.5.1 Prevention

After being the victim of identity theft, it is extremely difficult to straighten out one's record, let alone recover the stolen personal attributes. The best course of action is for individual defense. The following steps are considered minimal but effective:

   (i)   Shred all credit card receipts, canceled checks, and other financial
          documents.
  (ii)   Seek employer personal information protection plans.
 (iii)   We are leaking vessels of personal information. At every stop we make, we
          involuntarily give out crucial personal information such as sensitive finan-
          cial data, telephone numbers, Social Security numbers, and other vital per-
          sonal data.
  (iv)   Where possible, have all your payments deposited electronically in your
          bank account.
   (v)   Periodically check your credit report. It is better still if you review credit
          reports from all three credit bureaus for erroneous data on your personal
          credit report. When you get your credit report, look for things such as who
          is using your information. Check and make sure you know who requests for
          your information from these companies.
  (vi)   Shred all your credit card solicitations and all other mail that bears personal
          identification.
 (vii)   If you become a victim, report the incident to law enforcement personnel.
(viii)   Although not as effective so far, legislation is also important. The
          U.S. Congress recently passed a law that makes it a federal crime, punish-
          able by up to 5 years in prison, for anyone to misrepresent himself or herself
          to obtain someone's private financial data.

5.4   Ownership

As we discuss ownership in this section, and indeed in the whole book, we confine
ourselves to intellectual property ownership. Ownership of everything else other
than intellectual property is outside our present scope. An idea is novel if it is original, authentic, and new. Inventiveness, creativity, and discoveries are born of individual ideas. Good ideas are the source of substantial benefits to individuals and the
public. Before an idea can be useful, however, it must be put into utilizable form,
either as a process or as an application. It is this idea in a utilizable form that is the
core of intellectual property rights. In many countries the owner of such an application for the idea has a set of legal rights to its expression as a creation, work, invention, discovery, information, or any other form.

   Via the copyright law, the patent law, the trademark law, and trade secret statutes,
governments have indicated that they can protect owners' rights under certain conditions, and, therefore, legal ownership of creations, discoveries, information,
inventions, and the like, is protectable. As we have already seen, the domain of all
these rights constitutes intellectual property. Within this domain, these rights are
grouped into subsets defining specific areas of interests such as the right to make,
use, or sell one's works of discovery or creation. Each such subset is protected by
the four well-known instruments we discussed in Sect. 5.3.

5.4.1   The Politics of Ownership

Recently, much has been written about the concept of intellectual property rights, and the issue has been in the news, such as when the U.S. government negotiated with China, the country that many in the West believe has the highest rate of abuse of intellectual property laws. There have been many statements made about the effects of cultural differences between Western countries and other cultures of the world regarding the issue of intellectual property rights.

In fact, this issue alone has become a defining factor between Western and other cultures. Western culture emphasizes individuals, rewards individual achievements, and hence upholds intellectual property issues as a golden egg. Non-Western cultures, in contrast, which emphasize community responsibility, do not understand the West's focus on intellectual property rights. To many non-Westerners, a good manifestation of an idea that benefits a community should be enjoyed by the whole community, not just by one or a few members, because individuals make up the community.

As global economies become more and more intertwined, and as the West continues to keep the lead in technological development, many of the non-Western cultural underpinnings are likely to change as these cultures devour the new imported Western technology. Already a number of countries in Southeast Asia have been forced to abide by the intellectual property laws as dictated by the West.

In addition to the cultural politics of intellectual property issues, there is also a perception controversy. Many people believe the protection of the manifestation of one's ideas by copyrights, patents, trademarks, and trade secrets laws automatically constitutes a monopoly of the benefits that come with the ideas. Because of this misconception, the U.S. Congress and indeed other governments have passed antitrust laws to calm the public. The antitrust laws in themselves prevent or restrict patent, copyright, or trademark holders from collecting large loyalties beyond the term of the license by opening up the competition.

5.4.2   The Psychology of Ownership

Whether we grew up in a culture that rewards individual achievements or in those cultures that pride themselves on community achievements, we are aware of the distinct psychology about individual ownership. We tend to classify those items that we individually own, whether they are few or abundant, according to their intrinsic value to us. We may believe our self-worth and status in the community depend on the intrinsic value of the items we own. So the intrinsic value we attach to these items is one of the most important aspects of ownership. Another aspect of ownership is the tangibility of what we own. When what we own has a tangible form with glamour and value to others, whether it has any intrinsic value to us, it tends to raise our status in the community. We therefore gain the respect of others, which in turn affects our self-esteem and our egos.

5.5   Intellectual Property Crimes

An intellectual property crime (IPC) is the act of infringement on the rights of the owners of the intellectual property. IPC refers to all activities that involve infringement, counterfeiting, and piracy of products and services for profit. IPC also includes misappropriation, misrepresentation, cybercrimes, corruption and bribery, and espionage. The cost of intellectual property crimes to industry and nations is huge.

Technological advances have allowed these crimes to grow like wildfire in the past decade because committing these crimes is much easier and the field of crimes has become global, thus decreasing the threat of apprehension. Technology has also increased these crimes because duplicated products are easy to make and the costs are low.

5.5.1   Infringement

In Sect. 5.3 we discussed the legal protection over a domain of rights for an individual's manifested idea. This legal protection is offered in subsets of laws that define the boundaries within which such laws can be enforced. Anybody else with no rights within this domain is considered an infringer, defined as one moving within the protected domain to claim rights for the use of someone else's manifestation of an idea without permission from the holder of the rights.

This is an abstract concept, and the difficulty in understanding it illustrates the elusiveness of the boundaries of these rights. There are three types of infringements:

1. *Direct infringement*: The infringer knowingly or otherwise makes, uses, sells, or copies a protected item without any alteration.
2. *Inducement infringement*: The infringer intentionally supports infringement activities on a protected item without individually taking part in the infringement activities.
3. *Contributory infringement*: The infringer takes part in the infringement of a protected item. Let us now look at infringement under each one of the subdomains of the intellectual property domain.

5.5.1.1 Copyright Infringement

Copyright infringement is very difficult to prove. However, U.S. courts have provided guidelines that many courts follow [6]. Here are some of the items that courts look for in an infringement suit:

- Whether the infringer has knowledge or visual contact with the work
- Whether the individual claiming to be the owner has a valid copyright
- Whether the work under dispute is a major revision with substantially new contents of the original or just a variation

5.5.1.2 Patent Infringement

Similar to copyright infringement, patent infringement is also difficult to detect. Highly sophisticated methods of policing and investigative work need to be laid down and followed. No public law enforcement can be used in these cases. It is purely the effort of the owner of the patents, and he or she must meet all expenses incurred during the investigation and prosecuting of the infringer if caught. Once the infringer is caught and determined guilty by the court, a hefty settlement is collected from the perpetrator. There may also be punitive damages.

Because the policing and investigation can be difficult, lengthy, and expensive, patent owners tend to use a device that uses the public to do the policing for them. They achieve this by using patent markings on their products, for example "Pat." followed by the number of the patent. With this mark on the product, patent owners hope the public will police the marketplace and inform them if they suspect any patent infringement. If the patent owner confirms that an infringement on his or her patent has taken place, the first course of action is usually litigation to collect the damages and most importantly to send a message to the public and mostly to those who had intentions of infringing on the patent to keep off. Another channel of action open to the patent owner is through an independent arbitrator to obtain some compensation from the infringer.

5.5.1.3 Trademark Infringement

To prove infringement of a trademark, one must prove beyond doubt that the infringer's action was likely to confuse the public. Because of this, it is very difficult to prove trademark infringement. If the owner of the trademark can successfully prove and convince the courts that the infringer's mark has or is likely to cause confusion, then the infringer may be asked to pay any or a combination of the following: monetary awards based on the profits he or she made on the product displaying the mark, losses the owner supposedly incurred as a result of the infringement, and/ or punitive damages and legal fees.

5.5.2 The First Sale Doctrine

A copyright owner under the first sale doctrine has the right to distribute copies of copyrighted materials by means of sale, transfer of ownership, rental, release, or by any other means. In the United States, under the first sale doctrine section 109(a) of the Copyright Act, artists, authors, inventors, or discoverers can control subsequent use of their works through a lease or license. Anybody else who uses that work without either a lease or license is an infringer.

5.5.3 The Fair Use Doctrine

The fair use doctrine establishes a bridge between the protection of rights of artists, authors, inventors, or discoverers to benefit from their works and the basic rights of the community to gain from each member's contributions for the betterment of all and the upholding of the principle of economic competition. The use of copyrighted material is considered fair if it does not exploit the commercial value of the work. There are four ways to judge whether the use of an invention, discovery, or work is fair. We list them here and discuss them in depth in Chap. 12:

1. The purpose of use, whether commercial or educational
2. Nature of use
3. Percentage of use
4. The effect of use on the commercial value of the invention, discovery, or works

The fair use doctrine has also given rise to conflicts between the separation of free speech and copyrights. According to Strong [6], a "citizen may be free to speak, but he is not entitled to speak his mind in the same words as his neighbor. He is free to speak the idea if you will, but not the expression." There are so many exceptions and inclusions under the fair use doctrine that it is difficult to be sure what is fair use unless one talks to a copyright lawyer or other experts knowledgeable in copyright law. The rule of thumb advocated by many copyright lawyers is that any time you have to copy any part of a copyrighted work outside personal educational use, even in the case of just one copy, talk to somebody who knows the law.

5.6   Protection of Ownership Rights

In Sects. 5.3 and 5.5 we discussed the intellectual property rights instruments of protection and how they can be infringed. In this section we consider how an owner of these property rights can use these instruments. We approach this by discussing the domain, source and types, duration, and the strategies of protection.

5.6.1   Domain of Protection

During our discussion of intellectual property rights, we defined the domain as the set of all different rights enjoyed by the owner of a manifested idea. Within this domain, there are subsets of rights enjoyed by the owner, depending on the manifestation of the idea. These subsets are protected by the body of laws discussed in Sect. 5.3, namely, copyright, patent, trademarks, and trade secret laws. Under each of these subsets, different rights are protectable, as shown here:

1. *Copyrights*: Copyright laws protect all rights embodied within the copyrighted work by the copyright act of the particular country, including the right to use, transform, sale, copy, and modify.
2. *Patents*: Patent laws protect all rights embodied in the particular country's patent law.

3. *Trademarks*: Trademark laws protect all rights in the different trademark statutes depending on the state and country.
4. *Trade secrets*: Trade secret statutes and laws protect all rights within the different states, local authority, and the country's statutes.

Anything else outside these sets, except the various laws that protect personal identity, should be in the public domain and, therefore, is not protectable.

5.6.2   Source and Types of Protection

Because intellectual crimes have become global with the growing technological advances, there has been a realization that there must be protection of national interests. Thus, a number of national and global organizations have been put in place and national acts and international treaties signed to fight these crimes. In the United States, intellectual property rights are protected by the copyright and patent laws. Other intellectual property laws in United States include the following:

- The Antipiracy Act of 1976
- The Communication Act of 1984, The No Electronic Theft Act (NET Act)
- The Digital Millennium Copyright Act (DMCA)
- The Economic Espionage Act of 1996
- Money Laundering Act of 1956

These and a number of state statutes or local ordinances protect the IPR. But because neither federal nor state protection is extended outside U.S. borders, different organizations have over the years been set up to protect these rights. Among these:

- The World Trade Organization (WTO)
- Interpol
- The Universal Copyright Convention (UCC)
- Berne Convention
- The Trade-Related Aspects of Intellectual Property Rights (TRIPPS)
- The World Intellectual Property Organization (WIPO)

Remember that although intellectual property rights are protected by a body of laws, the burden of policing, detection, and prosecution in any country is squarely on the shoulders of the owner of the specific intellectual property rights protected.

5.6.3   Duration of Protection

As we saw in Sect. 5.3, the period during which intellectual property is protected depends on a number of factors, including the body of laws protecting your rights and your geographic region.

5.6.4   Strategies of Protection

The burden of safeguarding the intellectual property rights of an individual is with that very person owning the work. It is the duty of individual owners of copyrights, patents, trade secrets, and trademarks to devise strategies to safeguard these rights.

Various methods have been used by individuals and companies who hold these rights to defend themselves. Large companies and individuals have been known to use methods ranging from spying on competitors and suspected infringers using private undercover operatives to collaborating with government officials to check on imports and exports. Some companies call in their respective governments when they suspect foreign infringements. When governments step in, they negotiate joint policing within the respective countries and sign treaties to protect these rights. For example, the U.S. government has negotiated with and sometimes pressured foreign governments on behalf of U.S.-based companies to observe the intellectual property rights of U.S. technology companies after these companies suspected infringement by individuals and companies in these countries.

Within the United States, some corporations, especially software companies and computer chip manufacturers, have started using local law enforcement agencies to raid suspected infringers both in the United States and in other countries. Another approach used by private companies is a blitz of publicity about suspected countries and counterfeit products. Education campaigns via the mass media are also being used as a viable and effective protection strategy.

5.7   Protecting Computer Software Under the IP

We know that algorithms and ideas are not classified as intellectual property and, therefore, are not protected in any way. Ideas and algorithms belong to everybody, and no one can put a claim on them. Software, although it comes from and strictly follows an algorithm, is not considered an algorithm but rather a manifestation, an expression of that algorithm. Many people may have many different ways of expressing, and therefore representing, the same algorithm and hence have different programs that are considered clear intellectual property and are, therefore, protectable. But for computer software, there are no guidelines one can use to claim that because software is considered a derivation of an algorithm, it is, therefore, protectable. Computer products, in particular computer software, are more elusive and thus have been presenting many problems for those seeking protection under the intellectual property rights law. The difficulty with software protection comes from the difficulty in categorizing it. As we said earlier, software can be a product, a service, or a mixture of both.

5.7.1   Software Piracy

Discussing the intellectual property rights (IPR) one cannot fail to think about the modern wonder of technology, the computer software, and its relationship with IPR. The biggest problem concerning computer software and IPR is software piracy.

Generally speaking, we can define software piracy as the act of copying, distributing, or using proprietary software. This act is and has been illegal ever since software began to be protected by law after software manufacturers started filing for patents and copyrights for their products and creations. However, this has not always been the case. In the early days computers, mainly mainframe, came with software preloaded. There were few computers and few users, nobody cared about the software, the least understood component, let alone knowing how to use it and when to use it. With the miniaturization and widespread use of computers together with the high costs of production and purchase costs of software, this changed. A demand for software was created that lead to the piracy problems. We come around to this issue when we discuss the transnational software issues in the next section.

The issue of software piracy is a complex one. Several other issues complicate software piracy. Some people use illegal software without knowing that the copies they have are illegal. Others use it with the full knowledge that the copies they are using are illegal but they go ahead anyway. Others are confused by the software terminology that includes freeware, shareware, and commercial software. Yet others, especially those in educational institutions, are confused by the IPR principle of fair use. They cannot tell how much is fair. There is also a large percentage of illegal software users who do it purposely to 'get even' with software manufacturers that frequently upgrade software versions making older versions of the product obsolete. We discuss these and other issues in the coming section.

Is there a solution to this problem? Yes and no. Yes, in that software companies and governments are working together in efforts to eliminate or downgrade the problem.

5.7.2 Protection of Software Under Copyright Laws

Computer software, along with its documentation, can be protected under the copyright laws. According to Section 101 of the 1980 U.S. Copyright Amendment, a computer program is defined as "a set of statements or instructions to be used directly or indirectly in a computer in order to bring about a certain result" [10]. This statement automatically implies that such a set of instructions or statements is a written creative work by someone, hence a literary work. Therefore, copyright laws that protect creative works also protect computer programs, including technical manuals and documentation. The developer of a program thus has protective rights to authorize others of his or her choice to reproduce the format of the program en masse at any time, to update and upgrade the program, and distribute it for free, or to sell or transfer ownership. The copyright laws in this case protect the source code, the object code, and the executable codes, including the manuals and documentation, from illegal copying and piracy.

Although the developer has such rights, there are limitations or exceptions in some instances. For example, a buyer of such a program has some protected rights also. The buyer has the right to make another copy as a backup, provided that a copy is not used on another machine. Software registration for copyright, however, does not stop a software developer's worries because by registering software, the developer is opening up the secrets of the whole project as part of the requirements of the copyright issuance. According to Neitzke, there are two roadblocks in copyright registration in some countries:

1. Some courts have taken the position that copyright registration precludes maintaining software as a trade secret.
2. In some countries registration requires submitting at least the first and last 25 pages of the program for public inspection.

So before a developer goes ahead with a copyright application he or she should weigh the pros and cons of copyright protection.

5.7.3   Protection of Software Under Patent Laws

In Sect. 5.3.2 we defined a patent as the protection of the manifestation of an idea on condition that the patent owner discloses the methodology for the manifestation and workings of the product from the idea. In contrast to the copyright laws, however, patents protect the processing of the idea; they also protect the implementation of the idea as a machine, a manufacturing process, or a composition of matter or materials. Under these conditions, computer hardware components, by their very nature, are protected under the patent laws. Software also may be protected under the patent laws under certain circumstances. Under these conditions, how can software be protected?

This is a difficult question, and we must answer it first by explaining that patent issues for computer programs are not yet settled. There are various reasons for the debate, among which are the following:

1. The requirement of the patent system for total disclosure of all information pertaining to the application of the patent is still a big issue. Given that the patent protection lasts for 17 years and 2-year-old software is as old as software can get and still be really viable, requiring developers to disclose the secrets of their software before the 17-year deadline opens them up to stiff competition and better variations of the applicant's software format.
2. Most of the computer programs on the market are simple one-person ventures. Such persons, many of them independent-minded individuals, may not support yet let alone be able to afford the expense of the patent process application.
3. It has been and still is very difficult, as we saw earlier in this section, to prove to courts and patent offices that algorithms are processes and therefore a form of manifestation of an idea and not mere mental gymnastics that any human being can do and, therefore, not patentable because mental steps and mathematical formulas are not patentable items.

Although computer programs are not suited for patent protection, there have been successful applications that have received patents. For specific examples of some of these cases, see Gervaise Davis's book *Software Protection* [11].

5.7.4   Protection of Software Under Trademarks

In Sect. 5.3.4 we defined a trademark as a symbol or mark with financial value that helps customers connect to the product. The main purpose of a trademark is to make the product stand out against the competitors. All hardware companies and a few software concerns such as Microsoft have their trademark protected under the trademark laws and statutes. But how is a mark or symbol be used to protect computer programs?

The protection of computer programs by trademarks is achieved through self-realization by the infringer that it is not easy to copy, change, or redistribute copies of well-known software works. For example, it is not easy to make copies of Windows 9X, NT, or any other Windows product, and resell them, although there have been instances of this. So for big-name software developers, this realization by would-be infringers works far better than law enforcement. But the trick does not work all the time, especially in countries where this sort of realization does not have as much appeal because of lack of publicity of the products. Apart from these measures, software developers do include their symbols and marks within the product so that during use, the symbols and marks are displayed automatically. However, there are no effective global trademark laws to protect computer programs.

5.7.5   Protection of Software Under Trade Secrets

So far we have defined a trade secret as information one has about a manifestation of an idea and that no one should disclose or use for the benefit of themselves or a competitor. As pointed out in Sect. 5.3.3, there are basic laws to protect trade secrets. How do these laws help protect computer products, especially software?

The manifestation of an idea into a computer program usually starts with the blueprint and flowchart, as we saw earlier. This process then goes through the remaining stages of object code and executable code. One's knowledge of the process anywhere during these stages forms a trade secret and should not be revealed for personal gain or to a competitor.

It is generally known to computer programmers and software developers, as it is known to all hardware engineers, that once the blueprint and flowchart of a computer program are known, it is easy to develop a program. It is, therefore, of the utmost importance that at the early software development stages, the blueprint and flowchart not be known outside design circles. Typically the trade secret laws require an infringer, if caught, to stop, return the material under dispute to the rightful owner, and pay damages. But there are difficult cases, such as when former employees leave their employers without written material but with years of acquired knowhow of product development. Here the law is difficult to apply. Some companies make the employees sign nondisclosure contracts for a specific number of years after leaving the company. This method works to some extent, but it is very difficult to enforce except in high-profile and rich companies.

5.8   Transnational Issues and Intellectual Property

A number of studies concerning the international IP system show that there is an extensive and growing number of losses being incurred by businesses in the developed world as a result of nonenforcement of IP laws in the developing world. The developed world is charging that the lack of IP legislation in some development countries and the absence of enforcement in others are amounting to sanctioning pirates and leading to losses amounting to tens of billions of dollars' worth of goods of multinational corporations every year. Developing countries, however, are not amused with the charges lobbed on them. They argue that:

- The IP system, if instated in full in their countries, results in significant social costs on that country; this may include developing the cost of acquiring and maintaining the IP rights and defending those rights whenever there are international legal disputes.
- Country memberships in the present IP system are costly and exacerbate the costs of enforcement.
- Loosely enforcing the IP laws will speed their industrialization and development by enabling them to copy state-of-the-art technologies.
- The IP protection is not as profitable as was touted by developed countries. There is evidence that the innovation for developing countries is not visible. For example, the introduction or strengthening of patent protection for pharmaceutical products has not increased national or foreign direct investment, production, or R&D in developing countries. On the other hand, the Indian pharmaceutical industry became a global producer of active ingredients and medicines in the absence of patents on such products, which was only introduced in January 2005, at the expiry of the transitional period allowed by the TRIPS Agreement [1].
- The industrialized world, when in the process of development, did not depend on the patent system but rather the lack of the IP system, which promoted innovation.

So, the developing world is reluctant to accept the IP system wholesale without concessions unless the industrialized countries guarantee them greater access to their markets for their goods and agricultural products. There are other issues pertinent to the IP system, but we do not go into those here.

Discussion Issues

1. Do you think the developing world has relevant issues in this discussion?
2. Is the developing world being misled by a few powerful countries within their ranks?
3. What kind of concessions should the developed world make?

Exercises

1. Discuss the problems faced by software developers trying to apply for protection under trade secret statutes.
2. Why is it difficult to apply patent laws to software?
3. Why is it possible to apply patent law to software?
4. Is it possible to trademark software?
5. Discuss the ethical and legal issues surrounding software ownership.
6. There is a move to do away with the current copyright law. Why?
7. Why is the copyright law, in its present form, considered to be unenforceable?
8. What changes would you suggest in the current copyright laws to make it enforceable in cyberspace?
9. Has the Internet made software protection easier or more difficult? Why or why not?
10. There is a movement (that includes hackers) that is advocating for free software! Discuss the merits of this idea, if any.
11. Because of income disparities between north and south, and haves and have-nots, fair pricing of computer products is impossible. Discuss.
12. Most copyright violations are found in developing, usually poor, countries. Why?
13. Does the high price of software marketing in developing countries justify the high rate of software piracy in those countries? Why?
14. What do you think is the cause of the rising cost of software?
15. Is globalization a means through which the developed, usually northern, countries will enforce the copyright laws?

References

1. Glass A (1999) Cybersquatters frustrate political candidate. Cox News Service, 7 Sept 1999
2. Nasheri H. Addressing global scope of intellectual property law. http://www.ncjrs.gov/pdf-files1/nij/grants/208384.pdf
3. Johnson DJ (2009) Computer ethics, 4th edn. Pearson Education, Upper Saddle River
4. Prince J (1980) Negligence: liability for defective software. Okla Law Rev 33:848–855
5. Wikipedia. Work for hire. https://en.wikipedia.org/wiki/Work_for_hire
6. Strong WE (2014) The copyright book: a practical guide, 6th edn. MIT Press, Boston
7. Neitzke FW (1984) A software primer. Van Nostrand Reinhold, New York
8. Personal identity theft on the rise. USA Today, Tech Report. 09/14/00
9. Burge DA (1984) Patent and trademarks: tactics and practice, 2nd edn. Wiley, New York
10. Scott MD (1984) Computer law. Wiley, New York
11. Davis GG (1985) Software protection. Van Nostrand Reinhold, New York

Further Reading

Davis R (1992) A new view of intellectual property and software. Commun ACM 39(3):21–30

Oz E (1994) Protecting software as intellectual property. In: Ethics for the information age. Business and Education Technologies, Barr Ridge, pp 273–285

Samuelson P (1989) Information and property. Cathol Rev 38:365–410

Samuelson P (1991) Is information property? Commun ACM 34(10):15–18

Samuelson P (1992) Copyright law and electronic compilations of data. Commun ACM 35(2):27–32

Samuelson P (1992) Regulation of technologies to protect copyrighted works. Commun ACM 39(7):17–22

Suapper J (1995) Intellectual property protection for computer software. In: Johnson D, Nissenbaum H (eds) Computer ethics and social values. Prentice Hall, Englewood Cliffs, pp 181–190

Social Context of Computing

6

Learning Objectives

After reading this chapter, the reader should be able to

1. Interpret the social context of a particular software/hardware implementation.
2. Identify assumptions and values embedded in a particular computer product design, including those of a cultural nature.
3. Evaluate a particular computing tool implementation through the use of empirical data.
4. Describe positive and negative ways in which computing alters the modes of interaction between people.
5. Explain why computing/network access is restricted in some countries.
6. Learn the impact of the digital divide.
7. Understand how income, geography, race, and culture influence access to information technology and technology in general.
8. Analyze the role and risks of computing in the implementation of public policy and government.
9. Articulate the impact of the input deficit from diverse populations in the computing profession.

© Springer International Publishing Switzerland 2016
J.M. Kizza, *Ethics in Computing*, Undergraduate Topics in Computer Science,
DOI 10.1007/978-3-319-29106-2_6

Scenario 5: Electronic Surveillance and the Bodyguard
Jon Kiggwe is a young aggressive entrepreneur, with a bright future. With several businesses doing well and a few start-ups with promising financial status, Jon is on his way to making a million dollars before his 25th birthday. Jon's business meetings take him into tough neighborhoods. So, that he may feel secure, Jon uses a team of professional security bodyguards to shadow him almost 24 h a day.

In his big 10-million-dollar home, Jon receives a stream of guests, including both business associates and friends. His bodyguards, besides keeping an eye on him, also see to the orderly arrival and departure of the guests. Because of this, the bodyguards keep a permanent office and sleeping quarters at Jon's mansion.

Without informing them, Jon installed video recording and listening gadgets in the guards' office and sleeping quarters to record their every conversation and movement. He feels safe that way!

Discussion Questions

1. *Is Jon violating any law?*
2. *Do the bodyguards have any right to privacy on Jon's premises?*
3. *Does Jon have a right to know what the bodyguards are doing in his house?*

6.1   Introduction

In the past 5 years or so, we have witnessed an invasion of computers and computer-related equipment in workplaces, homes, and schools. The advent of the Internet, wireless communication, and mobile computer technology has considerably expanded this invasion into planes, trains, and automobiles. The widespread use of computers and computer technology in its present form has also resulted in a shift in computer usage. The computer started as a utilitarian tool but has now also been embraced as a social tool. Probably because of the popularity of the Internet, both young and old have found solace in computing devices everywhere. Playing this double role as a utility and an entertainment tool, the computer has become an integral part of our social fabric.

However, in the meantime, two worlds have been created for humanity: the unreal world of entertainment and a real computer technology-driven world, which augments our familiar environment and makes our daily activities easier and more enjoyable. This development in turn has led to an influx of computer technology into the workplace, schools, and the home. Indeed, the home has turned into a hub of technology. No one knows, as yet, the social, psychological, and intellectual implications that may result from this. Predictions abound that this will enhance our intelligence and improve our performance at whatever we do. This belief alone has been a driving force for the computerization of schools and homes, with parents hoping to produce young geniuses.

These beliefs about the value of technology, whether or not supported by scientific research, are not new. Ever since the beginning of the industrial age, when technology started entering the workplace and homes, the aim has been to utilize it to help us be wiser and more productive. It is, therefore, no wonder that as technology has developed, progress and fundamental changes have been taking place almost daily. Our focus in this chapter is on both the social and ethical effects of computer technology on people, whether we are at home, school, or work. We focus on the social and economic dimensions of computing as a result of the "digital divide," the workplace, workplace monitoring of employees, and the well-being of employees.

6.2 The Digital Divide

The technological inequalities among people in one country and between countries, commonly known as the digital divide, arose from the landmark 1994 U.S. Commerce Department's National Telecommunications and Information Administration (NTIA) report, "Falling Through the Net," commonly referred to as NTIA I. The NTIA I report used the Information and Communication Technologies (ICT) *access* indicator, one of the many digital divide indicators, to highlight sectors of the U.S. population that were technologically deprived. Since then, the digital divide debate has been raging, centered on a number of key critical issues including the following:

- Whether there is such a thing as a digital divide
- Indicators that should be used to measure such a divide if it exists, and
- The best ways to close such a divide

Much of the debate is the result of a lack of understanding about the digital divide—its origins, inputs, and responses to inputs. In general, in a broader sense, the study of the digital divide involves the study of the impact of the digital divide indicators. These indicators concern communication technologies such as radio, television, the press, fixed and cellular telephones, fax machines, computers, and connectivity to the Internet and participation in cyber activities for all members of a society. However, in its most basic definition, it is a discrepancy in access to information technology. What causes it? Why does it exist? Answers to these two questions can fill as many as two large books. There is a multitude of causes and enablers, and so long as these exist in any society, the digital divide will exist. Study after study, since the inception of the concept, have pointed to *social, economic, and geographic* factors as influencing the digital divide. More specifically, the following are enablers of the digital divide: *access, relevant technology, humanware (human capacity), infrastructure, and enabling environment.* These enablers fuel the following causes of the digital divide: *geography, age, education, income, race, and ethnicity.*

6.2.1 Access

Access is a crucial component in the digital divide: it involves obstacles that exist even if all the other remaining indicators are in place. Such obstacles may include, but are not limited to, costs involved in acquiring the technologies, availability of free or low-cost facilities in the neighborhood, the ability to travel to places where there are low-cost access points, such as libraries and community centers, and having the capacity needed to utilize the technologies. These obstacles can broadly be grouped into five categories: geography, income, ethnicity, age, and education.

6.2.1.1 Geography

According to the UN Human Development Report of 2011, there is a large digital divide between the rich, industrialized countries of the Northern Hemisphere and the poor, less industrialized countries in the Southern Hemisphere. The poor developing countries, geographically in the Southern Hemisphere and mostly in the southern axis of development, are more deprived of access to information, although mobile technology has improved this situation greatly in the last few years

ITU World Telecommunications/ICT databases (WTI) and UNDP for years 2000–2008 show us the digital divide that exists between countries. For example, in the highest ranked 30 or so countries of the HDI (the very high group), Internet users represent an average of 61.4 % of the population, whereas they represent an average of 1.8 % for the 20 or so lowest ranked countries classified as low human development (ITU 2009; UNDP 2008) [1].

Focusing on information communication technology (ICT), the main driver among the indicators of the digital divide, the picture, although improving some, remains the same in mobile cellular, mobile broadband, fixed broadband, and Internet technology (Fig. 6.1).

According to Caetano Notari [2], the status of global digital inclusion leaves much to be desired. For example, of the approximately 7 billion inhabitants of the earth (2011 estimates):

- 65 % are not digitally connected.
- 69 % of people in the developed countries have access to the Internet.
- 21 % of the people in developing countries have access to the Internet.

The divide is not only between the Northern and Southern Hemisphere nations, it also exists within individual nations. For example, within the U.S., Lennard G. Kruger and Angele A. Gilroy [3] report that although the number of new broadband subscribers continues to grow, the rate of broadband deployment in urban areas appears to be outpacing deployment in rural areas: 13 recent surveys and studies have indicated that, in general, rural areas tend to lag behind urban and suburban areas in broadband deployment. Consider the following surveys [1]:

- The Department of Commerce's "Exploring the Digital Nation" report found that although the digital divide between urban and rural areas has lessened since

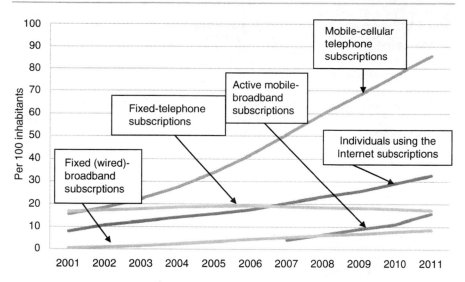

Fig. 6.1 World Information and Communication Technologies (ICT) Indicators (Source: World Telecommunication/ICT Indicators Database, http://www.itu.int/ITU-D/ict/statistics/)

2007, it still persists with 70 % of urban households adopting broadband service in 2010, compared to 57 % of rural households.

- Data from the Pew Internet & American Life Project show that the percentage of all U.S. adults with broadband at home is 70 % for non-rural areas and 50 % for rural areas.
- Data from the National Broadband Map (2011) indicate that 99.7 % of the population in urban areas have access to available broadband speeds of at least 3 Mbps (download)/768 kbps (upload), as opposed to 84.0 % of the population in rural areas.

However, this north–south technological divide is constantly changing for the better. Data from Table 6.1 show that although there is still a substantial rift between the Northern and Southern Hemispheres, it is rapid narrowing in at least in these four technologies.

6.2.1.2 Income
According to the most recent Pew Research Center study of the U.S. population, household income is the greatest predictor of the use of the Internet and other ICT technologies. Households earning more than $75,000 a year significantly outpace lower-earning households, particularly those making less than $30,000 a year [4]. In his Pew Research Center Report, "The Better-Off Online," Jim Jansen [5] reports that the analysis of several surveys conducted by the Pew Research Center's Internet & American Life Projects revealed significant key differences between those who live in households making $75,000 or more relative to those in lower-income

Table 6.1 Key statistical highlights: ITU data release June 2012

Mobile cellular:

Total mobile-cellular subscriptions reached almost 6 billion by end 2011, corresponding to a global penetration of 86 %

Growth was driven by developing countries, which accounted for more than 80 % of the 660 million new mobile-cellular subscriptions added in 2011

In 2011, 142 million mobile-cellular subscriptions were added in India, twice as many as in the whole of Africa, and more than in the Arab States, CIS, and Europe together

By end 2011, there were 105 countries with more mobile-cellular subscriptions than inhabitants, including African countries such as Botswana, Gabon, Namibia, Seychelles, and South Africa

Countries where mobile-cellular penetration increased the most in 2011 include Brazil, Costa Rica, Kazakhstan, Lao P.D.R., and Mali

Mobile broadband:

By end 2011, there were more than 1 billion mobile-broadband subscriptions worldwide

Mobile broadband has become the single most dynamic ICT service, reaching a 40 % annual subscription growth in 2011

Although developing countries are catching up in terms of 3G coverage, huge disparities remain between mobile-broadband penetration in the developing (8 %) and the developed world (51 %)

In Africa there are fewer than five mobile-broadband subscriptions per 100 inhabitants, whereas all other regions have penetration levels above 10 %

By end 2011, there were more mobile-broadband subscriptions than inhabitants in the Republic of Korea and Singapore. In Japan and Sweden, active mobile-broadband penetration surpassed 90 % by end 2011

In 2011, 144 million mobile-broadband subscriptions were added in the BRICS (Brazil, the Russian Federation, India, China and South Africa), accounting for 45 % of the world's total subscriptions added in 2011

Fixed (wired) broadband:

By end 2011, there were 590 million fixed (wired)-broadband subscriptions worldwide.

Fixed (wired) broadband growth in developed countries is slowing (5 % increase in 2011), whereas developing countries continue to experience high growth (18 % in 2011)

Fixed (wired)-broadband penetration remains low in some regions, such as Africa and the Arab States, with 0.2 % and 2 %, respectively, by end 2011

In 2011, 30 million fixed (wired)-broadband subscriptions were added in China, about half of the total subscriptions added worldwide, and fixed (wired)-broadband penetration reached 12 % in the country

Top performers, such as France, Denmark, the Netherlands, Norway, the Republic of Korea, and Switzerland, had fixed (wired)-broadband penetrations above 35 % by end 2011

Countries where fixed (wired)-broadband penetration increased the most in 2011 include Bahrain, Costa Rica, Ecuador, Mauritius, and Uruguay. However, among these, only Bahrain and Uruguay surpassed the 10 % fixed (wired)-broadband penetration by end 2011

Internet:

The percentage of individuals using the Internet continues to grow worldwide and by end 2011 2.3 billion people were online

In developing countries, the number of Internet users doubled between 2007 and 2011, but only a quarter of inhabitants in the developing world were online by end 2011

(continued)

Table 6.1 (continued)

The percentage of individuals using the Internet in the developed world reached the 70 % landmark by end 2011
In Iceland, the Netherlands, Norway, and Sweden, more than 90 % of the population are online
By end 2011, 70 % of the total households in developed countries had Internet, whereas only 20 % of households in developing countries had Internet access. Some outstanding exceptions include Lebanon and Malaysia with 62 % and 61 % of households with Internet, respectively

Source: ITU World Telecommunication/ICT Indicators Database. http://www.itu.int/ITU-D/ict/statistics/material/pdf/2011%20Statistical%20highlights_June_2012.pdf

households. The key findings in Jansen's report in three information communication technologies, namely, broadband at home, Internet use, and mobile cell phone ownership are as follows [5]:

- Broadband at home:
  - <$30,000   40 %
  - $30,000 to <$50,000   79 %
  - $50,000 to <$75,000   79 %
  - >$75,000   87 %
- Regularly use the Internet
  - <$30,000   57 %
  - $30,000 to <$50,000   80 %
  - $50,000 to <$75,000   86 %
  - >$75,000   95 %
- Cell phone ownership
  - <$30,000   75 %
  - $30,000 to <$50,000   90 %
  - $50,000 to <$75,000   93 %
  - >$75,000   95 %

6.2.1.3 Ethnicity

According to NTIA 2000 [6], one's ethnicity has a great influence on ICT access. For example, in the United States, blacks and Hispanics, the two main U.S. minority groups, are twice as likely as their white counterparts not to have a computer and access to the Internet.

Although there has been no comprehensive study of global ICT access based on ethnicity and race, there have been limited but revealing national studies. Nearly all these national studies point to results similar to those in the original NTIA 2000 report.

Since the NTIA 2000 report [6], however, there have been interesting changes in the issue of ethnicity and access to ICT technologies. These dramatic changes have been brought about by the rapid changes in modern communication technologies, more specifically Internet-able mobile communication technologies. Jesse Washington [6] reports in "For minorities, new 'digital divide' seen," that Latinos and blacks are now more likely than the general population to access the Web by cellular phones. Today, mobile technology has become an equalizer of sorts, in some aspects, as it brings computers and the ability to access the Internet and the Web, at the same rate as whites, to the hands of minorities such as Latinos and blacks. However, because these minorities have limited options to access the Internet and the Web, they are more likely than the general population to access the Web by cellular phones, and they use their phones more often to do more things. Aaron Smith [7] reports on a continuing a trend, first identified in 2009, that minority Americans lead the way when it comes to mobile access, especially mobile access using handheld devices. Nearly 64 % of African-Americans and 63 % of Latinos are wireless Internet users. It is also emerging that minority Americans are significantly more likely to own a cell phone than their white counterparts because 87 % of blacks and Hispanics own a cell phone, compared with 80 % of whites. Additionally, black and Latino cell phone owners use their cell phones in a wider array of functions compared to white cell phone owners.

Does this mean that the divide is over? Probably not! There is wide agreement that Latinos and blacks are becoming more challenged as they access the new technologies because the computing powers and functionalities of the current mobile technologies are still very limited. Thus, overreliance on them is creating a sort of new "digital divide" for these groups. For example, it is tough to fill out a job application on a cell phone. Also, blacks and Latinos are increasingly using their mobile power more for entertainment than for empowerment.

Discussion Topic In what ways does mobile technology disadvantage minorities?

6.2.1.4 Age
There is a myth that young people use computers and the Internet far more than any other age group. There is also conventional wisdom that young people under age 18 do more surfing of the Internet than any other age group. However, this is not the case. There are consistent data from NTIA 2000 and the UCLA Internet Report showing that the highest usage of computers and the Internet is among people between the ages of 18 and 49 (Table 6.2). NTIA 2000, the UCLA Internet Report (Table 6.3), and the British Office of National Statistics report (Table 6.4) are consistently showing that older people and those under 10 years of age use computers

Table 6.2 U.S. households with computer and online access by age of inhabitants

Category (years)	%
Under 8	15.3
9–17	53.4
18–24	56.5
25–49	55.4
50+	29.8

Table 6.3 Age and Internet usage (UCLA report)

Age group (years)	12–15	16–18	19–24	25–35	36–45	46–55	56–65	65+
Average hours per week	5.6	7.6	9.7	11.3	9.4	10.3	8.5	6.8

Table 6.4 Internet users and non-users, UK, 2011, Q1–Q4

	Used Internet				Never used Internet			
	2011 Q1	2011 Q2	2011 Q3	2011 Q4	2011 Q1	2011 Q2	2011 Q3	2011 Q4
All	82.2	82.3	82.9	83.5	17.5	17.4	16.8	16.3
Age (years)								
16–24	98.8	98.8	98.6	98.7	0.9	0.9	1.1	1.0
25–34	97.5	97.7	97.8	98.0	2.1	2.1	2.0	1.8
35–44	95.4	95.4	95.6	95.9	4.3	4.3	4.1	3.9
45–54	89.5	89.9	90.2	90.5	10.2	9.8	9.5	9.5
55–64	79.0	79.2	79.9	81.1	20.8	20.6	19.8	18.7
65–74	57.1	57.6	58.7	59.8	42.6	42.1	41.2	40.0
75+	23.8	23.6	27.3	29.0	76.1	76.3	72.4	70.8

Source: British Office of National Statistics, http://www.ons.gov.uk/ons/publications/re-reference-tables.html?edition=tcm%3A77-250549

and online access far less than any other age group. Also, the latest figures from Media Metrix show similar global patterns with a bell-shaped curve pattern of usage peaking between 18 and 54 years [8].

More than 12 years after the NTIA 2000 report, advances in technology have changed the digital inclusion landscape. Now, instead of talking about the use of computers, cell phones, and Internet access, it is more about mobile phones and wireless access. So, the discussion now focuses on use of the Internet and mobile devices to access the Internet.

Although we do not have comprehensive data for global digital inclusion based on age, we can discuss data from the U.S. and Britain. According to Ian Clark [9], in the United Kingdom, the 2011 statistics from the Office for National Statistics (ONS) of Internet use by age reveal the highest percent of use for the 16- to 24-year-old group than any other age group. This figure then levels off as age increases. It is worrying to see that 71 % of those more than 75 years of age and 40 % of the 65- to 74-year-old age group have never used the Internet (see Table 6.3). There are a number of reasons why this is the case.

The data do not change very much when it comes to the U.S. Some 92 % of Americans aged 18–29 are online, according to the Pew Internet and American Life Project [7]. Again, in a similar fashion, the rate falls as the ages of users increase, showing 87 % for those aged 30–49 years and 79 % in the age range of 50–64 years, down to a low of 42 % for those over 65 years of age.

On wireless communication, the picture becomes more interesting. Aaron Smith [10] reports that nine in ten persons of 18–29 years old own a cell phone, and these young cell phone owners are significantly more likely than those in other age groups to engage in all the mobile data applications, as follows:

- 95 % send or receive *text messages*
- 93 % use their phone to *take pictures*
- 81 % *send photos or videos* to others
- 65 % *access the Internet* on their mobile device
- 64 % *play music* on their phones
- 60 % use their phones to *play games* or *record a video*
- 52 % have used their phone to *send or receive e-mail*
- 48 % have accessed a *social networking site* on their phone
- 46 % use *instant messaging* on their mobile device
- 40 % have *watched a video* on their phone
- 33 % have *posted a photo or video online* from their phone
- 21 % have *used a status update service* such as Twitter from their phone
- 20 % have *purchased something* using their mobile phone
- 19 % have made a *charitable donation* by text message

There is growing evidence that this love for mobile devices is also growing fast among those 30 to 49 years old.

6.2.1.5 Education

Ever since the NTIA I report showed that the higher the education level one achieves, the more likely one is to use a computer and, therefore, the Internet, study after study have shown the same thing. Data from NTIA 2000 and the UCLA Internet Report (Tables 6.5 and 6.6) show the same trend. For example, the very highly educated with advanced degrees, reported in both NTIA 2000 and the latest UCLA Internet Report, show 69.9 % and 86 % Internet usage, respectively, compared to 11.7 % and 31 % usage, respectively, for those with less than a high school diploma.

As we observed earlier, more than 12 years since the NTIA 2000 report, the rapid advances in technology have changed the digital inclusion landscape. When we talk about digital inclusion, understanding has shifted from using computers, cell phones, and Internet access, to having an Internet-able mobile device. Based on this

Table 6.5 U.S. households with computer and online access by education level

Category	Computer (%)	Online (%)
Elementary	18.2	11.7
High school diploma	39.6	29.9
Some college	60.3	49.0
College diploma	74.0	64.0
Postgraduate	79.0	69.9

Table 6.6 Internet use and level of education (UCLA report)

Education level attained	Less than high school	High school graduate	Some college	College graduate	Advanced degree
Percent using Internet	31.2 %	53.1 %	70.2 %	86.3 %	86.3 %

thinking, in the past 12 years since the NTIA 2000 study, the situation has changed considerably but has remained the same in that digital inclusion still favors high education. Look at the data from the Pew report 2010 on the U.S population [7]:

- Of all people with less than a high school education, 38 % have access to a wireless Internet-able mobile device.
- Of all people with a high school diploma, 48 % have access to a wireless Internet-able mobile device.
- Of all people with some college education, 68 % have access to a wireless Internet-able mobile device.
- Of all people who are college graduates, 76% have access to a wireless Internet-able mobile device.

6.2.2   Technology

The computer-driven technological revolution has brought the countries of the world closer together. In their study of the digital divide, Rodriquez and Wilson observed that all developing countries, including the poorest, are improving their access to the use of ICT [11]. In fact, technological progress in developing countries between the 1990s and 2000s has been very strong, outpacing that in developed countries by 40–60 %, according to data from the World Bank report, "Global Economic Prospects 2008: Technology Diffusion in the Developing World." The percentage change in technological achievements between the 1900s and the 2000s is given here [12]:

- High income $\approx$75 % change
- Upper middle income $\approx$110 % change
- Lower middle income $\approx$102 % change
- Low income $\approx$160 % change

But the gap between rich and poor countries is still very wide [13]. As Figs. 6.2 and 6.3 show, there is still a large, persistent gap between the industrialized north on one hand and the predominantly developing south on the other. This state of affairs is the result of a lack of broad-based technological skills and know-how. The acquisition of technological skills and, therefore, the development of a good technological base, depends a great deal on relevant inputs that include investment capital, infrastructure, and humanware (human capacity). However, the situation with technology input and output is no better. New technological innovations require huge amounts of money to be invested in research and development. Unfortunately, not enough capital investment is done in developing countries. According to the UN Human Development Report 1999, although developed countries have 21 % of the $(US) 21,000 billion GDP in 1999 invested, the least developed countries had 20 % of the $(US) 143 billion GDP invested [14]. Because capital investment in technology is usually in form of hardware and software, let us focus on those here.

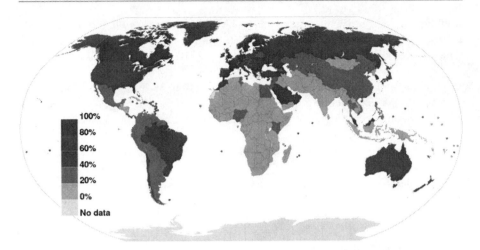

Fig. 6.2 Global technological divide [2] (Source: http://en.wikipedia.org/wiki/Global_digital_divide)

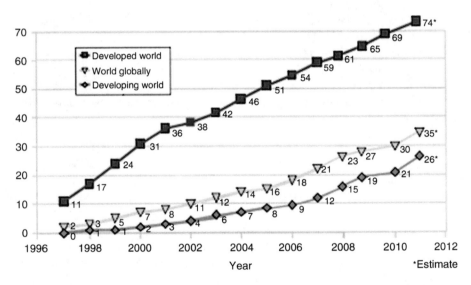

Fig. 6.3 Internet users per 100 inhabitants [2] (Source: http://en.wikipedia.org/wiki/Global_digital_divide)

6.2.2.1 Hardware

Although there has been a steady increase in the number of computers, telephones, and other modern communication technologies in almost all countries of the world in the last couple of years, as noted by Rodriguez and Wilson, the quantity, quality, and maintenance of these technologies is still a big problem that is challenging the narrowing of the ICT digital divide. There is a serious regression in hardware acquisition and maintenance. Computer components for example, are being acquired, but they are being disposed of at probably the same rate as they are acquired. Uncertain and unreliable power supplies contribute to the shorter lifespans of ICT products in developing countries; probably many of the unusable ICT products are so because they were hit by a power surge.

Replacement of the bad parts is hampered by the price of new ones. ICT parts are very expensive in a number of developing countries because governments either levy high tariffs on imports to raise local revenue or impose luxury taxes because these are classified as luxury items.

ICT products are also expensive because most outlet owners are not indigenous people; they are foreign investors who usually raise prices to cover their local and infrastructure expenses plus profits. In addition, similar to all equipment and software produced in developed countries and imported into developing countries, by the time such items arrive in the developing world, their prices have been inflated three to four times their original value.

6.2.2.2 Software

The problems presented by hardware are accompanied by the problems of software. For ICT equipment to be helpful, it must have good and relevant software. Countries that have seen benefits from ICT, such as those in OECD, either produce their own software or have enough financial capacity to source software with few problems. This is not the case in many developing countries. There is very limited humanware to have software locally produced. In addition, they do not have enough money to source the software from their northern counterparts where it is produced. Even if they have some money to buy software from developed countries, as we pointed out earlier, by the time software arrives in developing countries its list price is much higher. The end result, at least for the time being, is that most ICT software in developing countries comes with the bulk of the donated ICT equipment. However, the software shipped on donated company computers rarely meets the needs of the recipients. Consequently, the local people end up using a product that in most instances produces outputs that have very little value to them, irrespective of the inputs. In such a situation, that equipment ends up not benefiting the locals.

6.2.3   Humanware (Human Capacity)

In this section we consider the complex issues related to human capacity development. Availability and easy access to ICT does not always solve the digital divide problem. As Rodriguez and Wilson pointed out, it is only a partial solution to a complex problem. Even if we were to provide everyone on the globe with first-class ICT equipment, the reality would remain that only a few would be able to maintain and gainfully use the provided technology. This situation is likely to persist until there is a corresponding degree of technical capacity and knowledge acquired by the people intending to use the technologies so that they can maintain the equipment and derive value-laden outputs. The first problem is lack of humanware in developing counties to maintain the equipment. There is a shortage of teachers, technicians, and institutes to train them. The next challenge is to ensure that people can gainfully use ICT to add value to local inputs. People will take ICT seriously when it meets and serves their own local needs. Human capacity development is a complex multi-faceted endeavor consisting of many aspects, including these [15]:

- Creating awareness of the potential for ICT to meet one's needs
- Creating, developing, and strengthening capacity to use information and ICT effectively, using local inputs
- Building capacity to produce and package information so that it adds value to local inputs
- Ensuring ongoing technical capacity development and developing a format for sharing knowledge and information
- Preventing the local capacity from being drained to other, usually developed countries

The challenge, therefore, in tackling human capacity development is to take care of each of these issues so that the local persons using ICT may find useful answers to their local problems. ICT capacity development should take into account equity, fairness, and cultural and other contextual factors at the local levels.

6.2.4   Infrastructure

As noted by many, the digital divide infrastructure is related to access in many ways: both present obstacles to gaining access to ICT. For us, infrastructure will mean fixed communication structures. In those countries with good fixed communication structures such as electricity, telephones, good roads, and airports, ICT development is much faster. Lack of such resources hinders the development of ICT. In his communication to the Digital Opportunity (DIGOPP) discussion list, Robert Krech, drawing from his experience in Nepal, noted the enormous difficulties in "the logistics of reaching people located in remote rural areas with limited or no access to formal educational systems, healthcare, clean water, electricity or jobs related to the new information economy" [16]. Krech was expressing the necessity or lack of good fixed communication structures that are crucial to the development of ICT.

The availability of these resources helps to speed up the development of ICT structures such as Internet cafes. ICT access enablers such as personal computers, personal assistants, Internet-enabled cellular phones, and other miniature Internet-enabled gizmos in developed countries and the urban areas of developing countries, together with civic centers in developed countries and telecenters in developing countries, have all been hailed in advancing global communication. For these to work, however, there must be a basic communication infrastructure in place. So if digital communication is to be developed in the developing world, ICT-accessible points such as telecenters, civic centers, and Internet or cyber cafes must be opened up where there are none and expanded where there are only a few.

6.2.5 Enabling Environments

As Rodriguez and Wilson [11] noted, many countries with similar levels of per capita incomes and economic structures exhibit widely varying ICT performances. There are no good explanations for this except for the existence, or lack thereof, of enabling environments. An ICT-enabling environment is an environment in which ICT can thrive. Several things can bring about such an environment, including politics, public policy, and management styles.

6.2.5.1 Politics

According to Rodriquez and Wilson, ICT thrives in a good political environment that ensures:

- A climate of democratic rights and civil liberties conducive to ICT adaptation
- Respect for the rule of law and security of property rights
- Investment in human capacity
- Low levels of government distortions

One sure way of creating such environments in the different political systems that make up the landscape of the developing world is for the two leading nongovernmental organizations, the G8 Dot Force and the Commonwealth Expert Group on Information Technology, and other development organizations working toward the elimination of the digital divide, to develop a policy that charges governments in individual countries with the task of creating the enabling environments for ICT to thrive. One approach is to develop a Leadership Mobilization Strategy (LMS) to target and educate first the top political leadership at all levels within and outside government about the benefits of ICT to the country's development. These officials must understand the need for ICT and then articulate this need to others: this is crucial to convince leaders to mobilize people and bring ICT awareness to the general population. Although politics is conducive to a good ICT environment, much of ICT development also depends on good public policy and management styles.

6.2.5.2 Public Policy and Management Styles

Governments must put in place streamlined regulatory policies for the importation and licensing of ICT technologies. Laws must be enacted and enforced uniformly so that nongovernmental organizations (NGOs) and other organizations interested in investing in ICT economic activities can do so with ease.

In many developing countries, there are currently ICT-related laws and policies on the books that are not enforced. Such policies must be updated where necessary and enforced strictly and fairly. New competitive policies such as the liberalization of the telecommunication and energy sectors must be developed and the sectors must be staffed with competent managers with appropriate expertise. These ICT regulatory policies need to be efficient, predictable, and easy to understand. Licensing bodies need to be efficient and staffed with professionals. In addition, there must be government support for taxing policies that grant favors such as tax holidays to ICT equipment and investment firms. Finally, there must be transparency in government to create a moral bar for the rest of the country.

6.3   Obstacles to Overcoming the Digital Divide

Based on a number of studies and data, including those of Felix Bankole, Farid Shirazi, and Irwin Brown [17] titled "Investigating the Impact of ICT Investments on Human Development" and that of Kim et al. [18], indicating that digital inclusion is one of the agents of development, countries and policy makers are making every effort to expand the digital inclusion and thus decrease the digital divide within countries and across the global. However, minimizing the digital divide requires considerable effort and a plan in addressing the following types of access [19]:

- Physical Access: individuals need to be able to obtain access to computers, land-lines, and networks so they can access the Internet.
- Financial Access: the means to meet the costs of ICT devices, traffic, applications, technician and educator training, software, maintenance, and infrastructures.
- Political Access: the political environment that enables a faster growth of the Internet and other digital inclusion technologies.
- Cultural Access: availability of images and language to carry over the digital inclusion across different cultural lines.

6.4   ICT in the Workplace

The automation of the workplace has been the most vigorously pursued concept since the Industrial Age. Despite the original fear that workplace automation would mean the end to human work, except in a few areas workplace automation has proceeded hand in hand with increases in employment numbers [20]. This is, of course, not to deny that automation has caused some human displacements in the workplace. But overall numbers are steady, and according to the International Labor Office report, the introduction of computers into offices did not bring about any significant dismissal of personnel, nor did it result in a decline in the general level of employers [20]. Among all the different technologies that have thus far entered the workplace, computer technology has entered at an astonishingly high rate of speed.

6.4.1   The Electronic Office

We can define an electronic office as a technology-augmented office with knowledgeable employees. The technology in the environment may include computers and computer-driven devices that help in interpersonal oral and electronic communication, distribution, and receipt of correspondence; telecommunication devices with text-processing and storage capabilities to enable the office staff to design, develop, edit, and store material electronically; and other office support equipment to streamline decision-making tasks. The evolution of the electronic office began with industrialization but took giant steps beginning in the 1950s with rapid advances in computer technology and telecommunications. Since then the workplace has been undergoing a rapid transformation of its own. Gone are notepads, typewriters, large cabinets filled with manila folders, the rotary telephone, and rotary fans. Computers have replaced most of the filing cabinets, the files, and typewriters. Electronic notepads, automatic answering systems, office intercoms, copiers, and fax machines have moved in. Living plants and air-conditioning have become standard. Increasingly, office job descriptions at all levels and in all professions are being transformed to incorporate computer and telecommunication skills.

Two factors have been and are still fueling the growth of the electronic office. The first is the increasing productivity of office employees, both clerical and professional, to counter the rising costs of office operations, which according to Olson and Lucas [21] have been increasing faster than office employee productivity. The second is the acquiring of technology necessary to handle the ever-increasing complexity and modernization of office communication and decision-making processes.

6.4.2   Office on Wheels and Wings

As electronic gadgetry has been invading the office and the overall workplace, workers have been leaving the office in droves, a few of them replaced by the new technology, others transplanted by it, but many for the experience of working outside the confines of their original office.

The advent of laptop computers, tablets, cellular phones, and personal digital assistants (PDAs) have accelerated the mobility of the office. Busy executives, white-collar workers, and, this time around, blue-collar workers, especially those in the service industry, can be seen in airports, hotel lobbies, restaurants, and aboard airplanes and in trains, keying in data and putting in a day's work as they would have done previously in their offices.

Mail and package service company drivers are also keying in their locales and speed, transmitting the data to the company computers so a package can be continuously traced from the time of departure to within minutes of the estimated time of arrival. Many companies are embracing this new 'office on the go.' Among the industries that have found the edge in this phenomenon is the home service industry, which is utilizing the new office technology to improve services and of course increase business. Others include delivery services, home repair, and heating and air-conditioning services to keep workers on location and in the office in constant contact.

6.4.3   The Virtual Workplace

With the latest developments in telecommunication and computer technology, the virtual workplace is home to an increasing type of employees who work very briefly in their corporate workplaces, are mostly on the road, and often telecommute using personal or company-provided equipment. This breed of worker is rarely in a fixed workplace, but nevertheless he or she performs a full day's work even if at the beach.

According to Snizek [22], the most important element of the virtual workplace is the use of computers and other telecommunication devices to link employees with the massive worldwide databases of vital information and other human resources. As computer and telecommunication technologies improve and bandwidth and computer miniaturization increase, this will not only lead to more workers opting for the virtual workplace but will also increase vital information flow into the company and corporate offices, which may lead to companies gaining a higher level of vital data, employee expertise, and experience from colleagues around the globe. The increasing popularity of the virtual workplace is mainly the result of recent changes in computer and telecommunication technology and organizational changes coming from corporate downsizing and outsourcing. For example, for corporations to keep the same level of overall effectiveness and efficiency and even to surpass it sometimes with fewer employees, companies are increasingly encouraging virtual offices, and the trend is likely to continue [22].

There are other benefits of the virtual office in overhead savings and other costs. With virtual employees rarely in their offices, a number of other employees can share their office space and other office resources, thus saving millions of dollars in facilities and equipment costs. The company may no longer need to have a large workforce on a permanent full-time basis. Companies can now use a limited staff and seek out contract expertise on a case-by-case basis as the situation arises.

In addition to the transformation of traditional workers, the virtual office is also opening doors to a new group of workers such as the disabled, the homebound, and the elderly who have traditionally been left out of the work force.

It is probably too early to talk about the long-term effects of the virtual office on both employees and employer, but some difficulties are already visible in both the employee and employer communities. Because most employee time is spent outside the physical office, employees rarely meet face to face, so there is a lack of collegiality and of community spirit. Also, because most employees, especially experts, are not full-time employees of the corporation, there is a lack of belonging that affects employees and eventually undercuts their loyalty and hence their effectiveness. A company built on a transient work force lacks the moral force and legitimacy in the community in which its operations are based.

6.4.4   The Quiet Revolution: The Growth of Telecommuting

As workers have changed their work habits from working 40 h per week in the workplace environment to sharing those 40 h between being at the workplace and commuting to the workplace, the 9-to-5 time schedule for the majority of workers has started to crumble, with many moving their work locales outside the normal confines of time and space. Studies show that the largest number of workers doing their work outside their primary place of work do so in their homes. According to figures reported by Kraut [23], the percentage of home office workers or telecommuters in the total U.S. workforce by 1960 was 3 %, but numbers have been on the rise ever since. According to Michael L. Brown [24], in "Telecommuting a Growing Trend," telecommuting is a growing trend in the information age, with a current estimate that nearly 6 % of the American workforce (more than 8 million American workers) telecommute to work from their homes. The U.S. National Association of Home Businesses reported that the number of home-based workers increased more than seven times between 1984 and 1994. The association report said that there were 45 million telecommuters in 1994 compared to 6 million in 1984, a 750 % increase [22]. It is estimated that by year 2020 close to 30 % of the American workforce will be telecommuting [24]. This significant rise can be attributed to the growth in U.S. information-related work. In fact, JALA International [25], an international group of consultants in telework, telecommuting, and applied futures research, projects that more than 60 % of the U.S. workforce will be information related by 2020. The growth of telecommuting is also driven by advances in office technology and the plummeting of prices for computers and telecommunication devices, the diminishing sizes of communication devices, and the increase in speed and bandwidth of communication devices.

As office technology improves, a large number of workers outside the self-employed professions of artists, writers, and craftspeople are potentially able to work at home. The advances in technology are making many types of jobs that used to require a worker to stay in an office environment more mobile. This trend is being helped further by the shift in global economies from manufacturing based to information based.

6.4.4.1 Categories of Telecommuters

There are three categories of telecommuters. The first category of telecommuters consists of workers who use their homes as an adjunct to their conventional office jobs. These workers are usually in white-collar jobs in areas such as management, research, market studies, and education. They are highly motivated. For them, occasional work-at-home is a flexible alternative used most in cases of critical work that can best be done at home to avoid the office environment. Kraut [23], reporting on a study he did in 1983 and 1984 at AT&T Bell Laboratories, states that these workers put in a full day's work at the conventional office in addition to taking some of their office work home. They additionally work at home on weekends and in the evenings.

The second category of telecommuters consists of workers who use their homes as the base for their businesses. The majority of these are in telemarketing, small start-up companies, and human services such as child care and elderly care. In contrast to the first category, these individuals are less educated and less likely to use a fully equipped electronic home office. Others in this category are the dispatchers in the home service industry, who are more likely to use a telephone and a computer without much data transmission.

The third category of telecommuters consists of those who have full-time jobs with large companies, but prefer through their own initiative to work from home. This category includes computer programmers, sales specialists, editors, writers, and those whose work depends on a high degree of creativity such as artists, musicians, and composers. This third category is a mixed bag of highly educated, independent, and specialized workers, and those who are not so highly educated but are very talented and skilled.

As computers and telecommunication technology become cheaper, and people obtain more access to smaller more portable computers, and other communication devices become more readily available, the home is becoming more and more a place of refuge for conventional office workers. Although it is not possible to predict the future direction of the home office, it is likely that if the technology that has caused the increase in the home office keeps on track, the number of telecommuters is likely to continue growing, with the majority of workers remaining in home offices for economic benefits and convenience.

6.4.4.2 Company Role in Telecommuting

To many, the home office is a revisit to the cottage industry of the fifteenth through eighteenth centuries in Europe: Raw materials were dropped off at the workers' cottages and finished products later picked up for market. Ever since industrialization, factories and later companies have been using home workers. Thus, company experimentation with their employees telecommuting is not a new idea.

The home office has always been prompted by new advances in technology and by the need of businesses to become more productive with minimum expenditures. As the Internet and globalization open up new international competition and as new technologies make telecommuting more acceptable to employees, company-sponsored telecommuters will increase.

By the 1960s, according to Kraut [23], telecommuters accounted for 3.6 % of the U.S. workforce, and a small portion of this was company sponsored. But by the late 1970s and early 1980s, big companies such as IBM and AT&T were deeply involved with telecommuting experiments. Kraut estimates that by 1983 IBM had more than 8000 employees telecommuting. These big companies and other smaller ones spent money in this experiment, expecting a benefit in return. The experiments were also meant to provide information on the classification of work suitable for the home, to identify individual workers who could work at home, and to suggest how workers were to be monitored as they worked from their homes.

Although no study has yet reported big monetary benefits for companies from these experiments, some studies on other related issues have provided some results.

For example, on the issue of remote supervision, classification of jobs fit for telecommuting, and identifying individuals better suited for telecommuting, a study by Olson and Lucas [21] provided some partial answers. On the issue of classification of work, the study found that work with possible measurable milestones is most suited for telecommuting. On the issue of identifying individuals most suited to telecommute, the study found that people who usually need less supervision at the office and those who do volunteer work are the most suited to telecommute. These conclusions are also influenced by the nature of the work, gender, age, and labor supply. The study also highlighted difficult issues such as the effect of telecommuting on the promotability of employees because visibility is key to promotion. There was also some clarification of the issue of pay. Telecommuters tend to be paid less because their pay is based on output, which makes output the real mechanism of monitoring telecommuters [21].

6.4.4.3 Effects and Benefits of Telecommuting

Whenever there is a change in the environment of workers, there are always some social, psychological, and financial effects on both employee and employer. If the effects are financial, they become benefits. However, if they are psychological, they become health issues; if they are social, they become organizational issues. In this section we concentrate on social and financial issues.

An employer–employee-arranged home office is supposed to reap benefits for both parties. Let us start by qualifying our discussion to include only those telecommuters who are company employed, have traditional offices at the company premises, and through mutual arrangements with their companies have decided to work from their homes. This group truly exemplifies the benefits, if there are any, for both the employer and the employee. Because these workers have a choice of either staying at the office or working from home, they can only work only from their homes if they experience a benefit and the companies can only let them work from their homes if the companies expect a benefit from the arrangement. For those working at home with no choice except to work at home, such as those in the majority in the second category (see earlier), the benefits are already clear. Defining benefits for telecommuters is not easy because each participant in the arrangement perceives the benefits the way they would like them to be. For example, the company may see the benefit as savings on office space so that other workers can use the space, or as savings in office supplies, or a reduction in the likelihood of employee risks while on company premises. The employee may see benefits as spending more quality time with their loved ones at home, or spending less time in traffic commuting to and from work, or the flexibility and independence in decision making concerning the work the employee has to do. The value of benefits from this arrangement depends on individual circumstances as discussed by Kraut [23] and reported as follows:

1. *Gender*: Women have traditionally given care to children and the elderly, the two groups most homebound; women would therefore draw maximum benefits from telecommuting arrangements with their employees, if their primary objective for telecommuting is to take care of their families.

2. *Nature of work*: *managerial, clerical, sales, or service*: The nature and type of
   work one does also influences the kind of benefits one obtains. For example,
   clerical work tends to be more supervision intensive than managerial and professional work. In those types of work where supervision is not so intensive, there
   is a high degree of latitude for one to make decisions. However, jobs that are
   supervision intensive are less likely to be moved into home environments. If
   such jobs are to be moved to a home environment, chances are that the company
   may not garner any benefits, but employees may benefit by getting more freedom
   and flexibility in their work routine and in decision making.
3. *Labor supply*: When there is a limited supply of one type of worker, companies
   try to find innovative ways of attracting and keeping workers in those limited-
   supply areas. For example, in 1981, IBM, anticipating a demand in programmers
   and engineers, started a telecommuting program to attract young talented programmers and engineers. Members of such groups usually garner great benefits
   with such an arrangement.
4. *Age*: Age may be a factor in home office productivity. For example, in sales,
   young people are more productive outside of offices than older workers. In management, older people are more productive in offices than outside offices.
   Women in their childbearing years are more productive when they telecommute
   than when they work in company offices. So, using the age factor, both employer
   and employee can benefit from a home office.

The U.S. Department of Transportation summarizes the benefits of telecommuting
for both employees and employers as follows [26, 27]:

- An individual benefits from telecommuting because he or she immediately
  eliminates the time, trouble, and expense of physically commuting to work. This
  change gives the average person an extra hour per day, right off the top, to use for
  the thinking, writing, telephoning, planning, and reporting work that keeps the
  business organization moving forward.
- The benefits of telecommuting also translate directly and immediately into more
  discretionary time, less stress, and general health improvements.
- More autonomy in work decisions and having more control over time and more
  flexibility in job variations.
- Decreased commuting expenses for the individual.
- More quality time with family with less or no frustration at home.
- Employers benefit from the extra productivity, reported to be consistently at
  10–15 % in many studies in the past two decades. Employers also save on
  expenses through having fewer employees on company premises. Such savings
  come from the daily need for offices, desks and chairs, restrooms, copy machines,
  parking spaces, heating and lighting, and all the rest.
- In addition, telecommuting helps the best and satisfied employees stay longer,
  thus saving on recruiting and training costs.
- Society benefits from telecommuting through benefits to the environment.

However, the overall benefit to employers of home office workers is evaluated through such measures as the productivity of the employee. According to the report of the National Academy of Sciences and Electronic Services Unlimited [23] conducted in 1984, productivity among both clerical and managerial telecommuters of the 24 projects evaluated in the report increased about 15–25 %. Reductions in expenses come from office space, equipment purchases and wear, and office supplies. Businesses also reduce costs by hiring contract workers as the need arises, hence reducing the overall worker benefit expenses. Beside the reductions in overhead costs, by employing contract home workers, companies tap into the scarce resources of the professional expertise they would not otherwise find.

Telecommuting is not all positive, however. Among the issues that negatively affect the company image are employee morale and alienation. Because of the lack of professional contacts, employee morale may suffer and they may feel abandoned by the company. If this happens, productivity falls. Another negative impact is the public's perception of the company when they see an employee mowing the lawn at 3 p.m. on a workday.

6.4.5 Employee Social and Ethical Issues

Mention of the phrase *office automation* used to conjure up nightmarish images of less control, helplessness, joblessness, and the stagnation of humanity. Within the context of office automation, the concept implies the idea of massive layoffs because offices with intelligent machines may require fewer people. Besides the fear of layoffs, workplace automation has also been plagued with the issue of *deskilling*, meaning stripping an employee of job skills as a result of changes in either job content or procedures. Deskilling, according to Attewell and Rule [28], can either be intraoccupational, in which case the skill content of the job decreases over time, or inter-occupational, in which very few people gain the skills needed for the job, causing either low-paying jobs or layoffs. James Driscoll [3] expressed the fear of deskilling in a more sarcastic way by saying that the office of the future would "leave people in only two roles: bosses and garbage collectors." But so far these horrific fears of deskilling have not been realized, even with the heavy office automation of the past 10 years.

There have been some layoffs and deskilling of employees, but the numbers have been very small. Several factors such as the following have prevented this from happening:

1. The willingness of employees to retrain and use the newly acquired technology, which, of course, has led to the upgrading of skills in the workplace. In fact, according to Attewell and Rule, computerization has led to reskilling of employees rather than deskilling.
2. The historical patterns show that more efficient production techniques lead to expanded operations and added growth, which leads to more hiring rather than firing of existing employees.

3. In anticipation of automation, more employees are usually hired to cope with the
   new technology and to handle the expanded work capacity.

6.5   Employee Monitoring

In the past decade, most of the large industrialized economies have been shifting
from a heavy manufacturing base to an information management base. Along with
this shift has been stiff competition resulting from globalization. Competition is
coming from not only large economies but also from upcoming developing
countries. These developing economies with their cheap labor costs are making
this competition more costly for a number of older, more established and mature
economies.

This shift in the economies and the stiff competition have resulted in a shift in
management styles to bring more efficiency and quality in the established economies.
This is not the first time such management styles have shifted. Styles in management have been changing with shifts in economies since the dawn of the Industrial
Revolution. In those early days, management followed a style now commonly
known as Theory X, after Douglas McGregor. Theory X management, with all the
trappings of the industrial era, was characterized by a top-down autocratic style of
management in which the manager—literally from the top floor—commanded the
activities of the factory workers on the factory floor with almost omniscient and
demeaning power.

As economies grew larger and employees became more elite, a new management
style started to evolve that became known as Theory Y. Theory Y put more faith and
empowerment in the hands of the employees. The style was hierarchical with the
employee ranks broken down into small semi-independent units. Each unit was
headed by a supervisor. The supervisors themselves formed another top-down
hierarchy ending with the top management. Theory Y, or scientific management, as
this management style is commonly known because of its hierarchical structure,
gave more flexibility and partial decision-making powers to employees at different
levels of the management hierarchy. The workers themselves were more removed
from the top management, but at the same time they were closer to management
decisions and control from the smaller units. Scientific management has been in
effect for years.

With the recent shifts and globalization of world economies, however, scientific
management has been slowly giving way to a new style in which management is
trying to wrest control of the work process away from the workers and slowly bring
back the techniques of Theory X. Given the technological advances of recent years
and the abundance of educated and highly skilled workers, however, it would be
unwise for today's management to bring back these techniques. So, a new technique
in the works is called "fear management." It is aimed at keeping workers in line, just
like all other management styles, but with "voluntary" compliance by workers to
company management policies and practices they would normally have questioned
or challenged.

Differing from theories X and Y, which achieved worker control through autocratic and supervisory unit means, fear management uses both worker surveillance and control as enforcement means. Fear is transmitted to workers through policies such as "downsizing," "contingent workforce," and "outsourcing." To workers these policies spell disaster and fear of losing job security and being replaced by part-time, temporary, and contract workers. According to Karen Nussbaum [29], temporary workers now make up one-third of the U.S. workforce; less than one-half are covered by any pension, and many have no health insurance.

Management is using a wide array of surveillance gadgets and techniques, which include employees taking polygraph tests if they are suspected of a breach of any kind. Although compulsory use of the lie detector is banned in the United States, it is still used on a voluntary basis. Drug testing is widely used by many companies and is required of all U.S. government employees in some categories. Handwriting analysis, the honesty test, electronic monitoring, mind control, and many other techniques are also being used.

6.5.1   Workplace Privacy and Surveillance

The electronic office or workplace has provided management with a bonanza of new possibilities for monitoring employees in their drive to reduce ever-increasing workplace costs. The issue of employee monitoring is not new because of advances in computer technology. Ever since the Industrial Revolution, workers have been monitored for performance evaluation because its performance has been used as the basis for pay and for decisions about employee advancement. Monitoring has also been employed to control employees and impose overall discipline in the workplace. But before the advent of surveillance gadgets, workplace monitoring was done through human eyes—those of the supervisor.

As workplace modernization picked up speed with advances in technology, the techniques and debate surrounding employee surveillance intensified. The battles were fought on two fronts: those who see monitoring as good management control tools with plausible reasons such as increased production, more accurate assessment of employee performance, greater organizational control over employees, immediate feedback on individual employees (which can lead to high motivation), and more flexibility in work location, and those who see surveillance as an outright transgression of employee privacy, causing problems such as stress, decreased job satisfaction, and an affront to human dignity. The replacement of the human eye with an electronic one, on guard 24 h a day, 7 days a week, without taking a break, and easily concealed, started the real erosion of employee privacy.

Employers collect information from employees through two channels. The first is the voluntary channel in which employees surrender the information through forms, interviews, worker sessions, and worker get-togethers. The first work-related information collected from the employee by the prospective employer is collected from the job application, followed by more information surrendered by the prospective employee during the interviewing process. Most of the time this information is given voluntarily because the person wants to get a job and of course employers need employees they can trust. After being hired, especially during the first few days at the job, the new employee usually fills out myriad forms for an employee folder so the employer can pay for the new employee's benefits, taxes (part of them anyway), and salary.

The second channel is the private information the employer gathers through surveillance. The degree, rate, and method of surveillance depend on the employer and how much information is needed from the employee and the value of that information to the employer. The information collected is supposedly used solely for managerial decision making regarding employee work assignments, individual feedback, pay increases, bonuses, promotions, and other benefits, and, of course, termination. If most of this information, legitimately collected or otherwise, was used solely for employee benefits, very few would complain. But sometimes it is not, which is when employee privacy issues arise. For example, how much personal information is needed by the employer for employee benefits before it becomes an invasion of the employee's personal privacy? Are there restrictions on the use of that information? Does the employee have the right to view any information collected on him or her? Is employee surveillance legal, and if so, what legal avenues does an employee have?

According to Adler et al. [30], there are no general explicit constitutional rights to privacy in the United States except in a few states. The U.S. Privacy Act of 1974 has limited applicability, mostly to federal employees. Private employees are not adequately covered by this act; they are only covered by a threat to sue for libel, discrimination, and ethical consideration. In light of the limitation of both the U.S. Federal Privacy Act and state statutes, courts started to recognize independent torts, according to Adler et al. [30]. This judgment may be true in many other countries.

Is employee surveillance an invasion of employee privacy? That depends. Notice that invasion of privacy does not mean collection of information on an individual without the individual's knowledge but rather the disclosure of collected information on an employee without legitimate reason or interest. An employer can gather information from the employees with whatever means so long as that information is not used maliciously. For example, an employer can collect information from an individual employee through covert actions such as electronic monitoring and use that information solely to further business interests without disclosure to the employee. According to Adler et al. [30], this procedure is legal, and most courts have recognized it as a legitimate business interest and have sided with employers.

Adler et al. cite a case that further clouds the employee privacy issue. An employer was requested by a court to provide an employee's records. In such a case the employee may not have any legal rights regarding the information the employer has. If the employer refuses the request, the employer can be cited for contempt of court. But if the employer obliges, he or she may be charged with violating the employee's privacy rights.

Why are the employee privacy issues becoming so important? As the U.S. and many other economies shift toward information-based economies, the value of owning information for economic advantages becomes even greater. Many companies are trying to obtain information on individuals to market their products, to approve loans, to offer audits, and many other revenue sources. Because companies such as insurance, banks, loan assurance, and legal investigations want the information on their clients to be as accurate as possible (their businesses depend on it), information-gathering companies see the employer as their best source of such accurate and reliable information.

Individual information has become valuable not only to banks and insurance companies that want security for their money but also to a cross section of manufacturing and service companies. These companies want to find new markets for their products. To do that, they need a source from which to launch their marketing and get a foothold in specialized markets. This kind of information can best be acquired from employers. Once a company has gathered that information about individuals, it can model its market strategies around the characteristics exhibited by these individuals. Such information may include income levels, leisure activities, foods, favorite wines and beers, whether one eats chili, and so on.

In this rush for personal information, the employer takes center stage as the best source of such intriguing tidbits. Statistics show that the workplace is second only to the home as a place where we spend most of our time. It is common sense, therefore, that the workplace should be the next best place to look for information on an individual.

6.5.2 Electronic Monitoring

Electronic monitoring is generally the monitoring of employees using electronic devices such as video cameras, computer equipment, audio devices, and many other concealed gadgets. In most cases it measures the quality and usually the quantity of work and the ability and effectiveness of the worker. In other cases it also measures the worker's habits on and off the work premises because some employers believe these habits have a great bearing on employee performance. For example, if the employee is a drug user, the effects of drugs will eventually affect the quality of that employee's work.

Electronic monitoring of employees is characterized by workers' ignorance that they are being monitored, fear of the ever-watching eyes of the supervisor, and fear of how much that supervisor knows about them. Let us illustrate these fears by two short examples from Nussbaum [29]. She first cites the case of *Mary Williams* v. *United Airways* in which Mary Williams was first disciplined for her remarks to a coworker, sent to a psychiatrist, and subsequently fired from her work at United Airlines because she confided to a coworker about an obnoxious customer while management was listening. In another example in the same paper, Nussbaum cites a New York data processor whose boss kept flashing the message "you are not working as fast as the person next to you" on her computer screen.

There are thousands of cases similar to these two arising from employee monitoring. Although there are no comprehensive studies on the spread of electronic monitoring in the workplace, it is generally believed that electronic monitoring of employees is on the rise and is already enshrined in the banking, insurance, and airline industries, to name but a few.

As technology becomes cheaper, therefore more affordable, smaller, and easier to conceal, the trend is likely to pick up momentum as the pressure for quality, quantity, and standards increases because of global competition. This pressure is likely to force more companies to resort to electronic monitoring as a way to control employees to extract more performance, compliance, and probably more money. In fact, in some sectors of employment the percentages are already high. For example, according to Grant et al. [31], in the United States 25–35 % of all clerical workers are electronically monitored for work performance.

6.5.2.1 Effects of Electronic Monitoring on Employees

Recently, I watched a British television comedy in which the theme was employee monitoring. The setting was a department store. The managers of the store found out they were losing merchandise and decided the employees were the most likely culprits, so they hired a security guard to check all employees' bags and pockets at the end of each day as the employees left the premises. They also installed video cameras throughout the store, including the restrooms. With the cameras in place, all human movements could be monitored in the comfort of the manager's office. Employee morale and performance declined considerably because employees, already aware of cameras watching their every move and carefully recording their every word to customers, were more concerned about being seen sweet-talking their customers and looking smart than actually working. Employees neglected those parts of the store where they could not be seen "working" by management. Also there were fights between employees to take those strategic places. Funny as the television episode was and indeed as it was intended to be, it illustrates a number of issues research has shown to exist among electronically monitored employees.

In research conducted by a North American insurance company reported by Grant et al. [31], results similar to those portrayed in the television comedy were observed. The research studied a monitored group of the group claims-processing division of the insurance company and a non-monitored group of the same division. In these two groups, the researchers included some supervisors and department managers. The monitored group was responsible for entering and paying claims using an automated claim-processing system and interacting directly with subscribers answering their questions and settling their disputes so far as payments were concerned. Their work included printing checks and talking to customers on phones.

The computer "monitor" counted the number of checks produced by an individual on a daily basis. According to the findings of the research, the group that was monitored considered the number of checks printed as the most important part of their work. In fact, they thought that talking to subscribers was an impediment to their job of printing checks. These employees, just like those in the British comedy, focused on those parts of their jobs they thought were being monitored and neglected all other essential parts. Although the monitored group did their work this way, the researchers found that the employees in the non-monitored group had a different perception of their work. This group thought that interacting with customers was the most important part of their work.

Another research project conducted by Irving et al. [10] compared two groups of employees working in insurance companies, financial institutions, and government. One group was electronically monitored and the other was not. The researchers considered the effects of monitoring on issues such as job satisfaction, what employees consider as a measure of performance, amount and usefulness of feedback, and relationships among employees and between employees and supervisors. The results of the study were very similar to those of Grant's study and the British television comedy. Employees put much more emphasis on quantity as a measure of performance; there was no significant usefulness in the timely individual feedback; rewards were based on electronic performance evaluations in the monitored group, and those in the monitored group felt, and rightly so, that they were more supervised than any other group in the company. From these studies two important issues emerged.

1. Very often an intended goal of a monitoring program may be clouded by a different goal perceived by the monitored group. Therefore, without a well thought out electronic monitoring program, the intended goal of the company may be lost in the resulting perceptions of the employees.
2. The psychological effects on the monitored employees may be more severe than previously thought and anticipated. The philosophy that "if it isn't counted, it does not count" should not be allowed to flourish among employees. Besides what has been observed in Grant's study and the British comedy, there are social, ethical, and mental effects on the monitored employees.

6.5.2.2 Consequences of Electronic Monitoring

The most devastating effect of electronic monitoring on employees is fear of losing their jobs. For many of us a job is the only source of livelihood and any sign of losing it triggers fear. In addition to fear of job loss, electronic monitoring also causes the following problems:

- *Reduced task variety*: The type of work monitored most is of a low-skilled, repetitive nature. In these jobs employees take the quota to be the measure of work and usually cannot afford to take a break, let alone slow down, thus increasing the monotony of their activities.
- *Lack of individual initiatives*: Most monitored jobs do not require personal creativity because they are of a low-skilled, repetitive nature. The employee usually is not allowed to vary the procedures but must follow them to the letter.
- *Reduced or no peer social support*: Monitored groups are always given separate stations where gadgets can monitor them in full view. Thus, an employee must remain where he or she can be "seen."
- *Lack of self-esteem*: The isolation, the monotony of work, the lack of creativity, and the lack of freedom to vary job steps lower employee morale and consequently self-esteem.

- *Lack of interest in the job*: With low self-esteem, many people definitely lose interest in their jobs.
- *Lack of trust among workers, between workers and supervisors, and between supervisors and management*: This lack of trust can result in low company morale, and later production levels may begin to fall. As employee morale plummets and dislike of the employer rises, workers turn to litigation, filing privacy suits against their employers. Nussbaum reports that in the United States there were twice as many lawsuits of workplace privacy filed between 1984 and 1987 as between 1978 and 1980. In the courts, although workers' privacy rights have not been successful in the number of lawsuits filed, there is a growing recognition of workplace privacy rights. A number of states in the United States and indeed in other countries have been working on legislation to protect workers. The trade union movement has also been actively negotiating languages in worker contracts to help curb unnecessary workplace monitoring.
- *Alienation*: Sociologists define the concept of worker alienation as lack of worker freedom and control, purpose and function, and self-involvement in their work. Alienation, according to Shepard [32], is lower among workers in industries with automated technologies.

6.6   Employee Health and Productivity in the Workplace

Productivity of workers depends on the quality of their physical and mental state. Employers have always striven to make their workers happy, healthy, and productive.

There is now a movement to improve employee work environment as companies start to add facilities such as employee gyms, cafeteria, daycare centers, and worker facilities for their employees. For example, currently Google, Inc., is cited by many reports to be the top company in this movement. There has always been a feeling of powerlessness among employees to control the state of working conditions because they lack freedom and control. According to Shepard [32], a worker has freedom and control at work if he or she can vary steps involved in doing the job, determine work methods and workload, and increase or decrease speed at which the work is done. With the changing work environment caused by advances in computer technology, employers are finding themselves achieving what has eluded them for years, offering their employees happiness, healthier environments, and high productivity through empowerment.

Human beings always want to feel they are in control of their work and other aspects of their lives. The changing work environment gives the workers the choice to work either in a traditional office or from home. Choice brings commitment and obligation. When people make a choice of their own, they tend to commit to the requirements of their choice. The commitment to work always translates into higher productivity quotas. Although computer technology has given workers more control in decision making, it has also given them new dangers in the workplace. These dangers are collectively discussed next as ergonomics.

6.6.1   Ergonomics

Ergonomics is an applied science concerned with designing human–machine interactions that offer and maintain a safe, comfortable, healthy, and habitable work
environment. With the increasing automation of the workplace, our dependence on
machines is on the rise, and the field of ergonomics is correspondingly expanding.
It now covers a wide array of work environments and factors that influence the
employee's health and wellness through prevention of occupational diseases. In particular, ergonomics studies the design of human work and production because when
the demands for human performance of a task exceed human capacity then ergonomic injuries start to occur and human wellness declines.

An ergonomic injury results when the demand on a person to perform a task
exceeds that person's working capacity. Examples of ergonomic injuries include
work accidents that occur because of the overwhelming demand for performance and
all work-related musculoskeletal disorders such as back pain, neck, and shoulder
pains, and repetitive strain injuries (RSI), with most studies now focusing on RSI.

6.6.1.1 Repetitive Strain Injuries

RSI is a set of work-related musculoskeletal disorders caused by repeated and pro-
longed body movement resulting in damage to the fibrous and soft body tissues
including tendons, nerves, and muscles. Some RSI conditions are well known in
medical communities, but a number of others are still very obscure and difficult to
diagnose because they present with different and very often unpredictable patterns.
RSI as a disease is not new; it has been affecting people performing repetitive
motions, such as cashiers, musicians, and assembly and data entry workers for
years; it has just recently gained prominence because of the rise in computer availability and widespread computer use. Recent studies have isolated some of the main
causes of RSI as repetitive motion, forced gripping, performance stress, alienation,
static loading, fixed posture, deviated wrists, and boredom. Computer users of keyboards, mouse, tracking balls, touchscreens, and the foot mouse are among the
groups most prone to RSI. RSI attacks those body parts such as tendons, wrists,
shoulders, nerves, and arms, and sometimes the neck, that receive tremendous stress
exerted by body movements. This condition, which has come to be known by a
string of names such as occupational overuse syndrome (OOS), cumulative trauma
disorder (CTD), carpal tunnel syndrome (CTS), and upper limb disorder (ULD),
causes serious pain and if not treated early may even cause permanent disability. As
a result of the damage to the nerves, wrists, arms, tendons, and muscles, the disease
also causes eyestrain, fatigue, headaches, usually back pain, tingling, coldness,
hand numbness, and stiffness and discomfort in body movement, especially of the
fingers, arms, and head. When RSI is caught in time, it can be cured with proper
care and prescriptions that emphasize changes in individual work styles and techniques. Among the suggested changes in work styles and techniques are the
following:

1. *Use ergonomically correct work equipment.* Such may include chairs, tables, and computer equipment like new keyboards, monitors, new software, and new lightning in the workplace.
2. *Use a light touch on the keyboard to place less stress on body parts.* Also keep the wrists straight in line with your arms.
3. *Take frequent breaks from your work.* Do not work for long hours without a break. Once you get a break, walk around and do some stretching exercises.
4. *Educate yourself about RSI.*
5. *If necessary, reduce the time you spend at the computer terminal.*

Improvements in the design of human work and occupational environments can result in benefits to the employee and the employer. Among such benefits are the following:

• Reduced medical bills
• A higher level of self-esteem
• Increased productivity because of fewer employee errors. High attendance rate and retention skills increase per capita output

Studies have shown dramatic increases in the range of 20 % to 50 % in increased productivity after effective ergonomics remedies were implemented for people working with visual display units (VDU) [33].

6.6.1.2 Stress

Besides RSI, stress has also recently drawn public attention as a work hazard. Similar to its counterpart RSI, stress has been targeted to explain much worker discomfort and frustration that may lead to poor job performance, strained interpersonal relationships, and erratic employee behavior. Stress is believed to have its origins in environmental inputs, and it appears through symptoms such as fear, anxiety, and anger. Anything that increases the stress level of an individual ultimately endangers that individual's health.

In the work environment stress is mainly caused by a variety of factors including impending deadlines, long hours at work, uncooperative colleagues, lack of management support and understanding, constantly changing requirements, and lack of job capacity because of changes in either work procedures or the workplace environment. Stress onset affects individuals differently depending on the environment they are in, and different individuals react differently to stress. For example, Ivancevich et al. [34] report that under stress women consume less coffee than men, shout less but consume more aspirin, and visit doctors more frequently than men.

Employers can significantly reduce employees stress by enhancing the overall work environment, keeping consistent work schedules, giving fewer deadlines, and making fewer management demands. Health awareness and knowledge of the causes of stress are always the first step in controlling it.

Exercises

1. Discuss the effects of telecommuting on family life.
2. If there are benefits to the employer for telecommuting, why is it that not many companies have embraced telework?
3. Ergonomics is turning into a multimillion-dollar business. Discuss.
4. Electronic monitoring has more negative effects on both employers and employees. Discuss.
5. Work productivity is directly related to the well-being of the employee. Discuss.
6. Has automation caused any massive worker layoffs?
7. Has technology in the workplace created jobs or trimmed job rolls?
8. There has been a debate on the existence of the digital divide. What is your opinion? Is there one or not?
9. Is there anything like equal access to computing technology? If otherwise, is it achievable in any society?
10. The concept of telecommuting has not realized its earlier potential and, therefore, has not been successful. Is this a true statement? Why or why not?
11. Has the Internet, together with new developments in telecommunications, increased the value of telecommuting?
12. Have the Internet and related technologies helped to lessen the problems experienced by the telecommuter?
13. Discuss the social implications of telecommuting.
14. What, if any, are the ethical implications of telecommuting?
15. What are the benefits, if any, of employee monitoring?
16. What are the social and ethical problems resulting from employee-mandated drug and polygraph testing?
17. Why do you think employee monitoring is such a hot issue?
18. There are benefits to employee monitoring! Discuss.
19. Should employees sacrifice their privacy because of fear of losing a job?

References

1. Kruger L, Gilroy A. Broadband internet access and the digital divide: federal assistance programs. Congressional Research Service. http://www.nationalaglawcenter.org/assets/crs/RL30719.pdf
2. Notari C. What is the status of global digital inclusion. http://search.babylon.com/imageres.php?iu=; http://intelligentinclusion.com/wp-content/uploads/2012/05/document-head_info-graphics_1.jpg&ir=; http://intelligentinclusion.com/2012/05/what-is-the-status-of-global-digitalinclusion/&ig=; http://t0.gstatic.com/images?q=tbn:ANd9GcSGZdrLBcFhRCdS7hYh el3X4YRuaZ0rVam8FAZsod9Tu1XtN0S-N_GSvU3I&h=361&w=500&q=global++digital+i nclusion&babsrc=HP_ss
3. Driscoll J (1982) Office automation: the dynamics of a technological boondoggle. In: Landau RM, Bair JH, Siegman JH (eds) Emerging office systems. Ablex, Norwood
4. Wayne T (2010) Digital divide is a matter of income, er 12, 2010. The New York Times, 12 December 2010. http://www.nytimes.com/2010/12/13/business/media/13drill.html?_r=1

5. Jansen J (2010) The better-off online. Pew Research Center Internet & American Life Project, 24 November 2010. http://pewresearch.org/pubs/1809/internet-usage-higher-incomeamericans

6. National Telecommunications and Information Administration, Technical Report 2000 (NTIA) (2000) Falling through the net: toward digital inclusion. http://www.ntia.doc.gov.ntiahome/ttfn00/front00.htm

7. Smith A (2010) Mobile access 2010. Pew Research Center Internet & American Life Project, 7 July 2010. http://www.pewinternet.org/Reports/2010/Mobile-Access-2010/Summary-of-Findings.aspx

8. Rickert A (2000) The dollar divide: web usage patterns by household income. Media Metrix, August 2000. http://www.mediametrix.com/data/MMXI-USHHI-0600.pdf

9. Clark I. Age, disability and the digital divide. http://infoism.co.uk/blog/2012/04/age-disabilityand-the-digital-divide/

10. Irving RH, Higgins CA, Safayeni FR (1986) Computerized performance monitoring systems: use and abuse. Commun ACM 29(8):794–801

11. Rodriguez F, Wilson EJ (1999) Are poor countries losing the information revolution? Info DEV. The World Bank, Washington, DC

12. World Bank Global economic prospects 2008: technology diffusion in the developing world. http://siteresources.worldbank.org/INTGEP2008/Resources/4503313-1199473339970/Technological-progress-(large).gif

13. World Bank Global economic prospects 2008: technology diffusion in the developing world. http://en.wikipedia.org/wiki/Global_digital_divide

14. United Nations Human Development Report (1999) United Nations Development Program. http://www.undp.org/hdro/; http://www.ntia.doc.gov.ntiahome/net2/falling.html

15. DIGOPP Working Group of the Education Development Center. http://www.edc.org/GLG/Markle/dotforce/digopp/

16. Krech R (2001) Email communication to DIGOPP, 8 March 2001. http://www.edc.org/GLG/Markle/dotforce/digopp/

17. Bankole F, Shirazi F, Brown I (2011) Investigating the impact of ICT investments on human development. Electron J Info Syst Dev Ctries 48(8):1–19

18. Kim YJ, Kang H, Sanders GL, Lee ST (2008) Differential effects of IT investments: complementarity and the effect of GDP level. Int J Inf Manag 28(8):508–516

19. Wikipedia. Global digital divide. http://en.wikipedia.org/wiki/Global_digital_divide

20. Gottieb CC, Borodin A (1973) Social issues in computing. Academic Press, New York

21. Olson M, Lucas H (1982) The impact of office automation on the organization: some implications for research and practice. Commun ACM 25(11):838–847

22. Snizek W (1995) Virtual office: some neglected considerations. Commun ACM 38(9):15–17

23. Kraut R (1994) Predicting the use of technology: the case of telework. In: Huff C, Finholt T (eds) Social issues in computing: putting computing in its place. McGraw-Hill, New York, pp 312–334

24. Washington J (2011) For minorities, new 'digital divide' seen. Associated Press, 1 November 2011. http://www.rolandsmartin.com/blog/index.php/2011/01/11/for-minorities-new-digital-divide-seen/

25. JALA US workforce, http://www.jala.com/usworkers.php

26. Benefits of telecommuting. U.S. Department of Transportation's Departmental Office of Human Resource Management. http://dothr.ost.dot.gov/Telecommuting/benefits_of_telecommuting.htm

27. Boyd P. Six organizational benefits of telecommuting. http://pw2.netcom.com/~pboyd/org-bens.html

28. Attewell P, Rule J (1984) Computing and organization: what we know and what we don't know. Commun ACM 27(12):1184–1193

29. Nussbaum K (1991) Computer monitoring: a threat to the right to privacy. In: Dejoie R, Fowler G, Paradice D (eds) Ethical issues in information systems. Boyd & Fraser, Boston

30. Adler PA, Parsons LK, Zolke SB (1994) Employee privacy: legal and research developments and implications for personal administration. In: Huff C, Finholt T (eds) Social issues in computing: putting computing in its place. McGraw-Hill, New York, pp 312–334
31. Grant R, Higgins C, Irving R (1994) Computerized performance monitors: are they costing you customers? In: Huff C, Finholt T (eds) Social issues in computing: putting computing in its place. McGraw-Hill, New York, pp 312–334
32. Shepard J (1971) Automation and alienation. MIT Press, Cambridge, MA
33. Grandjean E (1987) Ergonomics in computerized offices. Taylor & Francis, London
34. Ivancevich J, Napier A, Wetherbe J (1983) Occupation stress, attitudes, and health: problems in the information systems professions. Commun ACM 26(10):800–806

Further Reading

Bailyn L (1989) Towards a perfect workplace. Commun ACM 32(4):460–471
Flynn L (1993) They are watching you: electronic surveillance of workers raises privacy concerns. *San Jose Mercury News,* June 13, 1993, p. 1F
Payser M (1995) When e-mail is oops-mail: think your private messages are private? Think again. *Newsweek,* October 16, 1995, p. 82
Sauter S, Gottlieb M, Jones K, Dodson V, Rohner K (1983) Job and health implications of VDT use: initial results of the Wisconsin NIOSH study. Commun ACM 26(4):284–294

Software Issues: Risks and Liabilities

Learning Objectives

After reading this chapter, the reader should be able to

1. Explain the limitations of software testing as a means to ensure correctness.
2. Describe the differences between correctness, reliability, and safety.
3. Discuss the potential for hidden problems in reuse of existing software components.
4. Describe current approaches to manage risk and characterize the strengths and shortcomings of each.
5. Outline the role of risk management in software systems design.

Scenario: Who Will Pay the Price for Flawed Software?

Peter Efon works as a programmer for a major software company. The company, Cybersoft, is launching itself to be a major Internet-based platform developer and it is soon to launch a web initiative. Peter is involved in the development of a crucial component of the initiative. The company has trust in Peter for he has worked for it since he left college 15 years ago. Since his arrival at the company, Peter has pioneered a number of major software development projects. Peter has followed, and is very much aware of, the losses suffered by other businesses due to defective software. He even knows that in 2000, US companies suffered a whopping $100 billion loss due to bad software. He and his company, Cybersoft, are determined to target quality as the major focus of their new web initiative. Peter dreams of the success of the web initiative and the recognition it might bring both to his company and him. However, a few days before the launch of the much-awaited initiative, as Peter makes his final quality checks, he discovers a flaw in the core component of the initiative whose magnitude he could not determine. To do so would mean a few weeks delay at best, a major blow to the company's efforts.

(continued)

© Springer International Publishing Switzerland 2016
J.M. Kizza, *Ethics in Computing*, Undergraduate Topics in Computer Science,
DOI 10.1007/978-3-319-29106-2_7

Scenario: (continued)

The company had mounted an advertising blitz on all major media outlets. Even a few weeks delay would cause major financial losses and the public's loss of confidence in the right company. This must never happen. Peter decides to see to it.

Discussion Questions

1. Is Peter Eflon wrong?
2. What damage would Cybersoft have suffered had there been a delay?
3. What do you think would have been the right course of action for Peter and Cybersoft?
4. Can you estimate the damage?

7.1 Definitions

Software is a set of computer programs made up of a sequence of short commands called instructions that tell the computer what to do. Normally, software is in one of two forms, either built into the computer's more permanent memory, called ROM (read-only memory), or loaded on demand in the less permanent but more volatile memory called RAM (random access memory). A *software producer*, or *developer*, creates or develops a set of programs to meet the specifications of a user, if there is a contract, or of a specific problem if it is general software. Developers are either individuals working alone or companies such as Microsoft, which employs hundreds of software engineers including analysts and programmers. *Software buyers*, or *customers*, obtain the finished software from the developer to satisfy a need, basing their decision on developer claims. The buyer may be an individual or a company.

In this chapter, we focus on the issues that arise from the relationship between the developer and the buyer, including claims, user expectations, and the legal ramifications that may follow an unhealthy relationship. The discussion touches on standards, reliability, security, safety, quality of software, quality of service of software products, causes of software failures, developer and buyer protection, and techniques for improving software quality. Let us begin by defining these terms.

7.1.1 Standards

Software developers must convey to buyers' satisfaction that their products are of high quality. The buyer, however, has little leverage in disputing the claims of the developer in these areas because there is no single universally acceptable and agreed-upon measure of software standards. But there are universal basic standards that a software product must meet. Such standards include the mutually agreed upon criteria and expectations of the buyer. In this case, the law imposes such standards, and if the product does not live up to them, the buyer has the right to pursue legal action. There is no one criterion that can be used to measure software standards but rather a collection of criteria such as development testing, verification and validation of software, and the programmer's professional and ethical standards.

7.1.1.1 Development Testing

According to Richard Hamlet [1], "programs are complex, hard to understand, hard to prove, and consequently often riddled with errors." But might not a small set of tests on a program pinpoint problems? Answering yes to this question has been the driving force behind testing, which helps reveal the discrepancies between the model being used and the real situation. Testing tries to assure that the program satisfies its specifications and it detects and prevents design and implementation faults. But testing is limited by an exponential number of states, which makes exhaustive testing very expensive and unworkable for large projects. Thus, a number of other selective testing techniques are being used. One such technique is *development testing*, which consists of a series of random tests on the software during the development stage. However, the use of mathematical techniques in developmental testing, which seems to offer good assurances and is widely used, does not ensure error-free code. Neither does refocusing verification of code to the underlying algorithm and basic computation, because not all errors may be in these areas. So, testing alone does not eliminate all the bugs.

7.1.1.2 Verification and Validation

The process of V&V involves static formal mathematical techniques such as proof-of-correctness and dynamic techniques such as testing to show consistency between the code and the basic initial specifications. It works from the specifications of the software and develops tests that can show that software under review is faulty. Tests are randomly chosen. But as any programmer will tell you, as the level of programming gets lower and lower toward machine code, software bugs get harder and harder to detect, and no amount of V&V is able to prevent those bugs from falling through the cracks.

7.1.2 Reliability

In contrast to hardware products whose reliability is measurable from age and production quantities, software reliability cannot be measured by wear and tear, nor can it be measured by copies produced at manufacture time, although experience has shown that it exhibits some degree of stochastic properties on unpredictable input sequences. A software product can fail to deliver expected results because of an unexpected input sequence. Reliability of software can, therefore, be defined in relation to these input sequences. According to Parnas et al. [2], reliability of software is the probability that such software does not encounter an input sequence that leads to failure. A software product, therefore, is reliable if it can continue to function on numerous unpredictable input sequences. Other measures of reliability include the number of errors in the code. But this also is difficult to take as a good measure because a program with fewer errors is not necessarily more reliable than one with many. Because no system can be certified as error free, including software systems, there have been, and will continue to be, numerous cases in which systems have failed and will fail the reliability standards.

Consider the example of the Denver International Airport baggage system [3]. When the city of Denver, CO, wanted to replace Stapleton International Airport, they contracted an automated baggage company, BAE Automated Systems of Dallas, to design and build a baggage delivery system. When BAE delivered the system, it failed all initial tests. Bags flew out of carts, and jams were frequent. After a number of failed test runs, and knowing they were running out of time, city officials hired another firm, which recommended a smaller, less expensive, but working manual system to run as a stand-alone alongside the automated system. When it opened, the airport was $2 billion over budget because of the delay caused mostly by this system.

In his book *Computer-Related Risks*, Peter Neumann gives numerous examples of system failures caused by unreliable products [4]. Similar to standards, reliability is another very difficult concept for a buyer or customer to understand because there are no universally accepted criteria for ascertaining the reliability of a product.

7.1.3 Security

In Sect. 5.3 we discussed the general concepts of system security including information security. In this section we focus on software security. As computer technology makes giant advances, our dependence on it increases, and so do our security concerns as more and more of the vital information that used to be secured under lock and key is now on giant computer disks scattered on numerous computer systems.

Software is an integral part of a computer system, and the security of such a system depends on its hardware but even more so on the software component. There are more security attacks on systems through software "holes" than hardware, mainly through piracy, deletion, and alteration of programs and data. Computer system software is secure if it protects its programs and data—in other words, if it does not contain trapdoors through which unauthorized intruders can access the system.

According to Neumann [5], improper encapsulation, inheritance of unnecessary privileges, and inadequate enforcement of polymorphism are the most common sources of software security flaws. Polymorphism is a state or a condition of passing through many forms or stages. Software development passes through many different forms. In addition to these as common causes of system insecurity is the human element. Computer system software can be protected from undetected modification through strong and sound design principles, enforcement of proper encapsulation, separation of all privileges, and ethical education of system developers and users about security issues.

The human and probably ethical side to system security, according to Ahl Davis [6], is that most computer crimes are not committed by hackers but by trusted employees, programmers, managers, clerks, and consultants in the company who know and can manipulate the working of the software. If Davis' observation is true, then computer security and hence system software security greatly depends on the education of system developers and knowledgeable users.

7.1.4 Safety

Recent advances in computer technology have resulted in wider computer applications in previously unthinkable areas such as space exploration, missile and aircraft guidance systems, and life-sustaining systems. In these areas the safety of software has become one of the most prominent components of the whole security system. Such a system cannot afford an accident or an error because of software failure without dire consequences to human life, property, and the environment.

A software system is unsafe if a condition is created whereby there is a likelihood of an accident, a hazard, or a risk. The function of software safety in system safety is that software executes within a prescribed context so as not to contribute to hazards or risk either by outputting faulty values and timing or by failing to detect and respond to hardware failures that may cause a system to go into a hazardous state.

According to Nancy Leveson [7], software safety depends on the design and environment in which such software is used. Thus, software that is considered safe in one environment may be unsafe in another. Because software is designed and produced by different people in different environments and used in different applications in a variety of environments, no one software product can conform to all requirements in all environments; in other words, one cannot assume that because a software product is hazard free in one environment it is hazard free in all environments. For example, according to Littlewood and Strigini [8], although the requirement for rate of occurrence of failures as a dependability measure is appropriate in systems that actively control potentially dangerous processes, the same measure is not as appropriate for life-critical processes in which the emphasis is on failure-free survival.

In the final analysis, good and safe software depends on good programming practice, which includes control techniques, application of various types of safety analysis during the development cycle, and evaluation of the effectiveness of these techniques. Whether these techniques are enough depends on the chosen and acceptable risk level, which tends to vary with the application environments [9]. For other dependability measures, consult Littlewood's article.

7.1.5 Quality

The emergence of a global software market, the establishment of powerful software development warehouses in different countries, and the improving standards of global software have all brought software quality to the forefront of software issues. A software product has quality if it maintains a high degree of excellence in standards, security, safety, and dependability. Many software vendors are starting to develop and apply quality improvement techniques such as total quality management (TQM).

A TQM technique that tries to improve software quality through a software development process known as the software quality function development (SQFD) represents a movement from the traditional techniques of TQM to the software development environment by focusing on improving the development process through upgrades in the requirement solicitation phase [10]. This technique focuses on this phase because software problems occur when user requirements are misunderstood, which causes overruns of development costs. Introducing design techniques that focus on user specification in this early phase leads to fewer design changes and reduces transfer errors across design phases.

7.1.6 Quality of Service

For a product, and in particular, a software product, quality of service (QoS) means providing consistent, predictable service delivery that will satisfy customer application requirements. The product must have some level of assurance that the customer's service requirements can be satisfied. For example, in the case of the Internet, QoS would mean that the network elements such as routers and hosts expect a high level of assurance that its traffic and service requirements can be satisfied. This requirement and expectations are important because the working and the architecture of the Internet are based on the "dumb" network concept, which at its simplest involves two smart end routers, one transmitting and one receiving, and no intelligence in between. Then, datagrams with source and destination addresses traverse a network of routers independently as they move from the sender to the receiver. Internet Protocol (IP) provides only an addressing mechanism and nothing else. It provides no guarantees of the delivery of any independent datagram in the network. So, QoS is needed in network protocols.

7.2   Causes of Software Failures

Failure or poor performance of a software product can be attributed to a variety of causes, most notably human error, the nature of software itself, and the environment in which software is produced and used.

7.2.1 Human Factors

In the human factor category, poor software performance can be a result of the following:

1. *Memory lapses and attentional failures*: For example, someone was supposed to have removed or added a line of code, tested, or verified, but did not do so because of simple forgetfulness.

2. *Rush to finish*: The result of pressure, most often from management, to get the product on the market either to cut development costs or to meet a client deadline, rushing can cause problems.
3. *Overconfidence and use of nonstandard or untested algorithms*: Algorithms are put into the product line before they are fully tested by peers because they seem to have worked on a few test runs.
4. *Malice*: Software developers, like any other professionals, have malicious people in their ranks. Bugs, viruses, and worms have been known to be embedded and downloaded in software, as is the case with Trojan horse software, which boots itself at a timed location. As we will see in Sect. 7.4, malice has traditionally been used for vendetta, personal gain (especially monetary), and just irresponsible amusement. Although it is possible to safeguard against other types of human errors, it is very difficult to prevent malice.
5. *Complacency*: When either an individual or a software producer has significant experience in software development, it is easy to overlook certain testing and other error control measures in those parts of software that were tested previously in a similar or related product, forgetting that no one software product can conform to all requirements in all environments.

7.2.2   Nature of Software: Complexity

Both software professionals and nonprofessionals who use software know the differences between software programming and hardware engineering. It is in these differences that many of the causes of software failure and poor performance lie. Consider the following:

1. *Complexity*: In contrast to hardwired programming in which it is easy to exhaust the possible outcomes of a given set of input sequences, in software programming a similar program may present billions of possible outcomes on the same input sequence. Therefore, in software programming one can never be sure of all the possibilities on any given input sequence.
2. *Difficult testing*: There will never be a complete set of test programs to check software exhaustively for all bugs for a given input sequence.
3. *Ease of programming*: The fact that software programming is easy to learn encourages many people with little formal training and education in the field to start developing programs, but many are not knowledgeable about good programming practices or able to check for errors.
4. *Misunderstanding of basic design specifications*: This lack affects the subsequent design phases including coding, documenting, and testing. It also results in improper and ambiguous specifications of major components of the software and in ill-chosen and poorly defined internal program structures.

As we already discussed in Sect. 7.1.4, the environment in which a software product is produced and tested has a great bearing on its safety.

7.3   Risk

The first step in understanding the nature of software is to study the concept of risk, software risk in particular. However, before we define risk, let us define *hazard*. A hazard is a state or set of conditions of a system or an object that, together with other conditions in the environment of the system, or object, will lead inevitably to an accident [7]. According to Leveson, hazard has two components; severity and likelihood of occurrence. These two form the hazard level. Risk is a hazard level together with the likelihood of an accident to occur and the severity of the potential consequences [7]. Risk can also be defined in simpler terms as the potential or possibility of suffering harm or loss; danger, in short. Peter Neumann defines risk as a potential problem, with causes and effects [4]. Risk can be both voluntary, with activities that we knowingly decide to undertake, or involuntary, with activities that happen to us without our prior consent or knowledge as a result of nature's actions such as lightning, fires, floods, tornados, and snowstorms. As our focus here is on the big picture of the dangers of software in particular and computer systems in general, we leave the details of the definitions at that.

How does risk function in software? Because we have defined risk as a potential problem with causes and effects, software risks, therefore, have causes and effects. Among the causes of software risks are poor software design, a mismatch of hardware software interfaces, poor support, and maintenance. Others include these [11]:

- Personnel shortfalls
- Unrealistic schedules and budgets
- Developing the wrong functions and properties
- Developing the wrong user interface
- Continuing stream of requirement changes
- Shortfalls in externally furnished components
- Shortfalls in externally performed tasks
- Real-time performance shortfalls
- Straining computer science capabilities

Because computers are increasingly becoming a part of our lives, there are numerous ways computers, and computer software in particular, affect our lives. In many of these encounters, risk is involved. For example, computers are used in medical care and delivery, in power generation and distribution, in emergency services, and in many other facets of life. So wherever we are, be it at work, on the way to or from work, or in our own homes, where there is direct or indirect use of computer software there is always a risk that an accident can occur.

For example, there is no way for a system manager to predict how and when a system failure or attack by hackers or viruses will occur. As our world become increasingly engulfed with computer and telecommunication networks, network-related threats by hackers, viruses, system overloads, and insider misuse are increasing to such a level that the risks involved are shaping the way we work. Appropriate and effective measures are needed to manage risk. Let us look at some here.

7.3.1 Risk Assessment and Management

Risk management is a process to estimate the impact of risk. It is an approach for system managers to measure the system's assets and vulnerabilities, assessing the threat and monitoring security. For software, we consider risk management both during the design phase and during use. Risk is an important aspect of the design process. Because it is so important, two constituent components must be included: assessment and control. To implement these two components, there must be a requirement that no software project may be delivered or accepted until and unless a risk assessment or risk control evaluation has been carried out. There must be documentation of the probability and consequences of hazards and accidents to help determine what the risks are and what to do about them.

The assessment aspects in the documentation should involve a list of all the potential dangers that are likely to affect the project, the probability of occurrence and potential loss of each item, and how each item ranks among all the listed items.

The control component in the documentation should consist of the following [11]:

- Techniques and strategies to mitigate the highest ordered risks
- Implementation of the strategies to resolve the high-order risk factors
- Monitoring the effectiveness of the strategies and the changing levels of risk throughout the design process

After the design process, when the software is in use, risk management then involves the following phases: assessment, planning, implementation, and monitoring.

7.3.1.1 Assessment
This step involves identifying the software's security vulnerabilities and may consist of a variety of techniques including question and answer, qualitative assessment, or methodology and calculation. A simple equation for calculating risk is

$$\text{Risk} = \text{Assets} \times \text{Threats} \times \text{Vulnerabilities}$$

7.3.1.2 Planning
Planning involves outlining the policies for security management.

7.3.1.3 Implementation
A good implementation may seek to match the security needs of the system with all available security tools.

7.3.1.4 Monitoring
Risk management is an ongoing process that needs constant monitoring: this helps to determine the necessary changes and new security applications to the system. The monitoring tools must be chosen based on the nature and applications of the system being protected. For example, if the system being protected is a network, the tools may include a firewall as well as intrusion detection and network forensics software.

7.3.2   Risks and Hazards in Workplace Systems

The workplace is second only to our homes in the amount of time we spend there. For most people with nine-to-five work schedules, work comprises about 40 h of the 168-h week. When you figure in commuting to and from work and other work-related activities, we spend on the average 84 h a week at home. Because we spend so much time outside our homes and in close contact with people from all walks of life and most often work with workplace machinery and people, which we call workplace systems, there is always a high risk associated with these systems, as well as with the commute to and from work.

In a workplace environment, accidents resulting from this three-faceted model of hardware, software, and humanware are caused by the intertwining of the components whereby each part affects the others. According to Leveson [7], an accident is then a coincidence of factors related to one another through this intertwining. Each component's contribution to system accidents depends on the environment of the system. Different environments may cause different types of accident. In some accidents, software may contribute more than the other two, whereas in others, humanware may contribute more, especially in cases where there is lack of effective training of the human component. There is a perception that humanware is more prone to errors in workplace systems than either hardware or software. According to Leveson, most workplace accidents are caused by what she calls a safety culture based on humanware—a general attitude and approach to safety consisting of overconfidence, complacency, placing low priority on safety, and accepting flawed resolutions of conflicting goals. To these we also add poor employee training and poor employee morale. In workplace systems where there is a transient human component, overlooking the human component for a critical safety decision-making process may result in high-risk system safety.

This perception is enhanced by the credibility problem and the myth about computers. People still hold the computer dear, that it is more reliable and creates less risk, that software testing eliminates software errors, that increased software reliability automatically implies increased safety, and that reusing software increases its safety level. All these are myths. Software safety is as unpredictable as its counterpart, the humanware.

For those with such perceptions, there is good news. The development of intelligent computer technology and communication devices may lessen the human component in the workplace. However, this does not mean that workplace systems will be error free. It will, however, shift the burden onto software because hardware errors are more readily predictable than those by humanware and software.

Hardware errors can easily be located and fixed. Software errors, on the other hand, may take many hours before they are found, and fixing them may take even longer. Yet software systems are becoming even more complex, with complicated codes and tight delivery schedules.

7.3.3   Historic Examples of Software Risks

In the maiden days of the "Wonder Machine," risk and vulnerability of both the computer user and data were not a problem. Software was unknown, the way we know it today, because it was embedded. Also, the computing system consisted more of hardware than software, and projects were small. As systems became smaller and less dependent on hardware, software came out of the hardware, and projects became bigger, more complex, and more dependent on software and humanware. Then, the problems of risk and vulnerabilities set in. Ever since then, major system mishaps in hardware, software, and humanware have been recorded that have given us a glimpse of the development of computer systems and the long road that system safety, vulnerability, and risk have taken.

In his book *Computer-Related Risks* [4], Peter G. Neumann, for many years the moderator of the online Internet group, "The Risk Forum," and contributor to ACM's "Inside Risk," has documented a wide collection of computer mishaps that address problems in reliability, safety, security, and privacy issues in day-to-day computer activities.

Numerous other authors have written about hundreds of incidents that have made headlines in their day. We cannot list them all. But we can look at the major history-making system safety incidents, a few among many that have dotted the computing landscape.

7.3.3.1 The Therac-25
The Therac-25 is a computer-controlled electronic–accelerator radiation-therapy system developed by Atomic Energy of Canada, Ltd. (AECL). Between 1985 and 1987 the system was involved in a number of accidents, some resulting in deaths because of radiation overdose.

The machine works by creating a high-energy beam of electrons targeted to the cancerous tumor, leaving the healthy tissue surrounding the tumor unaffected. The Therac-25 was not supposed to malfunction, but like all systems, there are many possibilities for errors. Therac-25 accidents did not occur until after 6 months of use, thus creating a high degree of confidence. And when malfunctions occurred, they were very irregular, and the system successfully worked on hundreds of patients in between malfunctions. Whenever malfunctions occurred, the Therac-25 could send through the patient readings in the range of 13,000–20,000 rads instead of the normal 200 rads. Anything over 500 rads can cause death. The Therac-25 used a software upgrade of the older model of the Therac-6. The manufacturers of the Therac-25, sure of the safety record of Therac-6, paid little attention to software. They were overconfident that it worked very well. So they simply upgraded it, adding in more parameters with few changes. In addition to endangering patients, the Therac-25 also endangered operators because of the stress that resulted from the situation. For the full account of the investigation into the Therac-25 accident, the reader is referred to the paper "An Investigation of the Therac-25 Accident" by Nancy G. Leveson and Clark S. Turner (*Computer*, vol. 26, #7, July 1993, pp. 18–41).

7.3.3.2 The Space Shuttle Challenger

On January 28, 1986, the US National Aeronautical and Space Administration (NASA) flight of mission STS 51–L using the *Challenger* spaceship burst into flames 72 s after takeoff. Flight 51–L of the *Challenger* spacecraft was scheduled originally to fly in July 1985, then it was postponed three other times until this fateful day. The accident left millions of people in shock, and it was a great setback for NASA and the prestige of the space program. The combination of these and other matters surrounding the accident, including problems within NASA, forced President Ronald Regan to appoint a commission of inquiry into the accident and the working of NASA so that similar future accidents could be avoided. The commission, chaired by William P. Rogers, former secretary of state under President Nixon (1969–1973) and attorney general under President Eisenhower (1957–1961), was expected to

> (i) [R]eview the circumstances surrounding the accident to establish the probable cause or causes of the accident; and (ii) develop recommendations for corrective or other action based upon the commission's findings and determinations.

In its deliberations, the commission interviewed more than 160 individuals, held more than 35 formal panel investigative sessions, and examined more than 6300 documents, totaling more than 122,000 pages, and hundreds of photographs.

On June 6, 1986, the commission handed their findings and recommendations to the President. In its executive summary report, the commission and other investigative agencies found that the loss of the *Challenger* was the result of a failure in the joint between the two lower segments of the right solid rocket motor. More specifically, the seals that prevent hot gases from leaking through the joint during the propellant burns of the rocket motor were destroyed, thus causing the joints to fail. Following are the commission's findings [12].

1. A combustion gas leak through the right Solid Rocket Motor aft field joint initiated at or shortly after ignition eventually weakened and/or penetrated the External Tank, initiating vehicle structural breakup and loss of the Space Shuttle Challenger during STS Mission 51-L.
2. The evidence shows that no other STS 51-L Shuttle element or the payload contributed to the causes of the right Solid Rocket Motor aft field joint combustion gas leak. Sabotage was not a factor.
3. Evidence examined in the review of Space Shuttle material, manufacturing, assembly, quality control, and processing on nonconformance reports found no flight hardware shipped to the launch site that fell outside the limits of Shuttle design specifications.
4. Launch site activities, including assembly and preparation, from receipt of the flight hardware to launch, were generally in accord with established procedures and were not considered a factor in the accident.
5. Launch site records show that the right Solid Rocket Motor segments were assembled using approved procedures. However, significant out-of-round conditions existed between the two segments joined at the right Solid Rocket Motor aft field joint (the joint that failed).

(a) While the assembly conditions had the potential of generating debris or damage that could cause O-ring seal failure, these were not considered factors in this accident.

(b) The diameters of the two Solid Rocket Motor segments had grown as a result of prior use.

(c) The growth resulted in a condition at time of launch wherein the maximum gap between the tang and clevis in the region of the joint's O-rings was no more than 0.008 in. and the average gap would have been 0.004 in.

(d) With a tang-to-clevis gap of 0.004 in., the O-ring in the joint would be compressed to the extent that it pressed against all three walls of the O-ring retaining channel.

(e) The lack of roundness of the segments was such that the smallest tang-to-clevis clearance occurred at the initiation of the assembly operation at positions of 120° and 300° around the circumference of the aft field joint. It is uncertain if this tight condition and the resultant greater compression of the O-rings at these points persisted to the time of launch.

6. The ambient temperature at time of launch was 36 °F, or 15° lower than the next coldest previous launch.

(a) The temperature at the 300° position on the right aft field joint circumference was estimated to be 28° ± 5 °F; this was the coldest point on the joint.

(b) Temperature on the opposite side of the right Solid Rocket Booster facing the sun was estimated to be about 50 °F.

7. Other joints on the left and right Solid Rocket Boosters experienced similar combinations of tang-to-clevis gap clearance and temperature. It is not known whether these joints experienced distress during the flight of 51-L.

8. Experimental evidence indicates that as the result of several effects associated with the Solid Rocket Booster's ignition and combustion pressures and associated vehicle motions, the gap between the tang and the clevis will open as much as 0.017 and 0.029 in. at the secondary and primary O-rings, respectively.

(a) This opening begins upon ignition, reaches its maximum rate of opening at about 200–300 ms, and is essentially complete at 600 ms when the Solid Rocket Booster reaches its operating pressure.

(b) The External Tank and right Solid Rocket Booster are connected by several struts, including one at 310° near the aft field joint that failed. The effect of this strut on the joint dynamics is to enhance the opening of the gap between the tang and clevis by about 10–20 % in the region of 300°–320°.

9. O-ring resiliency is directly related to its temperature.

(a) A warm O-ring that has been compressed will return to its original shape much more quickly than will a cold O-ring when compression is relieved. Thus, a warm O-ring will follow the opening of the tang-to-clevis gap, whereas a cold O-ring may not.

(b) A compressed O-ring at 75 °F is five times more responsive in returning to its uncompressed shape than is a cold O-ring at 30 °F.

(c) As a result it is probable that the O-rings in the right solid booster aft field joint were not following the opening of the gap between the tang and clevis at time of ignition.

10. Experiments indicate that the primary mechanism that actuates O-ring sealing is the application of gas pressure to the upstream (high-pressure) side of the O-ring as it sits in its groove or channel.

(a) For this pressure actuation to work most effectively, a space between the O-ring and its upstream channel wall should exist during pressurization.

(b) A tang-to-clevis gap of 0.004 in., as probably existed in the failed joint, would have initially compressed the O-ring to the degree that no clearance existed between the O-ring and its upstream channel wall and the other two surfaces of the channel.

(c) At the cold launch temperature experienced, the O-ring would be very slow in returning to its normal rounded shape. It would not follow the opening of the tang-to-clevis gap. It would remain in its compressed position in the O–ring channel and not provide a space between itself and the upstream channel wall. Thus, it is probable the O-ring would not be pressure actuated to seal the gap in time to preclude joint failure caused by blow-by and erosion from hot combustion gases.

11. The sealing characteristics of the Solid Rocket Booster O-rings are enhanced by timely application of motor pressure.

(a) Ideally, motor pressure should be applied to actuate the O-ring and seal the joint before significant opening of the tang-to-clevis gap (100–200 ms after motor ignition).

(b) Experimental evidence indicates that temperature, humidity, and other variables in the putty compound used to seal the joint can delay pressure application to the joint by 500 ms or more.

(c) This delay in pressure could be a factor in initial joint failure.

12. Of 21 launches with ambient temperatures of 61 °F or greater, only 4 showed signs of O-ring thermal distress, that is, erosion or blow-by and soot. Each of the launches below 61 °F resulted in one or more O-rings showing signs of thermal distress.

(a) Of these improper joint sealing actions, one-half occurred in the aft field joints, 20 % in the center field joints, and 30 % in the upper field joints. The division between left and right Solid Rocket Boosters was roughly equal.

(b) Each instance of thermal O-ring distress was accompanied by a leak path in the insulating putty. The leak path connects the rocket's combustion chamber with the O-ring region of the tang and clevis. Joints that actuated without incident may also have had these leak paths.

13. There is a possibility that there was water in the clevis of the STS 51-L joints because water was found in the STS-9 joints during a destack operation after exposure to less rainfall than STS 51-L. At time of launch, it was cold enough that water present in the joint would freeze. Tests show that ice in the joint can inhibit proper secondary seal performance.

14. A series of puffs of smoke were observed emanating from the 51-L aft field joint area of the right Solid Rocket Booster between 0.678 and 2.500 s after ignition of the Shuttle Solid Rocket Motors.

(a) The puffs appeared at a frequency of about three puffs per second. This rate roughly matches the natural structural frequency of the solids at liftoff and is reflected in slight cyclic changes of the tang-to-clevis gap opening.

(b) The puffs were seen to be moving upward along the surface of the booster above the aft field joint.

(c) The smoke was estimated to originate at a circumferential position of between 270° and 315° on the booster aft field joint, emerging from the top of the joint.

15. This smoke from the aft field joint at Shuttle liftoff was the first sign of the failure of the Solid Rocket Booster O-ring seals on STS 51-L.

16. The leak was again clearly evident as a flame at approximately 58 s into the flight. It is possible that the leak was continuous but unobservable or nonexistent in portions of the intervening period. It is possible in either case that thrust vectoring and normal vehicle response to wind shear as well as planned maneuvers reinitiated or magnified the leakage from a degraded seal in the period preceding the observed flames. The estimated position of the flame, centered at a point 307° around the circumference of the aft field

joint, was confirmed by the recovery of two fragments of the right Solid Rocket Booster.

(a) A small leak could have been present that may have grown to breach the joint in flame at a time on the order of 58–60 s after liftoff.

(b) Alternatively, the O-ring gap could have been resealed by deposition of a fragile buildup of aluminum oxide and other combustion debris. This resealed section of the joint could have been disturbed by thrust vectoring, Space Shuttle motion, and flight loads inducted by changing winds aloft.

(c) The winds aloft caused control actions in the time interval of 32–62 s into the flight that were typical of the largest values experienced on previous missions.

In conclusion, the commission stressed that the *Challenger* accident was the result of failure of the pressure seals in the aft field joint of the right Solid Rocket Booster. The commission also concluded that the failure, therefore, was a result of a faulty design unacceptably sensitive to a number of factors that include temperature, physical dimensions, character of materials, the effects of reusability, processing, and the reaction of the joint to dynamic loading.

During the commission's hearing, information emerged indicating that engineers at Morton Thiokol, Inc., the Utah company that designed the Rocket Booster joints in the *Challenger*, warned management against the launch of the space shuttle because of the predicted low temperatures. They feared that the predicted low temperatures would stiffen the O-rings.

Against their company's guidelines to give "yes" or "no" answers to the commission's questions, three engineers, Allan McDonald, Arnold Thompson, and Roger Boisjoly, broke ranks with management to reveal the warning. The three, led by Roger Boisjoly, told the commission that they warned management that the temperature of 18 °F (−8 °C) predicted the morning of the launch may make the booster O-ring stiff, preventing them from sealing the gases properly. They presented evidence to the commission to show that at 53 °F, in one of the past launches, one of the two redundant joints had not sealed. It was learned that although Morton Thiokol's management had not previously approved any launch at temperatures below 53 °F, on this occasion, management changed their position under duress from NASA, after previously postponing the *Challenger* launch four times. NASA argued that there were never any such data on the booster joint acceptable range of temperatures and they were, therefore, ready to go. Up to the last moment of launch, engineer Allen McDonald, the Morton Thiokol resident engineer at the Kennedy Space Flight Center, fought NASA to postpone the launch, but he did not succeed and the launch went ahead—at least for 27 s [13].

7.3.3.3 The Indian Bhopal Chemical Accident

The Union Carbide industrial accident in Bhopal, India, illustrates many of the elements of this safety culture. In December 1984, an accidental release of methyl isocyanate killed between 2000 and 3000 people and injured tens of thousands of others, many of them permanently. The accident was later blamed on human error. The official report stated that water was let into the storage tank of methyl isocyanate through an improperly cleaned pipe ([7], p. 40). According to Leveson, Union

Carbide management, including scientists, believed that because of the modern technology they had at the plant, such an accident could not happen there. It did.

7.3.3.4 The Chernobyl Nuclear Power Accident

The 1986 Chernobyl nuclear power accident in northern Ukraine, then a republic of the USSR, was the worst nuclear accident that has ever occurred. For a number of days after the accident, the Soviet government kept the world guessing at what was happening. But when details started to spill out, it was discovered that things started going bad on April 26, 1986, when during an experiment to determine the length of time the turbine and the generator could supply the emergency cooling system with electricity if an accident were to occur, the experiment went haywire and the operators started to notice a decline in the power output.

On noticing the decline, the operators turned off two automatic systems that were supposed to activate the controller rods in an emergency. At the same time they pumped more water into the reactor tank. When the water in the reactor tank stopped boiling, they then decreased the freshwater flow into the reactor tank—a bad mistake.

This action resulted in an unprecedented power upsurge in a very short time when the water in the reactor tank started to boil again. This overwhelming power, generated in only a couple of seconds, overheated the nuclear fuel, and a third of the core exploded from the inside. The quick upsurge in power and the subsequent explosion resulted from the fact that the steam from the boiling reactor tank water reacted with the graphite in the reactor and formed carbon dioxide and hydrogen, generating high steam pressure that lifted the lid off the reactor tank and quickly reacted with the air outside to cause the huge explosion. Immediately after, radioactive emissions were blown by the wind and quickly covered the surrounding areas and threatened western Europe [14].

7.4   Consumer Protection

Asset purchasing is a game of wits played between the buyer and the seller. Any time you make a purchase, remember that you are starting at a disadvantage because unlike the seller you do not have all the cards to win the game; the seller does. He or she always has more information about the item for sale than you, the buyer. As the game progresses the seller picks and chooses the information to give to the buyer.

In the case of software purchases, the buyer needs to be even more careful because many software products do not always work as the seller claims they do, or at least as the buyer would like them to do. Software products may not work as expected because the buyer has unrealistic expectations about the product, the environment in which the product is supposed to work is inadequate, the seller exaggerated the capacities of the software, or the software is simply faulty. So what can buyers do if the product just purchased does not live up to expectations? It usually depends on how much buyers know about their rights. Without claiming to be lawyers, let us begin this section by defining the legal jargon buyers need to press for their rights and to take legal action if nothing else works. Legal action should be the last resort, however, because once filed, a lawsuit takes on a life of its own in expense, time, and outcome.

7.4.1 Buyers' Rights

What are our rights as purchasers of a software product that does not live up to our expectations? The first step is to review the available options by contacting the developer of the product. If the developer is not the seller, then start with the vendor from whom you bought the product. Sometimes the vendor or seller may replace the product with a new one, depending on the elapsed time and warranties, or may refer you to the developer.

When talking to the developer, explain specifically and clearly what it is that you want, why you are not satisfied with the product, and what you want to accomplish. Although developers claim to help unsatisfied customers, computer software is more difficult to handle once it has been opened, and you may have to do more than you would with a different kind of product to convince both the vendor and the developer that their product is not satisfactory. Developers typically have technical teams to help customers with problems, and most of the problems are solved at this level. However, if you are still not satisfied with the service, other options are open to you, such as the following:

- *Product replacement*: You may demand a product replacement if you think it will solve the problem. Most developers usually do replace faulty products.
- *Product update*: When the product is found to have a fault that the provider was not aware of at the time of shipping the product to market, the producer may fix the fault by providing a patch or an upgrade of the product that can either be downloaded or shipped to all customers who report that fault (e.g., the Netscape case and the Intel Pentium chip debacle).

In the Netscape case, a serious flaw in the then just released Netscape Communications Corporation's browser was uncovered by a small Danish software company called Cabocomm. The bug made it possible for web site operators to read anything stored on the hard disk of a PC logged on the web site. Netscape acknowledged the error and offered to send upgrades to its customers [15].

The Intel Pentium chip situation was very much like that of Netscape, Inc., except that for Intel it was a hardware problem. A mathematics professor using a Pentium-based office PC found that at a high level of mathematical computation, the chip froze. He reported his discovery via e-mail to a colleague, and the word spread like wildfire. But unlike Netscape, Inc., which immediately admitted fault, Intel did not at first admit it until the giant IBM and other small PC companies threatened not to use the chip in their line of products. Intel then accepted responsibility and promised to send upgrades to all its customers [16].

If none of the options already discussed proves viable, the next and probably last step is legal action. A liability suit is filed in civil court against the producer of the product for damages. In some cases, if the product has resulted in a casualty, a criminal suit against the producer can also be filed if the customer believes there was criminal intent. If you decide to file a civil liability suit, two avenues are open to you—the contract and/or tort options (see Sects. 7.4.3 and 7.4.4). For a successful outcome in a software case, you need to proceed with care to classify what was purchased either as a product or a service. The decision of the courts in a purchase lawsuit depends heavily on this classification.

7.4.2   Classification of Computer Software

As we explained earlier, computer software falls into three categories: product, service, and a mixture of both service and product.

7.4.2.1 What Is a Product?

A product must have two fundamental properties. First it must have a tangible form, and second it must have a built-in intrinsic value for the buyer. Look at a few examples. Consider a lottery ticket you have just bought for which the jackpot is $100 million. Suppose you paid $1 for your ticket. The ticket has a form that everyone can see and touch; it is tangible. Now suppose your grandmother, who is visiting with you, lives in a state with no lottery. She finds your ticket lying on the kitchen table. To her, although the ticket has a tangible form because she can see and touch it, it has no value to her. To you, however, the ticket not only has tangible form, it also has an intrinsic value worth millions of dollars.

For a second example, suppose you have a splitting headache, which your physician tells you can be cured by a certain tablet. For you this tablet has a tangible form because you can see and touch it, but it also has an intrinsic value because you believe it will cure your headache. To somebody else who does not have a headache, the tablet simply has a tangible form but no value beyond that. For software to be considered a product, it must have both a tangible form and an intrinsic value. Many software packages have these two properties and can therefore be considered as products. For example, when you buy a U.S. tax preparation package and you live in the United States, to you the package has both a tangible form and an intrinsic value. But to somebody else living in another country, the package, although it has tangible form, does not have any intrinsic value at all.

7.4.2.2 What Is a Service?

A service, in contrast to a product, has intrinsic value, but it does not have a tangible form. Because it has no tangible form, whoever wants a service must describe it. A service most often involves a provider–client or provider–customer relationship: The provider in this equation is the person offering the service and the client is the person receiving the service. For professionals, the relationship is always provider–client, where there is an imbalance of power in favor of the provider (e.g., an attorney–client relationship or a doctor–patient relationship).

In nonprofessional situations, it is often a provider–customer relationship and the power play here is in favor of the customer because customers must always get what they want, and the customer must always be satisfied. What the provider and customer receive in this relationship, however, has no tangible form—but it does have intrinsic value. The customer gets satisfaction with the service and this satisfaction is the value of the service. The provider in turn gets paid, and again that is the value of the service.

7.4.2.3 Is Software a Product, a Service, or a Mixture?

Now that we have differentiated between a product and a service, let us tackle the problem of classification of computer software. According to Deborah Johnson [17], courts do not always equate products with what is tangible. If we accept this line of reasoning, then software with no tangible form can be considered a product and therefore can be protected by patent laws that protect products. But we have to be very careful with this line of argument not to conclude too hastily that software is going to be accepted as a product because there are items with no tangible forms that even the courts cannot accept as products.

If we define software as a set of instructions describing an algorithm to perform a task that has intrinsic value for the buyer, this definition classifies software as a service. For example, suppose you want a software item to perform a certain task for your company but you cannot find the appropriate type on the market. You describe what it is that you want done to a software developer, and the software developer comes up with what you want. What has been produced can be considered a service performed; it has intrinsic value for you, but no tangible form.

But suppose you want a program to do a task for you, and instead of describing it to a software developer, you decide to go to your discount store where you know such software item is sold, and you buy a box containing that item. What you have just paid for is a product no different from that box of potato chips you picked up at the same store. Suppose further that when you open your potato chips you find them crushed to a powder, or suppose when you eat the potato chips they make you sick, and later you find they were contaminated. Legally you cannot sue the producer of the chips for malpractice or negligence, but you can sue for product liability. Similarly, then, you cannot sue for malpractice or negligence if the contents of a software box do not work properly. You should sue for product liability because in this case software seems to be an indisputable product.

There are interesting yet mixed views concerning the classification of software. Jim Price [18] defines three categories of software classes using the producer–market–customer relationship:

1. *Canned software*: Off-the-shelf software for a general market customer. Tax preparation software packages fall in this category.
2. *Customized software*: The software produced for a customer after the customer has described what he or she specifically needs to the software producer.
3. *Hybrid software*: Canned software that is customized to meet certain customer needs, but cannot be used to perform the whole task without focused modifications.

Price argues for a product classification of all software falling in category 1 on the basis of three principles:

1. The product was placed in mainstream commerce by the producer with the purpose of making a profit, and the producer therefore should be responsible for the implied safety of the product.
2. The producer has a better understanding of the product than the buyer, and therefore is in a better position to anticipate the risks.
3. The producer can easily spread the burden of the cost of product liabilities from injuries over the entire range of product customers without the customers knowing, thus minimizing the costs and risks to him or her [17].

With software in category 1, strict liability for a bad product, including negligence, can be raised by the customer seeking benefits from the producer. For software in category 2, customers can seek benefits from the producer resulting from injuries by using malpractice laws because software in this category is a service.

With these two categories, the distinction between a product and a service is straightforward. But this is not the case with software in category 3. Some elements in this category belong to a product classification (e.g., placing the item in the mainstream of commerce in a tangible form).

Also, because the software can be changed to suit individual needs, the principle that the producer can spread the burden of the cost of product liability because of injuries over all product customers does not apply anymore. This is what Johnson calls a mixed classification case because it belongs in two categories: the canned category and the customized category. Johnson suggests that such software should be treated in the following way. If there is an error in the canned part, then it can be treated like a product. And if it develops an error in the customized part, then it should be handled as a service. The problem with this line of thinking, however, is that for an average software user it is almost impossible to tell in which part the error originated.

As technology advances, new categories will definitely emerge, and ideally new laws will be enacted to cover all these new categories. We cannot keep on relying on old laws to cope with the ever-changing technological scene.

When you have successfully classified your software, then you can pursue the two possible options open to you: contract or tort.

7.4.3   The Contract Option

Lawyers define a contract as a binding relationship between two or more parties. A contract need not be in a physical form like a document; it can be oral or implied. For a relationship to be a contract, it must satisfy several requirements including mutual consent. Mutual consent is a meeting of the minds on issues such as the price bargained or agreed upon, the amount paid or promised to be paid, and any agreement enforceable by law.

In contract laws, a producer/developer can be sued for breach of contract. Contract laws also cover express and implied warranties, third-party beneficial contracts, and disclaimers. Warranties are guarantees that the product or service will live up to its reasonable expectations. Some warranties are not specifically written down but are implied, whereas others are merely expressed either orally or in some other form.

7.4.3.1 Express Warranties

Express warranties are an affirmation of a fact, a promise, or a description of goods, a sample, or a model made by the seller to the buyer relating to the goods and as a basis for payment negotiations. Express warranties are entered into between the customer and the producer when a producer agrees to supply the product to the customer. They also involve promises made by the producer through sales representatives and written materials on packaging attesting to the quality of the product and guidelines buyers must follow to get detectable errors corrected by the producer. These warranties are also included in the U.S. Uniform Commercial Code (UCC) and, unless specifically excluded by the seller, express warranties become enforceable immediately upon application of the UCC transaction.

Producers usually limit their liability on products by stipulating a timeframe on warranties and contracts. But in most cases, time limits do not apply, especially in cases of express warranties because of advertising and description of the product capacity on or in packages [19].

7.4.3.2 Implied Warranties

Implied warranties are enforced by law according to established and accepted public policy. For example, in the nonideal world we live in, we cannot expect a contract to contain everything the buyer and producer may want. Remember that the process of buying and selling is a game in which there is a winner, a loser, or a draw. In this game, as we pointed out earlier, the seller has more cards than the buyer.

On the buyer's side are quite a number of things they do not have to negotiate because they do not know as much and need time to learn the product. The law protects buyers so they do not have to negotiate every small detail of the product conditions. Implied warranties make such conditions always part of the package agreement even if they are not specifically written down in the contract. An implied warranty guarantees that a product is of average quality and will perform no less than similar products and that it is fit for the intended use. For buyers to benefit from implied warranties, proof must be given that the contract did not exclude some features and there is no time limitation for reporting defects; some companies, however, stipulate a timeframe in which defects must be reported. Implied warranties are advantageous to buyers because they enforce a degree of discipline on the producers and vendors to sell standard products for the intended purposes. They are also useful to the producer and vendors because they create a degree of confidence and trust in buyers, hence increasing sales of products. However, there is a downside to implied warranties; they tend to make software expensive because the producer anticipates the cost of the lawsuits that might be generated and passes such costs on to the customers.

7.4.3.3 Third-Party Beneficiary Contracts

If a software product injures a user other than the buyer, under a third-party benefi-ciary contract the user may sue the producer for benefits from injuries or loss of income resulting from the product. Third-party beneficiary contracts suits are not common because they are rarely found valid in courts.

7.4.3.4 Disclaimers

Producers try to control their liability losses by putting limits on warranties via disclaimers. Through disclaimers, producers preempt lawsuits from buyers by telling buyers in writing on the contracts the limits of what is guaranteed.

Many users see disclaimers as a way producers try to avoid responsibility. Producers see them as a way of informing the users of the risks before they buy the product, and they also like them because they put the burden of proof and risk taking squarely on the buyers: caveat emptor (the buyer beware), so to speak. Whether these disclaimers are recognized in courts depends on a number of factors including the belief that the disclaimers were made in good faith.

7.4.3.5 Breach of Contract

A contract entered into between two or more parties and not performed as promised by either party can be considered breached by the party not in compliance. If the complaint is not very serious, the breach may not cause the termination of the con-tract, but the breaching party may be asked to pay some damages. However, if the breach is considered serious by one of the parties, it may cause the termination of the contract. In this case the offended party may demand damages from the breach-ing party in the contract upon satisfactory proof that there were indeed damages resulting from contract breaching.

7.4.4 The Tort Option

If a buyer cannot seek benefits from the producer through contracts laws, another avenue of legal action is through tort. A tort is a wrong committed upon a person or property in the absence of a contract. A tort may include negligence, malpractice, strict liability, and misrepresentation. Torts fall into two categories: intentional and unintentional. For example, if you are passing by a construction site and somebody pours concrete on you, this act may be interpreted as intentional if the worker who poured the concrete knew it was you passing; otherwise, it is unintentional.

7.4.4.1 Negligence

Negligence can be used by the buyer to obtain benefits from the producer if there is provable evidence that the product lacked a certain degree of care, skill, and compe-tence in the workmanship. Carelessness and a lack of competence may be proved from the design stage through the testing, installation, and user training stages of the product. For example, suppose that the buyer of a computer software product is a large hospital and the product is life-sustaining software. If it causes injury to a patient because the hospital personnel using the software were not adequately trained by the producer of the software, and this can be proved beyond a reasonable doubt, then the producer can be sued for negligence. In other words, negligence in this case is holding the software producer party liable for the injuries he or she did not intend and even tried to avoid while making the software. Negligence cases apply mainly to services rendered.

7.4.4.2 Malpractice

Malpractice is a type of negligence. It is also applicable in cases involving services. For example, if you visit the doctor for a simple eye surgery and he or she cuts off your ear, you can sue the doctor for malpractice. Malpractice lawsuits are common in professional services. In the case of software, if it is taken as a service, then malpractice applies.

7.4.4.3 Strict Liability

Strict liability is a tort involving products. Any product sold in a defective condition that ends up endangering a person creates a case of strict liability to the seller of such a product even if the buyer did not make a direct purchase from the seller. In strict liability lawsuits, the burden of proof of negligence is shifted to the producer, and the costs incurred by defects in the product are squarely in the hands of the producer. Under strict liability, it is the product itself that is on trial. The product is examined and if it is found to be defective and dangerous, the buyer is awarded benefits. Strict liability laws are harsh. They ignore efforts made by the producer of the product to make the product safe for the reason that the producer was in a better position to know the risks [20].

7.4.4.4 Misrepresentation

Most computer software and other computer products are no longer sold by their original producers and developers but by third-party sellers and vendors. Examples of such third-party sellers are mail-order computer hardware and hundreds of software companies and many big brand name computer outlets. So, very few original manufacturers and software developers are selling directly to the buyer. To the buyer of a computer product, this situation may add another layer of bureaucracy and more problems. The problems are not one sided, however; indirect selling also causes additional problems for the producer. Many of the producer problems added by this layer actually come from misrepresentation of the product. Misrepresentation may be intentionally done by the sales representative to induce the buyer to buy the product or it may be just a genuine mistake. Consider car manufacturers, for example. Usually they buy back faulty new cars from customers when these cars have developed specific problems within a designated period of time. These cars are usually repaired and sent back to the dealers to be sold, not as new but as used products. Sometimes, however, car dealers sell these cars as new cars. Whether car manufacturers are aware of these sales practices or not, customers always end up suing the car manufacturers.

Before you sue the producer, however, determine first whether it was an intentional misrepresentation called fraudulent misrepresentation. To prove fraudulent misrepresentation, you need to prove that the vendor was aware the facts given were not true or that the vendor would have known the true facts but opted not to inform the buyer accordingly. You also need to show, and be believed, that you as a buyer relied on that information to buy the product. And finally you need to show that the product resulted in damage. If you can establish all these facts and be believed by the courts, then you have a case [17].

7.5   Improving Software Quality

The problem of software quality cannot be solved by courts alone. Software producers must themselves do more to ensure software quality and hence safety.

7.5.1   Techniques for Improving Software Quality

Reputable software standards, reliability of software, and software safety depend greatly on the quality of the software. If the quality is low, software is prone to errors, is therefore not reliable, and hence has poor standards. In Sect. 7.1.1, we stated that software can be enhanced by techniques such as developmental testing, V&V, and programming standards. But the quality of software cannot be assumed by looking at these factors only. According to Linger et al. [20], software cannot be made reliable by testing alone. Software quality can be improved through the following innovative new review techniques:

- *Formal review*: Presentation of the software product by a person more familiar with the product to others with competent knowledge of that product so they can critique the product and offer informed suggestions.
- *Inspection*: Involves checking the known specific errors from past products and establishing additional facilities that may be missing in the product to bring the product up to acceptable standards.
- *Walk-through*: Requires code inspection line by line by a team of reviewers to detect potential errors. Each review session is followed by a discussion of the findings by the members of the review team, usually with the creators of the code present.
- *Phased inspection*: Technique developed by Jack C. Knight and Ann Mayers [21]. It is an enhanced method combining the previous three methods by putting emphasis on the limitations of those methods. It consists of a series of coordinated partial inspections called phases during which specific properties of the product are inspected.

If care is taken by the software developer to improve the development process of software by improving validation, verification, and the survivability of the software, the liability on their part will be minimized, and software safety will be greatly improved. If software developers paid more attention to software quality using many of the techniques cited here during development, there would be little need to discuss consumer protection.

7.6   Producer Protection

In Sect. 7.4 we outlined user rights and protection mechanisms in the case of substandard software. In this section we focus on the other side of the same coin: the software producer's rights and protection mechanisms. Software producers need to protect themselves against piracy, illegal copying, and fraudulent lawsuits. But because of the high costs, time, and the unpredictability of the outcome of lawsuits, it is not good business practice for software producers to sue a single person making a copy of the software. It only makes sense to go after big-time and large-scale illegal copying. Software producers should be prepared to seek protection from the courts to protect the software itself from illegal copying, piracy, and also from lawsuits from customers. In addition, producers should be prepared to protect themselves from lawsuits filed by consumers. For this kind of protection, producers are advised to use the courts as much as possible and ask for advice from lawyers and business colleagues. There is no one single magic bullet approach.

Exercises

1. Discuss the difficulties faced by software producers.
2. Discuss ways software customers can protect themselves from substandard software products.
3. Discuss how the following are used to protect a software customer:
   - Implied warranty
   - Express warranty
   - Disclaimer
   - Strict liability
4. It has been said that software problems are a direct result of its differences from hardware. Discuss.
5. Discuss the elements of software quality. How can software quality be a solution to many of software's liability problems?
6. Do safe software systems imply reliable systems? Why or why not?
7. Software reliability, especially in critical systems, is vital. Discuss the necessary conditions for reliability.
8. With the development of scanning and snooping software, computer systems cannot be assured of security. Discuss what steps need to be taken to ensure system safety.

9. We discussed in this chapter that risk can be both voluntary and involuntary. Give examples in each case.
10. Why do we always take risk as a crucial design component? What two aspects must be considered?
11. In carrying out the risk assessment and control of a software product, what aspects must be considered and why?
12. Why is there a myth that computers (hardware and software) do not make errors?
13. Does the myth about computers complicate the safety issue?
14. How does humanware affect system safety?
15. If workplace systems were all automated, could this eliminate workplace system risks? Would it reduce it?
16. Why is software safety so difficult to attain? Can it be guaranteed?

References

1. Hamlet R (1988) Special section on software testing. Commun ACM 31(6):662–667
2. Parnas D, van Schouwen J, Kwan S (1990) Evolution of safety-critical software. Commun ACM 33(6):636–648
3. Taylor J (1994) America's loneliest airport: Denver's dreams can't fly. Kansas City Star, 25 August, 1994. NewsBank, Transportation, fiche 43, grids D12–14
4. Neumann P (1995) Computer-related risks. ACM Press, New York
5. Neumann P (1993) The role of software engineering. Commun ACM 36(5):114
6. Ahl DL (1985) Employee computer crime on the rise. Creat Comput 11(6):6, Washington, DC
7. Leveson N (1995) Safeware: system safety and computers. Addison-Wesley, Reading
8. Littlewood B, Strigini L (1993) Validation of ultrahigh dependability for software-based systems. Commun ACM 36(11):69–80
9. Ritchie D (1984) Reflections on trusting trust. Commun ACM 27(8):761–763
10. Haag S, Raju MK, Schkade LL (1996) Quality function deployment usage in software development. Commun ACM 39(1):41–49
11. Boehm BW (1989) Software risk management: principles and practices. IEEE Computer Society Press, New York
12. President's commission on the challenger accident report. http://science.ksc.nasa.gov/shuttle/missions/51–l/docs/rogers–commission/table–of–contents.html
13. Fitzgerald K (1990) Whistle-blowing: not always a losing game. IEEE Spectr 26(6):49–52
14. Nuclear accidents. Swedish Nuclear Power Generation. http://www.thn.edu.stockholm.se/projekt/energi/kk/index.htm
15. Young S. Netscape bug uncovered. CNNfn, 12 June. http://cnnfn.com/digitaljam/9706/netscape–pkg/
16. Computer stock tumble over chip flow. New York Times, 4 December, 1994, section D
17. Johnson D (1994) Computer ethics, 2nd edn. Prentice Hall, Englewood Cliffs, p 134
18. Prince J (1980) Negligence: liability for defective software. Okla Law Rev 33:848–855
19. Neitzke F (1984) A software law primer. Reinhold, New York
20. Linger C, Mills HD, Witts B (1979) Structured programming: theory and practice. Addison-Wesley, Reading
21. Knight J, Mayers A (1994) An improved inspection technique. Commun ACM 36(11):51–61

Further Reading

Banker R, Datar S, Kemerer C, Zeneig D (1993) Software complexity and maintenance costs. Commun ACM 36(11):81–94

Fetzer J (1988) Program verification: the very idea. Commun ACM 31(9):1048–1063

Gelperin D, Hetzel B (1988) The growth of software testing. Commun ACM 31(6):687–690

Grady R (1993) Practical results from measuring software quality. Commun ACM 36(11):50–61

Laprie J-C, Littlewood B (1992) Probablistic assessment of safety-critical software: why and how? Commun ACM 35(2):13–21

Leveson N (1991) Software safety in embedded computer systems. Commun ACM 34(2):34–46

Computer Crimes

8

Learning Objectives

After reading this chapter, the reader should be able to

1. Describe trends in computer crimes and protection against viruses and denial-of-service attacks.
2. Understand techniques to combat "cracker" attacks.
3. Understand the history of computer crimes.
4. Describe several different cyber-attacker approaches and motivations.
5. Identify the professional's role in security and the tradeoffs involved.
6. Develop measures to be taken both by individuals themselves and by organizations (including government) to prevent identity theft.

Scenario 7: All in the Open, My Friend—Be Watchful for You Will Never Know the Hour!

Josephine Katu owns a company that manufactures women's cosmetics. She has loyal and dedicated employees, and each one of them works very hard. Josephine has been good to them too. She compliments them and rewards them handsomely when the occasion presents itself.

However, Josephine has become suspicious of some of the employees, without knowing which one(s) in particular. She is also not sure what it is that is not right, but she suspects something is going wrong somewhere in her company and she is not happy. So she decides to do something about it.

During the Christmas season, Josephine buys each of her 20 or so employees a laptop for his or her home and she promises to pay for their online expenses. In addition, she also promises to take care of all system maintenance, using the company technician, if they ever need it. Josephine writes a

(continued)

© Springer International Publishing Switzerland 2016
J.M. Kizza, *Ethics in Computing*, Undergraduate Topics in Computer Science,
DOI 10.1007/978-3-319-29106-2_8

Scenario 7: (continued)

virus that she occasionally and selectively uploads to her employees' computer, which uploads the content of the machine.

The plan is working very well and Josephine is getting plenty of information whenever the virus is released. She is even planning on bringing in the press and the FBI.

Discussion Questions

1. *Is Josephine right to release a virus on her employees' computers?*
2. *Do the computers belong to her or to her employees?*
3. *Are the employees' rights being violated? What rights?*
4. *What are the social and ethical implications of Josephine's little tricks?*

8.1   Introduction

It is difficult to define a computer crime without getting tangled up in the legal terminology. We will try to make it simple for the rest of us nonlawyers. A computer crime is a crime like any other crime, except that in this case the illegal act must involve a computer system either as an object of a crime, an instrument used to commit a crime, or a repository of evidence related to a crime. With the Internet, the scope of computer crimes has widened to actually include crimes that would normally be associated with telecommunication facilities. Because of this, we want to expand our definition of a computer crime to be an illegal act that involves a computer system or computer-related system such as any mobile device, microwave, satellite, or other telecommunication system that connects one or more computers or computer-related systems.

Acts using computers or computer-related technologies that fall within the limits that the legislature of a state or a nation has specified are considered illegal and may lead to forfeiture of certain civil rights of the perpetrator. In the United States, local, state, and federal legislatures have defined such acts to include such as the following:

- Intrusions into Public Packet Networks
- Network integrity violations
- Privacy violations
- Industrial or financial espionage
- Pirated computer software
- Computer-aided fraud
- Internet/e-mail abuse
- Using computers or computer technology to commit murder, terrorism, pornography, hacking, and many other crimes.

Computer crimes target computer resources for a variety of reasons [1]:

- Hardware such as computers, printers, scanners, servers, and communication media
- Software that includes application and special programs, system backups, diagnostic programs, and system programs such as operating systems and protocols
- Data in storage, transition, or undergoing modification

An attack on any one of these resources is considered a computer or computer-related attack. Some of these resources are more vulnerable than others and are, therefore, targeted more frequently by attackers. Most computer crimes on the resources just listed fall into the three categories following. Our focus in this chapter is on the last category [1, 2]:

- Human blunders, errors, and omissions that are usually caused by unintentional human actions. Unintended human actions are usually the result of design problems. Such attacks are called *malfunctions*. Malfunctions, although occurring more frequently than natural disasters, are as unpredictable as natural disasters.
- Intentional threats that originate from humans caused by illegal or criminal acts from either insiders or outsiders, recreational hackers, and criminals. For the remainder of this chapter, we are focusing on this last category.

8.2 History of Computer Crimes

As we look at the history of computer crimes, we focus on two aspects of such crimes: viruses and hacking. These two have been the source of almost all computer crimes. Sometimes they become one when hackers use viruses to attack computer systems, as we discuss next. The term virus is derived from the Latin word virus that means poison [3]. Until recently, the term had remained mostly in medical circles, meaning a foreign agent injecting itself into a living body, feeding on it to grow, multiply, and spread. Meanwhile, the body weakens and loses its ability to fight foreign invaders and eventually succumbs to the virus if not treated.

In contrast to a biological virus, however, a computer virus is a self-propagating computer program designed to alter or destroy a computer system's resources. Like its cousin, it follows almost the same pattern when attacking computer software. It attaches itself to software, grows, reproduces many times, and spreads in the new environment. It spreads by attacking major system resources including data and sometimes hardware, weakening the capacity of these resources to perform the needed functions and eventually bringing the system down.

The word virus was first assigned a nonbiological meaning in the 1972 science fiction stories about the G.O.D. machine, which were compiled in a book *When Harlie Was One* by David Gerrold. Later, Fred Cohen, then a graduate student at the University of Southern California, associated the term with a real-world computer program he wrote for a class demonstration [4]. During the demonstration, each virus obtained full control of the system within an hour. That simple class experiment has led to a global phenomenon that has caused nightmares for system administrators, security personnel, and cyberspace users.

Hacking, as a computer attack technique, utilizes the Internet working between computers and communication devices. So long as computers are not interconnected in a network, hacking cannot take place. So, the history of hacking begins with the invention of the telephone in 1876 by Alexander Graham Bell, which has made internetworking possible. However, there was a long gap between the invention of the telephone and the first recorded hacking activity in 1971 when John Draper, commonly known as "Captain Crunch," discovered that a toy whistle from a cereal box could produce the precise tone of 2600 Hz needed to make free long-distance phone calls [5]. With this act, "Phreaking," a cousin of hacking, entered our language. With the starting of a limited national computer network by ARPANET, in the 1970s, a limited form of system break-in from outsiders started appearing. The movie "War Games," which appeared in 1983, glamorized and popularized hacking. It is believed by many that the movie gave rise to the hacking phenomenon.

The first notable system penetration attack actually started in the mid-1980s with the San Francisco-based 414-Club. The 414-Club was the first national news-making hacker group. The group named their group 414 after the area code of San Francisco were they were. They started a series of computer intrusion attacks via a Stanford University computer which they used to spread the attack across the country [6]. From that small but history-making attack, other headline-making attacks from Australia, Germany, Argentina, and the United States followed.

In the United States, these activities, although at a low level, started worrying law enforcement agencies so much so that in 1984 the Comprehensive Crime Control Act was enacted, giving the Secret Service jurisdiction over computer fraud. Also at around this time, the hacker movement was starting to get active. In 1984, *2600: The Hacker Quarterly*, a hacker magazine, was launched and the following year the electronic hacking magazine *Phrack* was founded. As the Internet grew, hacker activities increased greatly. Then, in 1986, the U.S. Congress passed the Computer Fraud and Abuse Act. Hacker activities that had only been in the United States started to spread worldwide. In 1987, the Italian hacker community launched *Decoder* magazine, similar to the United States' *2600: Hacker Quarterly* [5].

The first headline-making hacking incident involving a virus took place in 1988 when a Cornell graduate student created a computer virus that crashed 6000 computers and effectively shut down the Internet for 2 days [6]. Robert Morris's action forced the U.S. government to form the federal Computer Emergency Response Team to investigate similar and related attacks on the nation's computer networks. Law enforcement agencies started to actively follow the comings and goings of networks traffic and sometimes eavesdrop on the communications. This move did not sit well with some activists, who in 1990 formed the Electronic Frontier Foundation to defend the rights of those investigated for alleged computer hacking.

The 1990s saw heightened hacking activities and serious computer network "near" meltdowns, including the 1991 expectation of the "Michelangelo" virus that was expected to crash computers on March 6, 1992, the artist's 517th birthday, but which passed without incident. In 1995, the notorious, self-styled hacker Kevin Mitnick was first arrested by the FBI on charges of computer fraud that involved the stealing of thousands of credit card numbers. In the second half of the 1990s, hacking activities increased considerably, including the 1998 Solar Sunrise, a series of attacks targeting Pentagon computers that led the Pentagon to establish round-the-clock, online guard duty at major military computer sites. Also, there was a coordinated attack on Pentagon computers by Ehud Tenebaum, an Israeli teenager known as "The Analyzer," and an American teen. The close of the twentieth century saw heightened anxiety in both the computing and computer user communities about both the millennium (Y2K) bug and the ever-rising rate of computer network break-ins. So, in 1999 President Bill Clinton announced a $1.46 billion initiative to improve government computer security. The plan intended to establish a network of intrusion detection monitors for certain federal agencies and encourage the private sector to do the same [5]. The year 2000 probably went down in history as one of the years that saw the most costly and most powerful computer network attacks: it included "Mel-lisa," "Love Bug," "Killer Resume," and a number of devastating distributed denial-of-service attacks. The following year, 2001, the elusive "Code Red" virus was released. The future of viruses is as unpredictable as the types of viruses themselves.

The period between 1980 and 2001 saw sharp growth in reported incidents of computer attacks. Two factors have contributed to this phenomenal growth: the growth of the Internet and the massive news coverage of virus incidents.

8.3   Types of Computer Systems Attacks

A great number of computer system crimes are actually computer attacks. Major computer attacks fall into two categories: penetration and denial-of-service attacks.

8.3.1   Penetration

A penetration attack involves breaking into a computer system using known security vulnerabilities to gain access to a cyberspace resource. With full penetration, an intruder has full access to all that system's resources. Full penetration, therefore, allows an intruder to alter data files, change data, plant viruses, or install damaging Trojan Horse programs into the system. It is also possible for intruders—especially if the victim computer is on a network—to use it as a launching pad to attack other network resources. Penetration attacks can be local, wherein the intruder gains access to a computer on a LAN on which the program is run, or global on a WAN such as the Internet, where an attack can originate thousands of miles from the victim computer. Penetration attacks originate from many sources, including the following:

(i) *Insider Threat.* For a long time, penetration attacks were limited to inhouse employee-generated attacks to systems and theft of company property. In fact, disgruntled insiders are a major source of computer crimes because they do not need a great deal of knowledge about the victim computer system. In many cases, such insiders use the system every day, which allows them to gain unrestricted access to the computer system, thus causing damage to the system and/ or data. The 1999 Computer Security Institute/FBI report notes that 55 % of respondents reported malicious activity by insiders [7].

(ii) *Hackers.* Since the mid-1980s, computer network hacking has been on the rise, mostly because of the wider use of the Internet. Hackers penetrate a computer system for a number of reasons, as we discuss in the next section, including the thrill of the challenge, bragging rights in the hacker community, and illicit financial gain or other malicious purposes. To penetrate the system, hackers use a variety of techniques. Using the skills they have, they download attack scripts and protocols from the Internet and launch them against victim sites.

(iii) *Criminal Groups.* Although a number of penetration attacks come from insiders and hackers with youthful intents, there are a number of attacks that originate from criminal groups, for example, the "Phonemasters," a widespread international group of criminals who in February 1999 penetrated the computer systems of MCI, Sprint, AT&T, Equifax, and even the FBI's National Crime Information Center. A member of the group in the United States, Calvin Cantrell downloaded thousands of Sprint calling card numbers. He later sold the numbers to a Canadian. From Canada, the numbers found their way back to America and on to Switzerland and eventually ended up in the hands of organized crime groups in Italy [7].

(iv) *Hactivism.* Demonstrations have taken place in Seattle, Washington DC, Prague, and Genoa by people with all sorts of causes, underlining the new phenomenon of activism that is being fueled by the Internet. This activism has not only been for good causes, but it has also resulted in what has been dubbed *hactivism*—motivated attacks on computer systems, usually web pages or e-mail servers of selected institutions or groups by activists. A group with a cause overloads e-mail servers and hacks into web sites with messages for their causes. The attacks so far have not been harmful, but they still cause damage to services. Such groups and attacks have included the "Electronic Disturbance Theater," which promotes civil disobedience online in support of the Zapatista movement in Mexico; supporters of Serbia, during the NATO bombing of Yugoslavia; electronically "ping"-attacked NATO web servers; and supporters of Kevin Mitnick, the famed computer hacker who while in federal prison, hacked into the Senate web page and defaced it [7].

8.3.2   Denial of Service

Denial-of-service attacks, commonly known as distributed denial of service (DDoS) attacks, are a new form of computer attacks. They are directed at computers connected to the Internet. They are not penetration attacks and, therefore, they do not change, alter, destroy, or modify system resources. However, they affect the system by diminishing the system's ability to function; hence, they are capable of bringing a system down without destroying its resources. They first appeared widely in the summer of 1999. The year 2000 saw this type of computer attack become a major new category of attack on the Internet. Headlines were made when a Canadian teen attacked Internet heavyweights Amazon, Ebay, E*Trade, and news leader CNN.

Differing from penetration attacks, DDoS attacks typically aim to exhaust the network bandwidth, its router processing capacity, or network stack resources, thus eventually breaking the network connectivity to the victims; this is achieved by the perpetrator breaking into weakly secured computers. The victim computers are found by using freely available scan software on the Internet that pinpoints to well-known defects in standard network service protocols and common weak configurations in operating systems. Once the victims have been identified, the perpetrator breaks in and may perform additional steps that include the installation of software, known in the industry as a "rootkit," to conceal the break-in trail and make the tracing of subsequent activities impossible.

When the perpetrator has several victim machines under its control, the controlled machines are then used to mount attacks on other machines in the network, usually selected machines, by sending streams of packets, as projectiles, to the secondary line of victims. For some variants of attacks like the Smurf attack (which is discussed shortly), the packets are aimed at other networks, where they provoke multiple echoes all aimed at the victim.

Similar to penetration electronic attacks (e-attacks), DDoS attacks can also be either local, where they can shut down LAN computers, or global, originating thousands of miles away on the Internet, as was the case in the Canadian-generated DDoS attacks. Attacks in this category include, among others, IP-spoofing, SYN-Flooding, Smurfing, Buffer Overflow, and Sequence Number Sniffing.

8.4 Motives of Computer Crimes

Hacking has many dubious motives. More recently, however, we have seen more cases of hacking for illicit financial gain or other malicious purposes. It is difficult to exclusively discuss all the motives, but let us look at the following major categories [2]:

(i) *Political Activism.* There are many causes that lead to political activism, but all these causes are grouped under one burner—hactivism—as discussed in Sect. 8.3.1.
(ii) *Vendetta.* Most vendetta attacks are for mundane reasons such as a promotion denied, a boyfriend or girlfriend taken, an ex-spouse given child custody, and other situations that may involve family and intimacy issues.
(iii) *Joke/Hoax.* Hoaxes are warnings that are actually scare alerts started by one or more malicious persons, and are passed on by innocent users who think that they are helping the community by spreading the warning. Most hoaxes are viruses although there are hoaxes that are computer-related folklore and urban

legends. Virus hoaxes are often false reports about nonexistent viruses that cause panic, especially to the majority of users who do not know how viruses work. Some hoaxes can become extremely widespread as they are mistakenly distributed by individuals and companies with the best of intentions. Although many virus hoaxes are false scares, there are some that may have some truth about them, but which often become greatly exaggerated, such as the "Good Times" and the "Great Salmon." Virus hoaxes infect mailing lists, bulletin boards, and Usenet newsgroups. Worried system administrators sometimes contribute to this scare by posting dire warnings to their employees, which become hoaxes themselves.

(iv) *The Hacker's Ethics.* This is a collection of motives that make up the hacker character. According to Steven Levy, hackers have motivation and ethics and beliefs that they live by, and he lists six, as below [8]:

 • Free access to computers and other ICT resources—and anything that might teach you something about the way the world works—should be unlimited and total.
 • All information should be free.
 • Mistrust authority; promote decentralization.
 • Hackers should be judged by their hacking, not bogus criteria such as degrees, age, race, or position.
 • You can create art and beauty on a computer.
 • Computers can change your life for the better.

If any of these beliefs is violated, a hacker will have a motive.

(v) *Terrorism/Extortion.* Our increasing dependence on computers and computer communication has opened up a can of worms we now know as electronic terrorism. Electronic terrorism by individuals is targeting enterprise systems, institutions, and governments. But cyber-terrorism is not only about obtaining information; it is also about instilling fear and doubt and compromising the integrity of the data, which leads to extortion. In many countries, financial institutions, such as banks, brokerage firms, and other large corporations, have paid large sums of extortion money to sophisticated international cyber terrorists.

(vi) *Political and Military Espionage.* For generations, countries have been competing for supremacy of one form or another. During the Cold War, countries competed for military dominance. At the end of the Cold War, the espionage tuft changed from military to gaining access to highly classified commercial information that would not only let them know what other countries are doing but might also give them either a military or commercial advantage without spending a lot of money on the effort. It is not surprising, therefore, that the spread of the Internet has given a boost and a new lease of life to a dying Cold War profession. Our high dependency on computers in the national military and commercial establishments has given espionage a new fertile ground. Electronic espionage has many advantages over its old-fashioned, trench-coated, sunglasses-wearing, and gloved Hitchcock-style cousin.

(vii) *Business and Industrial Espionage.* As businesses become global and world markets become one global bazaar, business competition for ideas and market strategies has become very intense. Economic and industrial espionage is on the rise around the world as businesses and countries try to outdo the other in the global arena. As countries and businesses try to position themselves and be a part of the impending global cutthroat competition, economic and industrial espionage is beginning to be taken seriously by company executives. The Internet has created fertile ground for cyber-sleuthing, and corporate computer attacks are the most used business espionage technique. It usually involves physical system penetration for trophies such as company policy, as well as management and marketing data. It may also involve sniffing, electronic surveillance of company executive electronic communications, and company employee chat rooms for information.

(viii) *Hate.* The growth of computer and telecommunication technology has unfortunately created a boom in all types of hate. There is growing concern about a growing rate of acts of violence and intimidation motivated by prejudice based on race, religion, sexual orientation, or ethnicity. Hate is being given a new and very effective and global forum.

(ix) *Personal Gain/Fame/Fun.* Personal gain motives are always driven by the selfishness of individuals who are not satisfied with what they have and are always wanting more, mostly financially.

8.5   Costs and Social Consequences

Are nations, businesses, and individuals prepared for computer attacks? Are they ready to pay the price? The answers to both these questions at the moment are probably no. It is not that we are not aware of it. It is not that we do not talk about it. And it is not that it has not happened before. It has. In fact, there have been heated and sometimes furious debates about it. There have been newspaper reports, and television and congressional discussions about the United States' preparedness for a national electronic attack. Yet not enough is being done beyond discussions. Because there are not enough data collection and analysis by U.S. intelligence agencies, or business and financial communities that would have provided lead information, assessment, and preparedness of the nation for an electronic attack on the national information infrastructure, a good credible policy cannot be formulated. In fact, during 1996 Congressional hearings on "Intelligence and Security in Cyberspace," a senior member of the intelligence community in charge of collecting such data compared the efforts in place at the time to a "toddler soccer game where everyone just runs around trying to kick the ball somewhere" [9]. We have come a long way since that time. Now both the U.S. Congress and the President are committed to protecting the nation's cyber infrastructure and are making resources available for this purpose.

This problem is not limited to the United States only; country after country around the globe is facing similar problems. Very few countries, if any, have assessed and analyzed any information on their information infrastructure, on how an electronic attack can affect not only their national security but also other essential infrastructures such as businesses, power grids, and financial and public institutions. There are various reasons for this lack of information [2]:

- In nearly all countries there is no required reporting mechanism in government agencies, even the private sector, to detect intrusions and report such intrusions.
- In the private sector, there is very little interest in the reporting of any system-related intrusions, a result of the fear of marketplace forces that would expose the management's weaknesses to the shareholder community and competitors.
- The insider effect. Various reports point to a blank picture about the effects of insider intruders on the overall detection and reporting of electronic attacks or e-attacks. It is reported in some studies that a majority of all e-attacks are generated and started by inside employees, which makes the job of detection and reporting very murky. It is like having an arsonist working in the fire department.
- Many nations have no required and trained security agencies to fight e-attacks.

The danger is real. The ability to unleash harm and terrorize millions of people, thus causing widespread panic, is possessed by many. The arena to play the game is global, and there is no one who can claim a monopoly on such attacks. In the United States, and probably in other countries, most attacks originating from outside the country are directed, for the moment, toward military and commercial infrastructures, for obvious reasons. Although most reporting of attacks seem to come from government and public sources, there is a similar rate of attempt and probably success in the private sector. The good news is that private industry is beginning to become a partner with the public sector in reporting.

The universality of cyber attacks creates a new dimension to cyberspace security. In fact, it makes it very difficult to predict the source of the next big attack, let alone identify trouble spots, track and apprehend hackers, and put a price on the problem that is increasingly becoming a nightmare to computer systems administrators, the network community, and users in general.

Every survey of computer crime and computer attacks indicates a rising trend. There are several reasons to which we can attribute this rather strange growth of cybercrimes [2].

(i) *Rapid technology growth.* The unprecedented growth and merging of both the computer and telecommunication industries has enabled access to the Internet to balloon into billions of users. The growing wireless technology and mobile devices have made Internet access easier because people can now log on to the Internet anytime, anywhere. But this easy access has also made hiding places plentiful. From Alaska's snowcaps to the Sahara desert to the Amazon and Congo forests, cyber access is as good as in London, New York, or Tokyo, and the arena of possible cyber attacks is growing.

(ii) *Easy availability of hacker tools.* There are an estimated 30,000 hacker-oriented sites on the Internet advertising and giving away free hacker tools and hacking tips [10]. As the Manila-generated *"Love Bug"* demonstrated, hacking prowess is no longer a question of affluence and intelligence but of time and patience. With time, one can go through a good number of hacker sites, picking tips and tools, and come out with a ready payload to create mayhem in cyberspace.

(iii) *Anonymity.* The days when computer access was only available in busy, well-lit, public and private areas are gone. Now as computers become smaller and people with these small Internet-able gizmos become more mobile, hacker tracing, and apprehension have become even more difficult.

(iv) *Cut-and-paste programming technology.* This phase has removed the most important impediment that prevented many would-be hackers from trying the trade. Historically, before anybody could develop a virus, one had to write a code for it. The code had to be written in a computer programming language, compiled, and made ready to go. This means, of course, that the hacker had to know or learn a programming language! Learning a programming language is known to be more than a 1-day job. It takes long hours of studying and practicing. Well, today this is no longer the case. We're in an age of *cut-and-paste programming*. The pieces and technical know-how are readily available from hacker sites. One only needs to have a motive and the time.

(v) *Communications speed.* With the latest developments in bandwidth, high volumes of data can be moved in the shortest time possible. Thus, intruders can download the payload, usually developed by cut-and-paste offline, very quickly log off, and possibly leave before detection is possible.

(vi) *High degree of internetworking.* Global networks are becoming more and more connected in every country. Nearly all these networks are connected on the Internet. In many countries, with readily available and cheap Internet-able mobile devices, Internet access is available.

(vii) *Increasing dependency on computers.* The ever increasing access to cyberspace, together with increasing capacity to store huge quantities of data, increasing bandwidth in communication networks to move huge quantities of data, increased computing power of computers, and plummeting prices on computer equipment have all created an environment of human dependency on computers. This, in turn, has created fertile ground for hackers.

8.5.1 Lack of Cost Estimate Model for Cyberspace Attacks

As the prices of computers and Internet-able mobile devices plummet and Internet accessibility becomes global, cyber attacks are likely to skyrocket. Cost estimating cyber attacks in this changing environment is becoming increasingly very difficult. Even in a good environment, estimates of cyber attack crimes are difficult. The efforts to develop a good cost model is hindered by a number of problems, including the following [2]:

   (i) It is very difficult to quantify the actual number of attacks. Only a tiny fraction
       of what everyone believes is a huge number of incidents are detected, and
       even a far smaller percentage of that is reported. In fact, as we noted in the
       previous section, only one in 20 % of all system intrusions is detected, and of
       those detected only one in 20 % is reported [11].
  (ii) Even with these small numbers reported, there has been no conclusive study
       to establish a valid figure that can at least give us an idea of what it is that with
       which we must cope. The only few known studies have been regional and
       sector based. For example, there have been studies in education, on defense,
       and in a selected number of industries and public government departments.
 (iii) According to Terry Guiditis, of Global Integrity, 90 % of all computer attacks
       both reported and unreported are perpetrated by insiders [12]. Insider attacks
       are rarely reported even if they are detected. As we reported in Chap. 9,
       companies are reluctant to report any type of cyber attacks, especially insider
       ones, for fear of diluting integrity and eroding investor confidence in the
       company.
  (iv) Lack of cooperation between emergency and computer crime reporting
       centers worldwide. There are many such centers worldwide, but they do not
       cooperate with one another because most are in commercial competition [12].
   (v) Unpredictable types of attacks and viruses. Attackers can pick and choose
       when and where to attack. Also, the types of attacks and topography used in
       attacks cannot be predicted. Because of these factors, it is extremely difficult
       for system security chiefs to prepare for attacks and, therefore, reduce the
       costs of each attack, if it occurs.
  (vi) Virus mutation is also another issue in the rising costs of cyber attacks. The
       recent "Love Bug" and "Code Red" e-mail attacks are examples of a mutat-
       ing virus. In each incident the viruses started mutating within a few hours
       after release. Such viruses put enormous strain on systems administrators to
       search and destroy all the various strains of the virus.
 (vii) There are not enough trained system administrators and security chiefs in the
       latest network forensics technology who can quickly scan, spot, and remove
       or prevent any pending or reported attack and quickly detect system intru-
       sions. When there is a lack of trained and knowledgeable personnel, it takes
       longer to respond when an attack occurs, and to clear the system from such an
       attack in the shortest period of time possible, thus reducing the costs. Also,
       failure to detect intrusion always results in huge losses to the organization.
(viii) Primitive monitoring technology. The computer industry as a whole, and the
       network community in particular, has not achieved the degree of sophistica-
       tion that would monitor a computer system continuously for foolproof detec-
       tion and prevention of system penetration. The industry is always on the
       defensive, always responding *after* an attack has occurred and with inade-
       quate measures. In fact, at least for the time being, it looks as if the attackers
       are setting the agenda for the rest of us. This kind of situation makes every
       attack very expensive.

For organizations, the costs of a data breach resulting from a cyber attack are not only alarming but are rising on an annual basis. According to the Poneman Institute [13], the institute that annually estimates the U.S. Cost of a Data Breach, an average data breach resulting from a cyber attack in 2010 was $7.2 million, or $214 per customer record; this was a $10 per-record jump from 2009. The Institute also estimates, that in the year, incidences in which companies experienced breaches for the first time resulted in average costs of a whopping $326 per record in 2010, again up from $228 the prior year [14]. In 2012, the Institute reported the previous year's (2011) estimate costs to be up 56 % on last year's figures (2010), with an average cost of $5.9 M per year, ranging from $1.5 million to $36.5 million per year [15].

If anything, these figures, though worrisome, indicate a growing trend with no end in sight.

8.5.2   Social and Ethical Consequences

Although it is difficult to estimate the actual costs of e-attacks on physical system resources, we are making progress toward better estimates. What we cannot now do, and probably will never be able to do, is to put a cost estimate on e-attacks on individual members of society. This task is difficult because of the following reasons [2]:

(i) *Psychological effects.* These effects depend on the attack motive and may result in long-lasting psychological effects such as hate. Psychological effects may lead to individual reclusion and increasing isolation. Such trends may lead to dangerous and costly repercussions on the individual, corporations, and the society as a whole.

(ii) *Moral decay.* There is a moral imperative in all our actions. When human actions, whether bad or good, become so frequent, they create a level of familiarity that leads to their acceptance as "normal." This type of acceptance of actions formerly viewed as immoral and bad by society is moral decay. There are numerous e-attacks that can cause moral decay. In fact, because of the recent spree of DDoS, and e-mail attacks, one wonders whether people performing these acts seriously consider them as immoral and illegal anymore!

(iii) *Loss of privacy.* After headline-making e-attacks that wreaked havoc on global computer systems, there is a resurgence in the need for quick solutions to the problem that seems to have hit home. Many businesses are responding with patches, filters, intrusion detection (ID) tools, and a whole list of other "solutions." These solutions are a direct attack on individual privacy. This type of privacy invasion in the name of network security is a threat to all of us whose price we will never estimate and we are not ready to pay! The blanket branding of every Internet user as a potential computer attacker or a criminal,, until proven otherwise, is perhaps the greatest challenge to personal freedom yet encountered by the world's societies.

(iv) *Trust.* Along with the loss of privacy, trust is lost. Individuals once attacked lose trust in a person, group, company, or anything else believed to be the source of the attack or believed to be unable to stop the attack. Together with draconian solutions, e-attacks cause us to lose trust in individuals, and businesses, especially businesses either hit by e-attacks or trying to stop attacks forcibly. Such customer loss of trust in a business is disastrous for that business. Most importantly, it is a loss of the society's innocence.

8.6   Computer Crime Prevention Strategies

Preventing computer crime is not a simple thing to do because to do that one needs to understand how these crimes are committed and who is involved in these crimes. To prevent such crimes, therefore, we need to focus on three entities in the game: the computer as a tool used to commit the crimes, the criminal who is the source of the crime, and the innocent victim of the crime. Our approach to prevention will, therefore, involve strategies from all three.

8.6.1   Protecting Your Computer

For better protection of your computer consider the following measures based on a list by the San Diego Police Department [16]. Similar measures can be found at many police departments in many countries.

8.6.1.1 Physical Protective Measures
Install surface locks, cable-locking devices, and fiberoptic loops to prevent equipment theft.

- Locate the computer and data storage away from outside windows and walls to prevent damage from external events.
- Install strong doors and locks to the computer room to prevent equipment theft and tampering.
- Reinforce interior walls to prevent break-ins. Extend interior walls to the true ceiling.
- Restrict access to computer facilities to authorized personnel. Require personnel to wear distinct, color-coded security badges in the computer center. Allow access through a single entrance. Other doors should be alarmed and used only as emergency exits.

8.6.1.2 Procedural and Operational Protective Measures
- If you take the computer as the main tool in the execution of the crime, this leads us to find those elements of the computer that are more susceptible to being the good conduit. The list of these items may include data, software, media, services, and hardware.

- Using this list, analyze the dangers to each item on the list. Buy and install protective software based on the value of each item on the list.
- Classify information into categories based on importance and confidentiality. Use labels such as "Confidential" and "Sensitive." Identify software, programs, and data files that need special access controls.
- Install software access control mechanisms. Require a unique, verifiable form of identification, such as a user code or secret password for each user. Install special access controls, such as a call-back procedure, if you allow access through a dial-telephone line connection.
- Encrypt confidential data stored in computers or transmitted over communication networks. Use National Institute of Standards and Technology (NIST) data encryption standards.
- Design audit trails into your computer applications. Log all access to computer resources with unique user identification. Separate the duties of systems programmers, application programmers, and computer programmers.
- Establish procedures for recovering your operating system if it is destroyed. Store all backup data offsite.
- Review automated audit information and control reports to determine if there have been repeated, unsuccessful attempts to log on both from within and outside your facility. Look for unauthorized changes to programs and data files periodically.

8.6.1.3 Anti-Virus Protection
The following measures can help protect your computer from viruses:

- Do not bring disks in from outside sources.
- Scan demo disks from vendors, shareware, or freeware sources for viruses.
- Restrict use of electronic bulletin boards.
- Scan downloaded files for viruses. Avoid downloading executable files.
- Make regular backups to aid in recovery.

8.6.2   The Computer Criminal

There are two measures that I would consider as appropriate for the computer criminal.

8.6.2.1 Pass Computer Crime Prevention Laws
Local and national governments should pass laws directed toward computer crimes including computer tampering, computer fraud, and other computer crimes, so that if a person commits a computer crime offense, when knowingly and without the authorization of a computer's owner, or in excess of the authority granted that person, if found guilty, should serve a court sentence consonant to the extent of his or her crime. An increasing number of countries now either have such laws or are in the process of enacting them.

8.6.2.2 Enforcement of Criminal Laws

We cannot fight computer crimes, whether or not we have laws on the books, unless those laws can be enforced. Thus, one way of reducing computer crime is to aggressively enforce computer crime laws with just but stiff sentences that send a message to would-be criminals that they will pay the price if they perpetuate computer crimes.

8.6.2.3 Moral Education

Throughout this book, I have been advocating for computer ethics education. There is a need for computer ethics education that includes an ethical framework which may make the would-be criminal reflect on the pending act. Computer ethics education, just like all types of education, is a long-time investment especially in the youth, not only to build their character but also to guide their actions throughout their lives.

8.6.3 The Innocent Victim

The following measures should be focused on the victims of computer crimes [13].

8.6.3.1 Personnel Policies

- Monitor activities of employees who handle sensitive or confidential data. Watch for employees who work abnormally long hours, or who refuse to take time off. Many computer crime schemes require regular, periodic manipulation to avoid detection. Be aware of employees who collect material not necessary to their jobs, such as programming manuals, printouts for data, programs, and software manuals.
- Change security password codes to block further access by employees who leave or are fired. The latter become a high risk to your company for revenge or theft.
- Establish rules for computer use by employees, including removal of disks or printed output. All employees should sign and date a printed copy of these rules to indicate that he/she understands them.

8.6.3.2 Educating the Computer User

Just as we did with the computer criminal, we need to educate the user to be aware of possible sources of computer crime and what to do if and when one becomes a victim of a computer crime. This education can go a long way in reducing computer crimes if the users take crime preventive steps every time they use the computer and when owning a computer.

Exercises

1. List five types of computer attacks.
2. In a short essay, discuss the differences between a denial-of-service attack and a penetration attack.

3. Which attack type is more dangerous to a computer system, a penetration attack or a denial-of-service attack?
4. List and briefly discuss five attack motives.
5. Why do hackers devote substantial amount of time to their trade?
6. Discuss the challenges in tracking down cyber criminals.
7. Why is it so difficult to estimate the costs of business e-crimes both nationally and globally?
8. What is the best way to bring about full reporting of e-crimes, including costs?
9. Why do countries worldwide have very little information to help them combat cyber crimes?
10. Why are cyber crimes on the rise?
11. In addition to monetary costs, there are ethical and social costs of e-crimes; discuss these "hidden" costs.
12. Estimate the cost of cyber attacks in the past 2 years.

References

1. Section A: the nature and definition of a critical infrastructure. http://www.nipc.gov/nipcfaq. html
2. Kizza JM (2011) Computer network security and cyber ethics, 3rd edn. McFarland, Jefferson
3. Dictionary.com. http://www.dictionary.com/browse/virus
4. Forchet K (1994) Computer security management. Boyd & Fraser, Danvers
5. Timeline of hacking. http://fyi.cnn.com/fyi/interactive/school.tools/timelines/1999/computer. hacking/frameset.exclude.html
6. Denning PJ (1990) Computers under attack: intruders, worms and viruses. ACM Press, New York
7. Freeh LJ. FBI congressional report on cybercrime. http://www.fbi.gov/congress00/cyber021600.htm
8. Levy S (1984) Hackers: heroes of the computer revolution. Anchor Press/Doubleday, Garden City
9. Security in cyberspace: U.S. senate permanent subcommittee on investigations. June 5, 1996
10. Christensen J (1999) Bracing for guerilla warfare in cyberspace. CNN Interactive, 6 April, 1999
11. Alberts DS. Information warfare and deterrence–Appendix D: defensive war: problem formation and solution approach. http://www.ndu.edu/inns/books/ind/appd.htm
12. Hacker sittings and news: computer attacks spreading (19 November 1999). http://www.infowav.com/hacker/99/hack-11/1999-b.shtml
13. San Diego Police Department tips for businesses: computer crime prevention. http://www.sandiego.gov/police/prevention/computer.shtml
14. Trigaux R (1998) Hidden dangers. St. Petersburg Times, 16 June, 1998
15. Annual costs of computer crime rise alarmingly. Computer Security Institute. http://www.gocsi.com/prela11.html
16. Warwick A. The cost of cyber attacks is up 56 %, study reveals. http://www.computerweekly.com/news/2240105258/The-cost-of-cyber-attacks-is-up-56-study-reveals

Further Reading

2010 annual study: U.S. cost of a data breach compliance pressures, cyber attacks targeting sensitive data drive leading IT organizations to respond quickly and pay more. http://www.symantec.com/content/en/us/about/media/pdfs/symantec_ponemon_data_breach_costs_report. pdf?om_ext_cid=biz_socmed_twitter_facebook_marketwire_linkedin_2011Mar_worldwide_costofdatabreach

Anderson KE (1997) Criminal threats to business on the Internet: a white paper. Global Technology Research, June 23, 1997. This is a discussion of the increasing trend of criminal activity against information systems, from the low-level, amateur intruder to organized crime, and industrial and international espionage

Carnegie Mellon University. CERT Coordination Center CERT/CC statistics 1998–1999. http://www.cert.org/stats/cert-stats.html

Chaturvedi A et al (2000) Fighting the Wily Hacker: modeling information security issues for online financial institutions using the SEAS environment. INET JAPAN 2000 Conference, July 18, 2000. The paper discusses proposed methods to analyze the online risks faced by the financial industry

Computer attacks: what they are and how to defend against them, *ITL Bulletins,* May 1999. http://www.nist.gov/itl/lab/bulletins/may99.html

Computer Security Institute/Federal Bureau of Investigation (1998) Annual cost of computer crime rise alarmingly: organizations report $136 million in losses, Press Release, Computer Security Institute, March 4, 1998. This is a summary of the 1998 survey on computer crime

Counterintelligence Office of the Defense Investigative Service (1996) Industry CI trends, OASDPA/96-S-1287, December 26, 1996. This paper discusses threats and techniques used for low-level intelligence collecting by foreign companies and governments against U.S. DoD contractors

General Accounting Office (GAO) (1996) GAO executive report B-266140. Report to the Committee on Governmental Affairs, U.S. Senate, May 22, 1996. This gives a detailed report on attacks to U.S. Department of Defense computer systems with recommendations for improved security

Grampp F, Morris R (1984) Unix operating system security. AT&T Bell Lab Tech J 63(8, Part 2):1649

Grosso A (2000) The economic espionage ACT: touring the minefields. Commun ACM 43(8):15–18

Johnson E. The real cost of cyber attacks. http://www.theatlantic.com/sponsored/zurich-risk/archive/2012/02/the-real-cost-of-cyber-attacks/253186/

Kapor M (1991) Civil liberties in cyberspace: when does hacking turn from an exercise of civil liberties into crime? Scientific American, September 1991. This is a discussion of the various legal, social, and privacy-related issues within computer networks using the U.S. Secret Service's raid on Steve Jackson Games as a case study

Kizza JM (1999) Civilizing the internet: global concerns and efforts toward regulation. McFarland, Jefferson

National Counterintelligence Center (1998) Annual report to congress on foreign economic collection and industrial espionage, Annual Report to the U.S. Congress, 1998. This is a summary of the espionage threat to the United States Specific highlights include the interest in information security and information warfare

Neumann PG (1999) Risks of insiders. Commun ACM 42(12):160

Overill RE (1994) Computer crime–an historical survey. Defence Systems International, 1998. This paper discusses the historical development of computer crime. United Nations, "International Review of Criminal Policy–United Nations Manual on the Prevention and Control of Computer-Related Crime." *International Review of Criminal Policy,* No. 43 and 44, 1994. These are extensive documents reviewing all aspects of international computer crime

Section A: the nature and definition of critical infrastructure http://www.nipc.gov/nipcfaq.htm

U.S. Department of Justice (1998) News Release, March 1, 1998. Israel citizen arrested in Israel for hacking U.S. and Israel Government computers http://www.usdoj.gov/opa/pr/1998/march/125.htm.html

Cyberbullying

9

Learning Objectives

After reading this chapter, the reader should be able to

1. Understand circumstances surrounding cyberbullying.
2. Understand the legal definition of cyberbullying.
3. Describe the different types of cyberbullying.
4. Learn about the evolution of cyberbullying in tandem with the evolution of online social media.
5. Learn the evolving legislation landscape of cyberbullying.
6. Recognize the difficulties and effects of cyberbullying.
7. Be able to identify and recognize the victims of cyberbullying.
8. Acquire the techniques and skills of handling cyberbullying.
9. Recognize the difficulties of managing cyberbullying.

9.1   Definition

In Chap. 11, we fully define and discuss the evolution of online social networks. But before then, and to be able to discuss and understand fully cyberbullying and its effects on society, we briefly define and give a brief 'exposé' of the evolution of online social networks. As we see in Chap. 11, a social network is a theoretical mesh network, where each node is an individual, a group, or an organization that independently generates, captures, and disseminates information and also serves as a relay for other members of the network; this means that individual nodes must collaborate to propagate the information in the network. The links between nodes represent relationships and social interactions among individuals, groups, organizations, or even entire societies. In reality, each network connection begins with an individual, using a digital device, reaching out to another individual or group for a social relationship of sorts, and it snowballs into a mesh of social relationships connecting

© Springer International Publishing Switzerland 2016

195

J.M. Kizza, *Ethics in Computing*, Undergraduate Topics in Computer Science,
DOI 10.1007/978-3-319-29106-2_9

many individuals or/and groups. Many online social network groups have become established, with household names such as *Facebook, Myspace, Friendster, YouTube, Flickr,* and *LinkedIn.*

The rapid growth of the Internet, together with ever-plummeting prices and increasing miniaturizations of digital devices popularized by easy mobility and fast access to online services, have all contributed to the creation of an exciting, seemingly unlimited virtual environment in which anything is possible with the least effort. To make things more complicated, within this environment, anonymity and telepresence are almost assured, although this is an illusion, but very few understand it. In fact, the combination of these two creates a certain degree of individual confidence that may sometimes reach realms of danger, because with this combination individuals in these virtual environments may be tempted to become reckless, knowingly or otherwise. This attitude is one of the key causes and perpetuators of cyberbullying. But let us first define *cyberbullying.*

Since its debut as the ugly side effect of the online social networks, much has been written about cyberbullying and consequently many definitions have been proposed. According to Wikipedia [1], *cyberbullying* is an action of harming or harassing an individual or individuals, mostly in the online social network environment, which we refer to most commonly in the public commons as social media, but also via any other digital networks, in a repeated and deliberate manner.

9.1.1 Legal Definition

According to Wikipedia [1], cyberbullying is defined in legal glossaries as these actions:

- Actions that use information and communication technologies to support *deliberate, repeated, and hostile behavior by an individual or group, that is intended to harm another or others.*
- Use of communication technologies for the *intention of harming another person.*
- Use of Internet service and mobile technologies such as Web pages and discussion groups as well as instant messaging or SMS (short message service) text messaging with the *intention of harming another person.*

In all these foregoing legal definitions, I have highlighted what is common and disturbing, that is, the prior and deliberate intention to intimidate, harm, control, manipulate, put down, falsely discredit, or humiliate the recipient.

9.1.2 Cyberstalking

Stalking, a cousin of bullying, is defined as unwanted and/or obsessive attention given to an individual or group by a perpetuator or perpetuators. Cyberstalking, a cousin of cyberbullying, then is digital stalking, usually using online media.

Cyberstalking comes in many versions, including but not limited to, sending threatening messages to the victim, monitoring the victim, extortion, false accusations, altering a victim's information, identity theft, and the list goes on. The actions of a cyberstalker are usually repeated, persistent, and often illegal.

As Mariam Merritt notes in her essay, "Straight Talk About Stalking" [2], what is interesting and of course disturbing is that stalking is often perpetrated not by strangers but by someone known by the victim. Of course, the list of known people is long, including one's ex(s), former friends, and acquaintances.

9.1.3 Cyber Harassment

According to Merriam-Webster's dictionary, to *harass* is to continuously and persistently annoy someone: to create an unpleasant or hostile environment for that individual, especially by uninvited and unwelcome verbal or physical conduct, and also to make repeated attacks against a victim [3]. Based on these definitions, then *harassment* is the act of doing one or more of the foregoing, intended for disturbing, tormenting, or annoying the victim. When these acts are done by a person or a group of people using online digital technology, then we have *cyber harassment*.

9.2 Types of Cyberbullying

Because of the flexibility, ease of use, anonymity, and telepresence of virtual online technologies and environments, the online environment offers many different ways harassment can be perpetuated. *End to Bullying Organization* [4] outlines five different types of cyberbullying:

9.2.1 Harassment

As we have already pointed out, harassment is the act of knowingly, purposely and repeatedly annoying; creating an unpleasant or hostile environment, especially by uninvited and unwelcome verbal or physical conduct; and making repeated attacks against the victim.

9.2.2 Flaming

Flaming is "burning fiercely inside and emitting flames" by someone as a way to express annoyance. In online networks and in social media, this may involve exchanged e-mails, instant messaging, or chat rooms among the parties involved. So if it is directed to an individual by a person or group of people, it is a form of harassment.

9.2.3 Exclusion

Exclusion harassment is slightly more difficult to define, but it involves the intentional exclusion of an individual or a group by another individual or group from an online space for the purpose of using that space to harass the victim(s).

9.2.4 Outing

Outing is the unwanted and uncalled-for online display in the public commons of a victim's information and other attributes for no other purpose than harassment.

9.2.5 Masquerading

Because the digital online environment supports anonymity and telepresence, both of which can enable an individual or a group to hide their true identity, to acquire false identities, and to masquerade online with the intention of harassing others, online environments support masquerading as a form of cyberbullying.

9.3 Areas of Society Most Affected by Cyberbullying

Although the growth and popularity of communication technologies has equally affected all of us, user preferences of these technologies is stratified by a number of factors including age group, income level, and geographic location. Consequently, user activities are following these divisions. Divisions such as these have seen vices such as cyberbullying taking root in specific divisions of society. For example, cyberbullying is more prevalent in school-age youth and in the working communities, especially among white-collar workers. So let us look at cyberbullying in these areas.

9.3.1 Schools

According to the report "Facing the Screen Dilemma: Young Children, Technology and Early Education" by the Campaign for a Commercial-Free Childhood (CCfC) [5], on any given day, 64 % of babies between 1 and 2 years of age watch TV and videos for an average time span of slightly more than 2 h; that in 2011 there were 3 million downloads of just Fisher Price apps for infants and toddlers; that estimates of how much time preschoolers spend, on average, with screen media range from at least 2.2 h to as much as 4.6 h per day. Even though there is no research showing the benefits of introducing children to new technologies in the first years of life, parents of young children are increasingly uploading new technologies to their young children in the belief that technology will make their children smarter. With this thinking, educators and school districts and authorities at every level are facing increasing pressure to increase both the technology and the amount of time children spend with digital technologies in early childhood settings.

Children growing up with these ever-increasing and evolving technologies have acquired a high degree of easiness of their use, far superior than that of their parents, yet with limited or no guidance and counseling on the vices of these technologies.

The rapid growth of technologies, their increasing and ubiquitous use, the early acquired ease of use of new and powerful smartphones and laptops, the lack of counseling, and the ever-present curiosity of youth are all driving an increasing number of young people to try out these new technologies in online social media. While all this is going on, there is limited—or no—parental control and guidance. This attitude is resulting in an increase in cyberbullying in schools, which in turn is leading to increased suicides of young people.

9.3.2 Cyberbullying in the Workplace

Bullying in the workplace is not new. Bullying has been present in workplaces since long before the invasion of cybertechnology. Bullying is a character trait in an individual that may be aided by the different characteristics of technology such as anonymity, speed, reach, and ease of use. It is motivated by the bully's own lack of self-esteem rather than the specific actions, appearance, or personality of the victim [6]. Because of their internal shortcomings or weaknesses, many bullies feel threatened that they cannot cope with certain aspects of what they are supposed, expected, or required to do. This threat, many times, may lead them to take defensive actions by trying to remove the source of the threat, which may be done in several different ways. Technology then, through its attributes such as anonymity, scope, and ease of use, help them to achieve whatever desired action they want. The increasing use of workplace "bring your own devices" (BYOD), take-home work-related digital devices, along with increasing use of online social media, have all increased the channels of harassment.

9.4   Legislation Against Cyberbullying

As we have pointed out earlier, bullying, as a vice, is not new. It is as old as humanity itself. Of course, its definition has changed over the years as our expectations, living conditions, and social status have changed. As these things changed, our tolerance of the vice has also evolved as awareness became more widespread. In the past, big kids in schools, and big and powerful people in places of work, and even in families, would administer large doses of what is today considered harassment as they "picked on" or "singled out" those who seemed to be less powerful and less threatening, and nothing happened to these bullies. However, matters are not the same today because of the high levels of awareness of these evils and the high levels of reporting of such incidents.

With more awareness and better reporting, direct bullying activities had been declining, until the Internet brought in a medium that supported both the anonymity and telepresence of the bully. So, anonymity, telepresence, and the ubiquity of the use of mobile technology have all led to a rapid growth of the vice, thereby increasing the number of victims and indeed even the number of suicides of young victims. This situation has led to a call for legislation and public awareness. Several legislative bodies and institutions at different levels have been developing laws, statutes, and policies.

9.4.1 Federal Laws

Cyberbullying is a vice that affects all social strata and income levels. Because of this and the fact that it is emotional, because it affects mostly young people, there have been many efforts for legislations to mitigate it. Even so, legislation to combat cyberbullying at the federal level is still lacking as of this writing. However, even if no federal law directly addressing cyberbullying has been passed, there are some cases where bullying overlaps with *discriminatory harassment*, which is covered under federal civil rights laws enforced by the U.S. Department of Education (ED) and the U.S. Department of Justice (DOJ) [7]. These laws include the following [7]:

- Title IV and Title VI of the Civil Rights Act of 1964
- Title IX of the Education Amendments of 1972
- Section 504 of the Rehabilitation Act of 1973
- Titles II and III of the Americans with Disabilities Act
- Individuals with Disabilities Education Act (IDEA)

9.4.2 State Laws

There is a patchwork of state-sponsored cyberbullying laws. A great resource to learn about cyberbullying laws and legislations at the state level is the Cyberbullying Research Center [8]; also see Sect. 9.7 below for more resources. According to the Cyberbullying Research Center [8], at last count, 44 states have laws regarding bullying, and 30 of those included some mention of electronic forms of harassment. For the time being, all these laws, whether state or local ordinances, are simply directing school districts to have a bullying and harassment policy, without stating the actual content of such policies.

9.4.3 International Laws

The rapid growth of the Internet, which has quickly engulfed the globe, and the plummeting prices of Web-enabled smart mobile devices that are bringing the rest of humanity into cyberspace, have made cyberbullying into a global problem. So, the desire to contain it is also global. Although the need is there and is growing, only a few countries and regions have passed legislation to combat it. Among these are the European Union (EU), Canada, Australia, Spain, UK, France, and Germany, but it is slow going.

9.5   Effects of Cyberbullying

As we have been pointing out, cyberbullying is bullying using a new Internet-supported medium. Statistics from different countries are showing that the vice is growing, hampered only by massive awareness campaigns, and hence is affecting more and more people.

Similarly to all forms of bullying, cyberbullying affects everyone—the bully, the victim, and the bystanders—although in different ways. Thus, the effects vary by the type of bullying, the techniques used, and the role one plays in the bullying cycle. Thus, it is difficult to put the effects of cyberbullying into specific categories because different people react differently to the same causes. The major underlying effects, however, cutting across the board, are psychological, emotional, and physical stress. These types of effects affect people differently. For example, StopBullying.gov [9] reports the different effects in the bullying circle as follows.

Kids Who are Bullied
Kids who are bullied are more likely to experience:

- Depression and anxiety, increased feelings of sadness and loneliness, changes in sleep and eating patterns, and loss of interest in activities they used to enjoy. These issues may persist into adulthood.
- Health complaints
- Decreased academic achievement—by GPA and standardized test scores—and school participation. They are more likely to miss, skip, or drop out of school.

Kids Who Bully Others
Kids who bully are more likely to

- Abuse alcohol and other drugs in adolescence and as adults
- Get into fights, vandalize property, and drop out of school
- Engage in early sexual activity
- Have criminal convictions and traffic citations as adults
- Be abusive toward their romantic partners, spouses, or children as adults

Bystanders
Kids who witness bullying are more likely to

- Have increased use of tobacco, alcohol, or other drugs
- Have increased mental health problems, including depression and anxiety
- Miss or skip school

Indeed, as we pointed out earlier, what cuts across are psychological, emotional, and physical factors that can lead to the individual's overall well-being. This problem is not limited to schoolchildren alone, although they are more likely to suffer these effects than adults. These effects may influence an individual's health and psychological balance, which may lead to suicide, although it may not be the cause of it.

9.6   Dealing with Cyberbullying

Cyberbullying comes in many forms including pretense, masquerading, hacking into the victim's online account, and invading and bracketing of social media. Because of the varied ways cyberbullying is carried out, the means of handling it need to be carefully chosen to manage each of the many approaches of delivering bullying to the victims.

However, because most of the effects of bullying are based on psychological, emotional, and physical stress, we can take underlying and broad approaches that will cover the major source of cyberbullying and handle the different reactions to its effects, including the following.

9.6.1   Awareness

Find ways of developing massive education campaigns about what cyberbullying is, who is affected, and its consequences, which may include death. Broad mass and targeted education campaigns are essential. These mass awareness education campaigns are meant to focus on targeted audiences. For example, if the audience is a school or schoolgoing children, techniques must be found to deliver the message in quantities and proportions that are relevant and acceptable to the targeted age group. If it is targeted to a work environment, the delivery techniques of the message are different.

9.6.2   Legislation

Mass education and awareness programs, however targeted they are, can go only so far in the absence of policies, statutes, and laws with corresponding enforcement. Thus, legislation at either the state or federal level is necessary, at least for schools. In businesses, the best approach is for the companies to draw up operating policies that involve guidelines of behavior for all workers. Such company policies must be enforced to be effective.

9.6.3 Community Support

Communities should also become involved in cyberbullying reduction and prevention. Cyberbullying public awareness activities must be included in community public activities, especially those directed to youth in the community. Part of the package of community cyberbullying awareness campaigns should include some form of reporting. Without it, the efforts are not likely to succeed.

9.7 Resources

There are a number of resources to which one can go for help. Most of these resources are directed toward children, parents, educators, and adults, mostly in the work environment:

- The Cyberbullying Research Center: http://cyberbullying.us/. This is a great resource with materials for all categories of users. They also have current statistics on cyberbullying and additional reading resources and testimonials.
- Stopbullying.gov: http://www.stopbullying.gov/resources. This site provides tips, facts, toolkits, training materials, and more. You can access a trove of information on cyberbullying on this site by entering a topic related to bullying in the keyword search area. Their collection includes federal and nonfederal training materials, evidence-based program directories, articles, and other materials related to bullying.
- The National Crime Prevention Council: http://www.ncpc.org/topics/cyberbullying. This site gives a variety of information on both bullying and, in particular, cyberbullying:
  - What Parents Can Do About Cyberbullying
  - Cyberbullying FAQ for Teens
  - Cyberbullying PSA Contest
  - Training on Cyberbullying
  - Bullying and Intimidation
  - Professional training from NCPC for youth and adults on managing bullying situations
  - Products and Publications on Cyberbullying
  - Helping Kids Handle Conflict
  - Cyberbullying Banners for the Web
  - Rapid Response Outreach Tools on Cyberbullying
    - Cyberbullying Crime Flyer
    - Cyberbullying Crime Palm Card
    - Cyberbullying Crime Poster
    - Cyberbullying Research Brief
  - Programs on Cyberbullying
  - Be Safe and Sound in School

- The Human Rights Campaign: http://www.hrc.org/resources/entry/resources-on-cyber-bullying. This site gives the reader a list of organizations that focus on cyberbullying and provide the most up-to-date articles, fact sheets, and news stories on cyberbullying as well as specific education resources for parents, educators, and children:
  - Cyberbullying.org. This site is run by the Center for Safe and Responsible Internet Use, and provides a number of helpful resources for educators and parents, including an educator's guide to cyberbullying and information on legislation related to cyberbullying.
  - Cyberbullying.us. This online research is maintained by Justin W. Patchin and Sameer Hinduja of the Department of Criminology and Criminal Justice at Florida Atlantic University. They have written numerous articles and given several presentations across the country on the nature and extent of cyberbullying. This site includes extensive resources on cyberbullying as well as research, news, and events on the topic.
  - I-Safe is a nonprofit foundation dedicated to protecting the online experiences of youth everywhere. It incorporates classroom curriculum with dynamic community outreach to empower students, teachers, parents, law enforcement, and concerned adults to make the Internet a safer place.

The foregoing is in no way an exhaustive list. There are many more resources focusing on bullying and cyberbullying.

Exercises

1. Who are the victims of bullying? of cyberbullying?
2. Discuss the traits of a bully and of a cyberbully.
3. What is the legal definition of cyberbullying? Is there one?
4. Cyberbullying laws vary greatly depending on location. Discuss what would be common among all.
5. Discuss what type of enforcement of laws, statutes, and policies is possible, if any.
6. Describe the different types of cyberbullying.
7. Trace the growth of cyberbullying following the evolution of online social media.
8. Compare two or more state laws on cyberbullying with the laws in your state.
9. Cyberbullying may go on unnoticed: discuss efforts being taken to identify victims early in your state.
10. Discuss techniques and skills required to cope with cyberbullying.

References

1. Wikipedia [https://en.wikipedia.org/wiki/Cyberbullying]
2. Merritt M. Straight talk about stalking. http://us.norton.com/cyberstalking/article
3. Merriam-Webster's. http://www.merriam-webster.com/dictionary/harass
4. End to bullying organization, http://www.endcyberbullying.org/5-different-types-of-cyberbullying
5. Campaign for a Commercial-Free Childhood (CCfC). Facing the screen dilemma: young children, technology and early education, http://www.commercialfreechildhood.org/screendilemma
6. MONEYWATCH. Understanding the reasons for workplace bullying. November 13, 2007, http://www.cbsnews.com/news/understanding-the-reasons-for-workplace-bullying/
7. Stopbullying.gov. http://www.stopbullying.gov/laws/federal/index.html
8. Cyberbullying Research Center. http://cyberbullying.us/the-current-state-of-cyberbullying-laws/
9. StopBullying.gov. http://www.stopbullying.gov/at-risk/effects/index.html

New Frontiers for Computer Ethics: Artificial Intelligence, Virtualization, and Cyberspace

10

Although it is obvious that machines can perform some activities at a higher level than persons can; these tasks remain, by and large, highly specialized and therefore remote from the capacity of human intelligence for multipurpose activities.

– Michael R. LaChat, The Methodist Theological School in Ohio

Learning Objectives

After reading this chapter, the reader should be able to

1. Understand the value of ethics in automated decision making.
2. Identify and discuss the different forms of automated decision making.
3. Recognize the role ethics plays in artificial environments.
4. Be able to differentiate between virtual reality and software virtualization
5. Identify and discuss credible safeguards to ensure privacy concerns and prevent runaway computation resulting from autonomous agents.
6. Understand the role of autonomous agents in our daily lives.
7. Recognize and discuss the responsibilities of users of autonomous agents.
8. Recognize and discuss the responsibilities of users in virtual environments
9. Learn the complexity of cyberspace issues.
10. Learn the ethical framework of cyberspace

© Springer International Publishing Switzerland 2016
J.M. Kizza, *Ethics in Computing*, Undergraduate Topics in Computer Science,
DOI 10.1007/978-3-319-29106-2_10

Scenario 8: One for the Road—Anyone?

Florence Yozefu is a brilliant scientist who heads a robotics research laboratory at one of the top ten research universities. Florence has been developing wearable robotics gear that can take over the driving functions of a vehicle from a human operator when it is worn by the driver. In laboratory tests, the robot, nicknamed Catchmenot, has performed successfully whenever Florence and her assistants have worn the robot. However, no real-life experiment has ever been conducted outside the lab. Florence has been meaning to try it out one day, but has not got a chance as yet to do so.

For New Year's Eve, Florence has plans to visit her mother and sister, about 100 miles away. This was a good opportunity to show her mother and her sister what she has been up to these last few months. So she decides to take Catchmenot with her. She packs her car the evening before and on the morning of the trip, she passes by the lab to get her robot and put it in the car. She drives the 100 miles in a little under her usual time and arrives at her mother's house earlier than usual. In the evening, Florence bids her mother good-bye and passes by her sister's apartment as promised. But at her sister's apartment, she finds a few of her teen friends and they get right into a party mode. Florence drinks and dances and forgets about time. There are many stories to tell and to listen to. About 1:00 a.m., after the midnight champagne toast, she decides to leave and drive back to her apartment.

She had promised to accompany her friend to a preplanned engagement. Although she is very drunk, and against her friend's advice and insistence that she should not drive, Florence puts on Catchmenot and in a few minutes she is off. Thirty minutes later, she is cruising at 70 mph and she is also sound asleep.

She is awakened by a squirrel running all over her car at about 5:00 a.m. She is parked by the roadside in front of her apartment complex. She has made it home safely. She has no idea when and where she passed out and what happened along the way. She will never know. Although she is surprised, confused, and feels guilty, she is happy how well Catchmenot has worked. She decides to market it.

How much should she charge for it, she wonders.

Discussion Questions

1. *Why did Florence feel guilty?*
2. *Is Florence right to market Catchmenot?*
3. *If anything went wrong along the ride home, would Florence be responsible? Who should be?*
4. *Is it ethical to market Catchmenot?*
5. *Discuss the ethical implications of artificial intelligence based on Catchmenot.*

10.1 Introduction

"In the theistic tradition of Judeo-Christian culture, a tradition that is, to a large extent, our "fate," we were created in the *imago Dei,* in the image of God, and our tradition has, for the most part, showed that our greatest sin is pride: disobedience to our creator, a disobedience that most often takes the form of trying to be God. Now, if human beings are able to construct an artificial, personal intelligence—and I will suggest that this is theoretically possible, albeit perhaps practically improbable—then the tendency of our religious and moral tradition would be toward the condemnation of the undertaking: We will have stepped into the shoes of the creator, and, in so doing we will have overstepped our own boundaries."[1]

"The Hebraic attitude towards AI has been one of fear and warning: "You shall not make for yourself a graven image...", while that of the "Hellenic" has been fascination and openness." [1]

Artificial intelligence (AI) is an exciting technological frontier offering a novel environment with unlimited possibilities. The AI environment works with the possibilities of understanding and extending knowledge to create intelligent agents, perhaps with a human value base, intended to help solve human problems.

Virtualization is a process through which one can create something that is there in effect and performance but in reality is not there—that is, it is virtual. It is a physical abstraction of reality, a real phenomenon such as a company's computing resources including storage, network servers, and memory. Virtualization involves and absorbs participants into a virtual reconstruction of real-world entities into seemingly real images with corresponding in-depth information to turn these images into a high degree of realism. It is a process that embodies both abstraction and reconstruction to create a sense of complete participant immersion yet with autonomy of participants to vary their chosen new environments to suit individual liking. In other words, virtualization is a process that makes real entities, scenes, and events virtual mirror images of self; it is a virtualization of reality. In many ways it is a mediation of interaction through an electronic medium between humans and humans as well as between humans and machines [2].

Cyberspace, on the other hand, is a multidimensional space vision of pure information either at rest in large storage media or in motion between digital nodes that form a mesh.

The description we have given here of the technologies and environments are quite enticing to us humans who are naturally curious and drawn to investigate new phenomena whenever possible. Thus, the frontiers we discuss in this chapter have drawn a number of people, some for the experience to participate in cyberspace, others to experience the thrills of virtual reality, and yet others to investigate the application of knowledge in areas yet unknown. Wherever and whenever they are drawn to these environments, human beings are participatory: they try out things and get involved as they pursue individual social goals.

10.2 Artificial Intelligence

Artificial intelligence (AI) is a field of learning that emulates human intelligence. The recent development of AI and its seemingly unbounded potential to solve real-life problems has broadened computer technology applications into exciting areas that were thought to require deep human intelligence. Because human intelligent behavior is so varied, poorly defined, and difficult to predict, let alone understand, most artificial intelligence studies concentrate on a limited number of areas in which human abilities to think and reason are clear and the overall human intelligent behavior is well understood.

These areas exhibit those aspects of human intelligence that can be represented symbolically with first-order logic such as game playing and natural language understanding. Other areas that exhibit a high degree of human intelligence such as thought processes, pattern recognition, and concept formation are still abstract and scarcely understood. However, with the recent realization that most real-world problems that are usually not so difficult for human intelligence, but are still intractable for current machine intelligence, involve numerical computation, and with the improvement in the computation power of new computers, AI research is slowly shifting from those areas that use symbolic manipulation to numerical computation. This shift is bringing diversification and practicability to AI and increasing the repertoire of AI techniques. Because of the lack of incorporation of common sense into AI techniques, however, progress in real terms has been slow, except in areas such as robotics and machine learning in which there has been more excitement because of the practicability of the applications to our daily lives. However, the realization is opening new doors in AI research in areas such as neural networks and fuzzy logic theory, and it is causing scholars to take a new look at ways of achieving machine intelligence and at the same time start to study the social and ethical impact and where to place responsibility for such machines, if they ever come to be. In this section we look at the social and ethical implications in these active areas where AI techniques have made advances and are becoming established.

10.2.1 Advances in Artificial Intelligence

Starting with Alan Turing in his 1950 machine intelligence experiments, in which he proposed a game played between a computer and a human being that could demonstrate whether a machine, in this case a computer, could think, there has been a steady growth of interest in building intelligent machines, commonly known as *autonomous agents*, in those areas of AI in which intelligence can be modeled easily, such as in game playing, expert systems, natural language understanding, neural networks, and robots.

Autonomous agents are not new to AI. Since Turing, numerous scholars such as Marvin Minsky, Alan Key, and Rodney Brooks have at various times studied agents' behavior and sometimes constructed autonomous agents. An autonomous agent is a collective name encompassing both hardware and software intelligent agents. Autonomous agents can take different forms depending on the nature of the environment. For example, if the environment is real 3D, the agents are robots, whereas in 2D they are computer programs referred to as intelligent agents.

As progress is made in AI research, areas of application of autonomous agents are becoming more numerous. For example, robots have been used in a number of areas including surveillance, exploration, and in inaccessible and hazardous environments. More intelligent agent robots are being helped by better vision systems, sensors, and easier programming languages. The field of robotics is getting wider, involving areas such as perception, cognition, and manipulation in which success has been most apparent through industrial applications. Industries and the military are relaying more and more on these new technologies.

10.2.2 Artificial Intelligence and Ethics

Human beings by nature strive to create a good life for themselves through the acquisition of knowledge and the creation of intelligent machines to do most of the jobs that we either are not able to do or do not like to do. But according to George Lugar and William Stubblefield [3], the notion of human efforts to gain knowledge as a transgression against the law of God is deeply rooted in us, and we still believe that the human quest for knowledge must eventually lead to disaster. This belief has not been affected by current philosophical and scientific advances, but instead has produced the Frankenstein monster syndrome of fear of new advances in intelligence, particularly machine intelligence. It is this fear that has been the source of controversy in the field of artificial intelligence and has the potential to hinder its development.

Writers of fiction such as Isaac Asimov [4] have written about AI. The most positive has been Jack Williamson who, in "With Folded Hands" [5], portrayed a young scientist disillusioned by man's destructive nature who creates robots to follow the Asimovian Prime Directive [6]: "To serve and obey, and guard men from harm." In the story, robots replicate themselves and do all the jobs he wants them to do—until he realizes the mistake he has made. But it is too late. He has rendered himself useless. "Men sat with idle hands because there was nothing left for them to do." Science was forbidden because the laboratories were dangerous to man. There was no need to acquire knowledge because the robots could do anything and do it better. "Purpose and Hope were dead. No goal was left for existence." One would ask why the young scientist could not kill the robots. He tries, but they stop him because he is violating the Prime Directive. Meanwhile, they multiply.

Philosophers too have long expressed this fear. According to Weizerburm [7], it is immoral to use a computer system to replace human functions involving interpersonal respect, understanding, and love. Floyd believes that computers should only be used if "there remains sufficient scope outside the computer application for other human faculties and forms of experience not to degenerate" [7]. Marvin Minsky likens it to an old paradox dealing with slave education: "If you keep them from learning too much you limit their usefulness; if you help them become smarter than you, then you may not be able to trust them to make better plans than they do for you" [8].

To us all, AI represents a social and ethical paradox. We want the machines to do those things we are not able to do because we are not good at them, yet we do not want them to get too good. We probably would have no reservations and certainly no objections if only we could be assured that they are, to put it in Hans Moravic's words, "our very own mind-children" [8]: that is, that they share our own values, truths, and virtues. As these autonomous agents achieve better intelligence and become more widely used and acceptable, they will be taking on more and more responsibility and autonomy that only humans have been known to have. This development raises many questions about the future of these autonomous agents, their relationship with humans, their behavior, and emotions. Among such questions are the following:

- How will humans perceive these intelligent agents?
- How will the autonomous agents themselves feel about human beings?
- Will human beings let these intelligent "creatures" keep on getting more and more intelligent even though they are aware the ultimate end result would be to surpass human intelligence?
- How will they do what they are supposed to do?
- Will they do only what they are supposed to do?
- Who will be responsible for the actions of these agents?
- Will these agents outperform their owners?
- Will they eventually eliminate the need for human skills?
- And the most important of these questions is, how much power and autonomy should we give these creatures, and will these agents eventually take away human autonomy and consequently take control of human destiny?

According to Mitchell Waldrop [6], as these autonomous agents become more and more intelligent, we need a theory and practice of machine ethics that will embody a built-in code of ethics in these creatures in the spirit of Asimov's laws of robotics and Carbonell's hierarchy of goals [6, 9].

Isaac Asimov, in his book *I, Robot* (1950), created his fictional robot characters with an implanted code of conduct he called the Laws of Robots:

- A robot may not injure a human being or, through inaction, allow a human to come to harm.
- A robot must obey the orders given to it by human beings except when such orders would conflict with the first law.
- A robot must protect its own existence as long as such protection does not conflict with the first or second law [4].

According to Jim Carbonell [9], programs can be governed by a hierarchy of goals that act as a guide and a prescribed direction in the program's reasoning processing. This hierarchy should then be set up so that it inputs a code of ethics into the programs. The question, however, is whether it will be followed by the intelligent programs and robots, and to what extent? Is there a possibility that they can vary the code, however much we try to stop them from doing so? Carbonell's concept is good, but it creates many questions that still need answers.

Discussion Topics

1. Is the construction of a personal AI or a human-like robot an immoral experiment?
2. Does a personal AI or a human-like robot have rights?
3. Can an artificial intelligence be moral?

Can there be benefits to humans of these agents without infringing on our autonomy? There are those who see the future of AI as very beneficial to humanity. They see a fruitful partnership with the agents in which the agents are relieving us of all our dangerous and tedious tasks, making our lives a little easier and helping us reach our ultimate goal of the good life. They further believe that will we learn more about ourselves in the attempt to construct something like ourselves. Will we become better as human beings in what we do and how we do it? Will the success of AI and the creation of ourselves bring us to the full understanding of our inadequacies and belittle our human experience? There is a possibility that this may bring us to transcend our human experience altogether and lead us to the post-human. At that stage we will be thinking big of ourselves able to transcend all our human fears that something can go wrong and looking forward to unimaginable possibilities—if it comes to pass, that is!

But again, as Michael R. LaChat [1] said, if we do not make a human-like robot to pass the famous Turing Test, then perhaps little of our effort will be lost and this might eventually bring us to the brink of our mysticism that has, at least, been partially "tested." Will that make us feel more "special"? What will this do to our moral and ethical beliefs?

10.3 Virtualization

The immersion aspects of virtualization create a multimedia that simulates the physical presence of participants with autonomy accorded to them. In fact, the process of immersion is created by software-based computer simulations that artificially create either computing environments or environments representing sensory experiences, which can include sight, hearing, touch, smell, and taste. We refer to these later environments as virtual reality (VR) environments.

10.3.1 Simulated Computing Environments

VMware.com, a software developer and a global leader in the computing virtualization market, defines virtualization of computing resources as a process in which software creates virtual machines (VMs), including a virtual machine monitor called *hypervisor,* that allocate hardware resources dynamically and transparently so that multiple operating systems, called *guest operating systems,* can run concurrently on a single physical computer without even knowing it [10]. For example, using software virtualization, one can, using the existing underlying hardware and software resources like operating systems, create and run several independent virtual machines on top of one physical operating system using the existing hardware resources to execute independent system tasks. Hardware virtualization also takes the same concept wherein several servers or client machines can be created based on one underlying hardware. The virtualization concept has been with us for some time.

The potential power of computing resources virtualization in substantially increasing the performance of computing systems, such as hardware and software through division of the underlying physical computing resources into many equally powerful virtual machines, has increased the popularity of the technology in the past 20 years, and this love continues today. The rush to virtualization is driven by its resulting server consolidation, creating savings to be invested in new IT initiatives such as cloud computing, mobility, data analytics, and use of social media for business purposes. This rapid growth is a reflection of the changing benefits of virtualization from being used only as a tactical tool to drive consolidation and higher system utilization to leveraging the mobility of virtual machines to improving management and operations of IT environments. The computing virtualization concept now includes a host of new use cases that range from high availability and disaster recovery to hosted clients and true utility computing.

10.3.2 Virtual Reality

As we said in the previous section, virtual reality (VR) is a type of virtualization technology that employs computer-controlled multisensory communication capabilities that allow more intuitive interactions with data and involve human senses in new ways. Virtual reality is also a computer-created environment immersing users and allowing them to handle information more easily. The sense of presence or immersion, resulting from virtualization, is a critical feature distinguishing virtual reality from other computer-based applications.

VR started as a science without applications, and VR applications in real life were difficult to come across and develop, prompting many to label it a *solution in search of a problem* [11]. Today, however, VR applications are on the rise in several medical and scientific areas including visualization of scientific and simulation data. VR visualization is driving high-volume multidimensional scientific research and simulated data into 3D displays that offer a more accurate and realistic approach to the representation of the original numeric data and thus help with a better understanding of the abstract phenomena under study [12].

10.3.3 Different Types of Virtual Reality

As in computing resource virtualization, there are different types of virtual reality, including immersive, desktop, projection, and simulation [13].

10.3.3.1 Immersive

Immersive virtual reality involve the use of computer interface devices such as a head-mounted display (HMD), fiberoptic-wired gloves, position tracking devices, and audio systems providing 3-D (binaural) sound. The user is immersed in a new environment, which becomes their immediate personal experience. For example, being in a simulated airplane cockpit gives a first-person experience of flying an aircraft. Similar experiences may be achieved when one is wearing goggles and gloves or using a joystick in a simulated NASCAR drive. Many current video games already give these kinds of personal experiences to the gamers.

10.3.3.2 Desktop

With desktop virtual reality, the user at a desktop computer gets an immersive personal 3-D experience via the screen of the desktop by using a virtual reality tool connected to the desktop such as a mouse, a joystick, hand gloves, or head gear. Again, there are many examples of computer games creating this experience.

10.3.3.3 Projection

In a projected virtual reality, users are not directly immersed into the new environment. They are originally outside the environment but the environment is projected to them. By the users establishing communication with the new projected environment, they immerse into the environment and can take part in its activities, events, and objects. This kind of virtual reality is common in a number of video games in which a computer captures the user's image via a videocamera from which it extracts and incorporates the users' features such as their positions and movements in the environment [13]. There are several examples of these environments, including Virtual Actors (like Mario and Eggwardo) and environments (like CAVE) [13].

10.3.3.4 Simulations

Virtual reality environments are created via simulators creating personal experiences through the immersion. The illusion of presence in the virtual environment is created by the use of visual elements greater than the field of view, three-dimensional sound inputs, computer-controlled motion bases, and more than a bit of theater [13]. Simulated virtual reality has been popular in training and entertainment. Examples of these environments include California-based Fighter Town, which features actual flight simulators, and SIMNET, a networked system of cab simulators that is used in military training [13].

10.3.4 Virtualization and Ethics

As we stated earlier, VR is a new frontier. To many the image evoked by the word *frontier* rekindles a sense of free adventurism, unregulated and pure. The VR environment brings the user closer to this romantic vision. But illusion is illusion, and it brings forth two major social and ethical themes. One is the reactions and feelings of the occupant of the environment, and the other is the intention of the creator of the environment. Some of the factors and issues to consider include the following:

1. *The Emotional Relationship and the Feeling of Being in Control*: This is a major psychological problem that confronts many VR users while in, and even sometimes after they leave, the environment. Although users get to interact with the agents inside the VR environment and enjoy the emotional highs generated by the agents, they also tend to develop an emotional relationship with the agents. This relationship may take the form of a deeper attachment to the agents, which gives the user a sense of being in control and later creates a sense of responsibility and trust on the part of the user. The relationship may also take the adversarial form, in which case the user feels out of control and may become hostile both inside the environment and after he or she leaves. In both cases, there is a possibility that the user may take the character of one of the agents and try to live it outside the environment. The immediate question that arises out of this situation is who should be held responsible for the outcome of the VR environment.

2. *Safety and Security*: Besides the psychological and mental conditions that the user of the VR environment may develop, there is also the danger of security of the user while in the environment. With the ever-increasing intelligence of the agents in the VR environment, the agents may cause a feeling of, or the reality of, both bodily and mental harm to the user. The effects may be directly caused by the contacts of the user while in the environment or may be delayed for some time, perhaps weeks after the user has left the environment.

3. *Human–Agent Interaction*: The interaction between the user and the agents in the VR environment has many consequences including the nature of the interaction, the activities to be performed, and the reaction and emotions of the user and the agents. If the interaction is perceived as friendly by the user, it may not be problematic; otherwise, there might be an impression of superiority of the agents and the user may feel threatened because of the high level of intelligence associated with the agents. This experience may lead to the user going amok because of a loss of control and probable feelings of helplessness.

4. *The Intentions of the Creator*: The intentions are always very difficult to predict and in this direction may lie the greatest danger for the user. One will never be sure whether these environments are doing what they are intended to do. There may be some malicious intent in which the environment is used, for example, to collect information on the user for the creator or agents of the creator without the user ever knowing about it. It may be that the environment is used secretly by some authority for mental and psychological transformation of the user.

Unfortunately, in contrast to AI intelligent agents where a considerable number of people are reluctant to surrender to them, in VR there is an unquestionable willingness to give it all up upon first being asked because people are looking for pleasure. Because VR is a very new science, there have been no comprehensive studies focused on VR environment user behavior. It is worth research, and ideally as VR makes strides such studies may come. The question, however, is this: What should we do if there are problems? We can fight any sinister creator intentions and user irresponsibility by making the VR environment operate in an implanted code of ethics both in the software and in the hardware, as we discussed earlier in the spirit of Asimov. But as we pointed out earlier, there is no way to predict the outcomes of these VR agents with such embedded code. The question remains the same. Would the VR environment stick to the code or vary it? And to what extent? We will never know. So educating the users about responsible use of the VR environment can help in this regard.

This responsibility should be based on sound ethical and moral principles relating to VR. Beardon [7] outlines three traditional principles by famous philosophers that are quite relevant to VR:

- One should not do things with computers for which one should not accept responsibility without computers.
- Continuous exposure to VR will impoverish those aspects of life that determine social development, interpersonal insights, and emotional judgment.
- Computers should be used in applications where computation and symbol manipulation are adequate ways of dealing with reality.

To these let us also add deception, a Kantian ethical principle, because a user can masquerade as somebody else and deceive others. For example, consider the following VR scenario: You are happily married; you are aware of the problems with extramarital affairs, and you do not approve of them. You have a list of compelling reasons such as health (STDs such as AIDS, herpes, and syphilis), outcomes such as unwanted and probably illegitimate children, moral sanctions against infidelity, and your own self-respect. But in your next encounter with VR, you are paired with a very beautiful sexual partner and you find yourself getting involved in illicit sexual acts you would not have condoned in the real world. The VR environment has removed all your constraints about extramarital affairs; you can now justify your actions even using utilitarian ethical theory. Is this a confusion in the traditional ethical theories or a redefinition of these theories in the new realities of VR? This scenario reflects what Beardon has defined VR to be—a deep philosophical confusion [7].

10.3.4.1 Social and Ethical Implication of Virtualization

To comment on the social and ethical implications and consequences of virtualization to society, let us present the following arguments by some of the best minds in this area. First, one of the anticipated benefits of virtualization to society is to extend the known and relatively managed social spheres and social networks of humanity in an unprecedented way through opening up of virtual domains of social interactions, many with a degree of managed control [14]. Another good social aspect of virtualization is to avail society of tools to create new virtual social networks out of the old and dismantle old social ones [14]. These new tools are also making communication among and between these new virtual networks possible and easy. In addition, virtualization is bringing about easy creation of new human identities in the new virtual environments, which makes authentication more difficult but at the same time is creating unprecedented potential in self-creation and self-presentation: this may bring new opportunities to humanity. As Ronald Purser [15] puts it, virtualization, in principle, has the potentiality of either erasing or heightening our situated presence in the world. This happening, he believes, may lead to a new form of cultural expression, allowing an individual, or even groups of people, to project their own imagination into a collective space, thus empowering the average individual to be an artist in virtual reality. This consciousness-raising potential may facilitate the emergence of a new cultural aesthetic that would result in the rebirth of the collective imagination [15]. This will be good for society.

On the flip side, the foregoing developments may create mayhem in the social infrastructure as we know it today, just because individuals can literally decide to be who they wish to be with ease. Henceforth, these unparalleled opportunities of virtualization may come at a price to society [14], because true virtualization requires an absence of reality. Without that consciousness in individuals and groups, there is no accountability as individuals and groups are shielded from the real consequences of their actions. In fact, without a situated and embodied sense of individual or group responsibility, there is likely to be no commitment and no risk [14]. In such an environment, therefore, moral engagement is limited and human relationships become trivialized [15]. The result may be that society is not benefiting from virtualization.

10.3.4.2 Virtualization Security as an Ethical Imperative

The ethical approach entails us to making sure we devote our best and most thorough thinking to every weak spot in our interaction with the world. Virtualization as we have seen here, in all its forms, is a process and a technology that is bound to complicate and transform the social fabric of society. It is not only ethical but imperative that we attend to all its ethical and security loopholes through which both intentional and unintentional exploitations of the technologies can take place, as these exploitations are bound to have far-reaching consequences for humanity.

To understand virtualization security problems and appreciate the efforts being made to protect any virtualized infrastructure, one has to remember that virtualization technology is based on software. So, all security problems and vulnerabilities that have ever been encountered in any software product have the potential to be present in a virtualized infrastructure. This possibility opens up a very broad area of attachment for those interested in securing virtualized infrastructures. To narrow the focus, it is important and probably more feasible to concentrate on specific major components of a virtualization infrastructure such as the hypervisor, hosts, transducers, communication pathways, and probably users. These major focus points can be secured to the best of known security protocols and best practices. More specifically, the focus should be put on the understanding that all virtual infrastructures are based on physical port gateways, so if we tighten security on those entry points, we can go a long way in securing the virtual infrastructure. Thus our first points of interest are those points where certain types of network traffic go within the physical network. We focus on these first because network traffic into and out of the virtual infrastructure goes through these points. The restriction of traffic into and out of the virtual infrastructure through a few of these designated points also offers additional security of the virtual resources from unauthorized users from outside the virtual infrastructure access gateway ring. Security within the virtual infrastructure is also enhanced by the growing inclusion and migration into the virtual infrastructure of security components that were traditionally hardware based such as firewalls and VPN, thus ensuring that virtual infrastructure customers can themselves extend the enforcement of security and compliance requirements of their physical network into the virtual environments.

Perhaps the greatest threat presented by virtualization of computer networks is the fact that, using one physical computer, one can access many virtual infrastructures, a feat that is not so feasible in the physical networks. According to Gruman quoting Simard [16], "graphics cards and network cards today are really miniature computers that see everything in all the VMs." They could be used as spies across all the VMs, letting a single PC spy on multiple networks.

10.4 Cyberspace and the Concept of Telepresence

Cyberspace is a global artificial reality environment based on a global mesh of interconnected computer networks. This mesh allows and makes it possible for anyone using a point-of-entry device such as a computer, smartphone, or any other Internet-enabled electronic device to reach anyone else, with the potential to access the mesh, through a one-on-one, one-to-many, and many-to-one communication capabilities or through broadcasting via the World Wide Web. Cyberspace, because of immense capabilities and global reach, is used either in real time or otherwise, simultaneously by millions if not billions of people around the world. Through its specialized applications, users enter this virtual world electronically to get many services and perform numerous tasks via use of applications to benefit humanity.

When one is in cyberspace, there is a feeling of being in a location other than where one actually is. This is a notion of *telepresence*, a feeling one gets of being present at a place other than one's true location. This feeling and sometimes the ability to control a robot or another device at a distance gives cyberspace and in fact makes cyberspace a virtual environment with power of immersion, the kind of experience we discussed in the previous chapter. Whether in cyberspace or not, both telepresence and immersion, as a concept, require that the users' senses be provided with such stimuli as to give the feeling of being in that other location. Additionally, users may be given the ability to affect the remote location. In this case, the user's position, movements, actions, voice, etc. may be sensed, transmitted, and duplicated in the remote location to bring about this effect. Therefore, information may be traveling in both directions between the user and the remote location [17].

10.4.1 Securing Cyberspace

Keeping cyberspace users secure is a daunting job that requires advanced techniques and prevention methods. Both the detection and prevention techniques are changing very fast. The several known ways of doing this include the following:

10.4.1.1 Detecting Attacks in Cyberspace

A detection system deployed around a computer system or a computer network is a 24-h monitoring system to alert the owner or system manager whenever something unusual occurs, something with a non-normal pattern, different from the usual pattern of life in and around the system. The monitoring system is actually an alarm system that must continuously capture, analyze, and inform the system manager on the daily patterns of life in and around the computer system.

10.4.1.2 Vulnerability Scanning in Cyberspace

System and network scanning for vulnerability is an automated process where a scanning program sends network traffic to all network nodes or selected nodes in the network and expects receiving return traffic that will indicate whether those nodes have known vulnerabilities. These vulnerabilities may include weaknesses in operating systems and application software and protocols.

10.4.2 Social Issues in Cyberspace

The Internet and indeed cyberspace has become the largest repository of information and source of materials for almost anything worth the searching, whether it has value or not. Indeed, although one can find information for any food recipe of choice, it is also the source of all sorts of information on terrorism. As the Internet is a source of terrorism information from how-to to recruiting, there are calls for cyberspace censorship. Depending on the country, the rationales for censorship have varied from historical, social, political, and economic to cultural grounds.

But cyberspace censorship is proving to be both difficult and very expensive for those trying, and many governments and censorship bureaus are fighting a losing battle because of the exponential growth of the Internet. For governments and censorship bureaus to keep pace with this growth, they have to be continually hiring censors, which is very expensive.

In addition to the explosive growth, Internet content is becoming highly specialized and richer in graphics, which requires very expensive equipment and highly trained people to keep pace. Also, cyberspace's one-fits-all role of telecommunication, broadcast, and computer services is making censorship very difficult and expensive. Effective censorship calls for a better focus on at least one of these because not all three media carry the same materials. Censors may concentrate on materials of a broadcast nature like web pages, assuming that the content they are looking for is more likely to be in this kind of medium, but may find this is not the case. Contents of materials also change in nature and focus from time to time and from medium to medium.

And finally, applying geographically defined court jurisdictions in cyberspace, a physical boundary-less entity, is proving to be futile at best. Any attempt to enforce the law in one country means enforcing the same law in many others. Many cyberspace problems that lead to censorship have been brought about by the transient nature of membership in cyberspace communities. Users rarely stay in the same community with the same peers for long. These transitions are brought about by a number of factors including changing interests, job changes, changing lifestyles, and a host of others. Each cybercommunity is a moving target community. Transients do not have allegiance and, therefore, no responsibility and accountability.

If the ideal situation is to be realized for every community user worldwide, cyberspace needs to be a place of comfort and entertainment where one can be satisfied and one's curiosity and dreams fulfilled. It needs to be a decent place where children can log on without sparking fear in their parents that their offspring will stumble onto inappropriate material. How this wished-for security can be achieved in cyberspace is the focus of many governments and civic organizations around the globe. The question is how, without total censorship of cyberspace, can these governments and civic organizations do it? As pressure builds for some kind of action, governments have started formulating policies for cyberspace use, some of which is ending up as censorship. An array of measures is being debated in legislatures and government board rooms around the globe. Such measures include the following:

- Guidelines, usually issued by a government body, outlining the do's and don'ts for cyberspace users.
- Some governments are encouraging the filtering process, picking certain domains and specific names they deem suggestive of what they are looking for. This kind of filtering is usually delegated to system administrators and system operators.
- States are setting up cyberspace on-ramp services and, through low user fees, are encouraging users to opt for these instead of private services. They also urge all educational and research institutions to use these services for free.
- Other governments are encouraging cyberspace user groups to "self-censor" through appeals to patriotism and nationalism and asking users to refrain from using or downloading what they deem offensive materials and sometimes even to report whenever they see objectionable materials [18].
- The use of blocking gadgets is also on the table. An industry for these gadgets is emerging. The blocking software programs work by blocking unwanted cyberspace materials [19]. But blockers have a serious drawback: they can be very easily circumvented by smart programmers.
- And finally, some governments are either enacting laws or are amending existing laws.

In the U.S. Congress, over the course of several years now, lawmakers have been trying to come up with ways to regulate indecent activities on the Internet. Such efforts have of course yielded a series of acts and bills with the majority of them in 1995 and 1996, the 2 years that encompassed the widely debated Telecommunications Bill of 1996. This bill contained the controversial Communications Decency Act, now defeated in court, whose purpose was to provide protection to citizens, especially minors, against harassment, obscenity, and indecency by means of telecommunication devices such as computers. This was not the first legislative measure to censor the Internet. Other legislation includes the Protection of Children from Computer Pornography Act of 1995, the Comprehensive Terrorism Prevention Act of 1995, the Digital Millennium Copyright Act (2001), the Child Online Protection Act (1998), and the Children's Online Privacy Protection Act (1998). The intent of these efforts has always been to protect the helpless, such as children, from indecent and illicit activities on the Internet. But because of the borderless nature of cyberspace and the rapid growth of the technology these efforts are meant to fight, they have had little or no impact on their intended targets, and there are always new cries for more control. Individual governments' efforts are also complicated by other factors. Chief among them is the realization that because of the differences in political, social, cultural, and religious systems around the globe, what is considered politically offensive in one locale may not be so in another and whatever is considered tolerable in one culture may not be so tolerated in another.

10.4.3 Privacy in Cyberspace

In Chap. 4 we described a scenario in which Citizen X no longer has privacy. In fact, many have been questioning the very concept of personal privacy—whether it still exists at all.

According to recent studies, personal privacy is becoming the number-one social and ethical issue of concern for the information age. Advances in technology have brought with them gadgetry that has diminished individual private spaces through electronic surveillance and monitoring, transmission, scanning, tapping, and fast and more efficient means of collecting, categorizing, and sorting data. Among the current issues of concern are the following:

* Transmission, scanning, and tapping using computers and mobile phones.
* Information gathering as a result of better software and equipment. In this category, cyberspace is proving to be a fertile ground because of its powerful search engines and the volume and speed of data. Information gathering, especially from an individual, is now the most threatening and worrisome form of invasion of privacy because of its ever-increasing commercial value. With the right tools at the right time, one can gather all forms of information one needs about a subject in a matter of hours from sources that include county offices, auto registration offices, credit card bureaus, utility companies, postal records, telephones,

and satellites. In a day's work one can build an individual profile that in the past would have taken years, if not being outright impossible.

* Individual tracking through mobile and paging devices and computers. Many carrier companies are now using employee tracking to get up-to-the-minute information on what the employee is doing at any given moment.
* Private investigators (PIs) have found a new partner in cyberspace using satellites; PIs can track and report on any individual with alarming details.
* Information-gathering abuses by established information-gathering agencies. Governments and government agencies such as the National Security Agency (NSA), the Federal Bureau of Investigations (FBI), the Central Intelligence Agency (CIA), all in the United States; both UK's MI5 (the Security Service) and MI6 (the Secret Intelligence Service); and the Federal Security Service of the Russian Federation (FSB) in Russia, all gather information in the name of national security and crime fighting. In such cases information is gathered on an individual before even an arrest is made. The biggest threat from these established information-gathering agencies is that if not properly focused and supervised, they have the capacity and means to do whatever they like with individual freedoms, bringing us to the privacy paradox that too much individual privacy is very dangerous. According to Daniel Brandt [20], society consists of individuals; if each individual has total privacy, then society as a whole has zero security. Of course, no government can allow this to happen. Because no government can exist without security, somebody's privacy has to be sacrificed.

10.4.3.1 Privacy Protection

As a cyberspace community member, or cyberzen, you have to be proactive in protecting your privacy, which can be done through information control, property control, and use of anonymity. You are in control of your privacy and you decide on how much to give up. Individual privacy is threatened whenever you voluntarily surrender information through online transactions such as entering online sweepstakes or filling out online surveys. Make sure you surrender personal information only when you must and as minimally as possible. Controlling access and information about your personal property (e.g., car, house, or computer) can also help safeguard your privacy.

Exercises

1. Discuss the implications of the common knowledge problem on advances in AI.
2. Is the "mad scientist" syndrome justifiable? Discuss.
3. Why is the study of AI limited to only small arrears? Will this not hinder the study of human behavior in other areas?
4. Will the study of AI make us better understand human behavior?
5. Can the understanding of AI, if this ever happens, help to understand and model human behavior, and hence develop better techniques for teaching computer ethics?

6. As AI applications increase, as in the use of robotics, will the wider use of these "manlike" machines compromise our moral value system? Why or why not?
7. Is the Frankenstein Syndrome an exaggeration or it is real?
8. Is it possible to develop a robot with our own moral value system?
9. Will the development of more advanced intelligent systems improve the declining moral value?
10. Discuss the future of AI and its ethical implications
11. Discuss the social implications of virtualization.
12. Discuss the social implications of virtual reality.
13. Discuss the social and ethical implications to society of the virtualization technologies.
14. Discuss the social and ethical implications to your society of virtual reality.
15. Although there has been tremendous growth in the virtualization of computing resources, there are still many skeptics of the technology. List their concerns. Suggest ways to overcome those concerns.
16. Discuss the differences between virtualization and virtual reality.
17. Discuss the differences between virtualization and emulation, giving examples
18. Why was VR characterized as a science without applications?
19. Some people believe VR is the same as cyberspace. Support or reject the claim.
20. Discuss the social and ethical issues associated with VR.
21. VR was discredited as a science in search of a solution. Was/is this a fair characterization? Why?
22. Research the current VR projects and suggest how they contribute to social and ethical values of your society.
23. Why is it so difficult to censor cyberspace?
24. Suggest reasons why cyberspace should not be censored.
25. List the steps taken by governments to curb cyberspace ills.
26. Discuss the merits and demerits of censorship measures.
27. Discuss the civic roles of cyberspace.

References

1. LaChat MR (1986) (The Methodist Theological School in Ohio). Artificial intelligence and ethics: an exercise in the moral imagination. AI Mag 7(2)
2. Wikipedia. http://en.wikipedia.org/wiki/Virtualization
3. Luger G, Stubblefield W (1993) Artificial intelligence, 2nd edn. Benjamin Cummings, Reading
4. Asimov I (1964) The rest of the robot. Doubleday, New York
5. Williamson J (1978) With folded hands. In: The best of Jack Williamson. Ballantine, New York, pp 154–206
6. Waldrop M (1991) A question of responsibility. In: Dejoie R, Fowler G, Paradice D (eds) Ethical issues in information systems. Byrd & Fraser, Boston
7. Beardon C (1992) The ethics of virtual reality. Intell Tutor Media 3(1):22–28
8. Minsky M, Riecken D (1994) A conversation with Marvin Minsky about agents. Commun ACM 37(7):23–29

9. Carbonell J (1979) Subjective understanding: computer models of belief systems. University of Michigan Press, Ann Arbor
10. VMware.com
11. Singh G, Feiner S, Thalmann D (1996) Virtual reality: software and technology. Commun ACM 39(5):35–36
12. Bryson S (1996) Virtual reality in scientific visualization. Commun ACM 39(5):62–71
13. The handbook of research for educational communications and technology. http://www.aect.org/edtech/ed1/15/15-03.html
14. Purser RE. Virtualization of consciousness or conscious virtualization: what path will virtual reality take? http://online.sfsu.edu/~rpurser/revised/pages/iabddoc.htm
15. Wikipedia. Phenomenology, ethics and the virtual world. Technoethics. http://en.wikipedia.org/wiki/Technoethics#Phenomenology.2C_Ethics_and_the_Virtual_World
16. Gruman G (2008) Virtualization's secret security threats: virtualization can be both a blessing and a curse, serving up improved security while at the same time hiding dangers. InfoWorld, 13 March, 2008. http://www.infoworld.com/d/security-central/virtualizations-secret-security-threats-159?page=0,0
17. Wikipedia. Telepresence. http://en.wikipedia.org/wiki/Telepresence
18. Lewis P (1996) Limiting a medium without boundaries. New York Times, 15 January, 1996, D1
19. Bhimani A (1996) Securing the commercial internet. Commun ACM 39(6):29–35
20. Brandt D (1993) Cyberspace wars: microprocessing vs. big brother. NameBase NewsLine 2, July–August 1993. http://ursula.btythe.org/NameBase/NewsLine.02/

Further Reading

Barlow J (1991) Electronic frontier: private life in cyberspace. Commun ACM 34(8):23–25

Bates J (1994) The role of emotion in believable agents. Commun ACM 37(7):122–125

Boden M (1994) Agents and creativity. Commun ACM 37(7):117–121

Cowie J, Lehner W (1996) Information extraction. Commun ACM 39(1):80–91

Green M, Halliday S (1996) A geometrical modelling and animation system for virtual reality. Commun ACM 39(5):46–53

Hayes Roth F, Jacobstein N (1994) The state of knowledge-based systems. Commun ACM 37(3):22–39

Kanade T, Read M, Weiss L (1994) New technologies and application in robots. Commun ACM 37(3):58–67

Munakato T, Jani Y (1994) Fuzzy systems: an overview. Commun ACM 37(3):69–75

Norman D (1994) How might people react with agents? Commun ACM 37(7):68–71

Poston T, Serra L (1996) Dextrous virtual work: introduction. Commun ACM 39(5):37–45

Riecken D (1994) Intelligent agents: introduction. Commun ACM 37(7):18–21

Schoppers M (1991) Real-time knowledge-based control systems. Commun ACM 34(8):27–30

Singh G, Fisher S, Thalmann D (1996) Virtual reality software and technology: introduction. Commun ACM 39(5):35–36

Webe J, Hirst G, Horton D (1996) Language use in context. Commun ACM 39(1):102–111

Wilkes M (1992) Artificial intelligence as the year 2000 approaches. Commun ACM 35(8):17–20

Wilkes Y (1996) Natural language processing. Commun ACM 39(1):60–62

Ethical, Privacy, and Security Issues in the Online Social Network Ecosystems

11

Learning Objectives

After reading this chapter, the reader should be able to

1. Understand computer networks.
2. Understand social networks.
3. Understand online social networks.
4. Understand privacy issues affecting online social networks.
5. Discuss privacy issues in social networks.
6. Discuss ethical issues in online social networks.
7. Discuss security issues in online social networks.
8. Discuss the limitations of the legislation network to manage online social, privacy, and security issues.

11.1 Introduction

Because we intend to focus on online social networks in this chapter, it is imperative that the reader has a good grasp of network infrastructure upon which the online social network is anchored. So, we start this chapter with a brief introduction of the concepts of a computer network. Some knowledge of the computer network infrastructure will help the reader understand how these online social network services, discussed in Sect. 11.4.3, work. Thus, an introduction to computer networks follows.

Definition: An ecosystem is a localized group of interdependent organisms together with the environment that they inhabit and on which they depend.

© Springer International Publishing Switzerland 2016   227
J.M. Kizza, *Ethics in Computing*, Undergraduate Topics in Computer Science,
DOI 10.1007/978-3-319-29106-2_11

11.2   Introduction to Computer Networks

A *computer network* is a distributed system consisting of loosely coupled computing elements and other devices. In this configuration, any two of these devices can communicate with each other through a communications medium. The medium may be wired or wireless. To be considered a communicating network, the distributed system must communicate based on a set of communicating rules called *protocols*. Each communicating device in the network must then follow these rules to communicate with others. A standard wired computer network resembles the network in Fig. 11.1.

Individually, network elements may own resources that are local or global. Such resources may be either software based or hardware based. If software, it may consist of all application programs and network protocols that are used to synchronize, coordinate, and bring about the sharing and exchange of data among the network elements. Network software also makes possible the sharing of expensive resources in the network. The hardware components of a computer network consist of a collection of nodes that include the end systems, commonly called *hosts*, and intermediate switching elements which include hubs, bridges, routers, and gateways.

11.2.1 Computer Network Models

Several network configuration models are used in the design of computer networks, but the two most common are the centralized and distributed models shown in Figs. 11.2 and 11.3. In a centralized model, all computers and devices in the network are connected directly to a central computer through which they can interconnect to

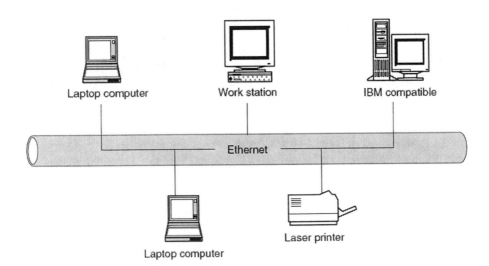

Fig. 11.1 A computer network

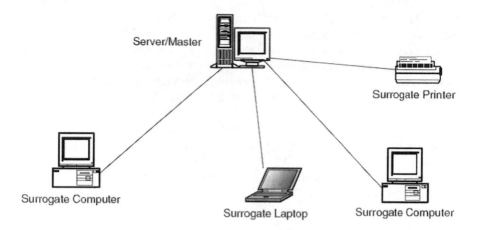

Fig. 11.2 A centralized network model

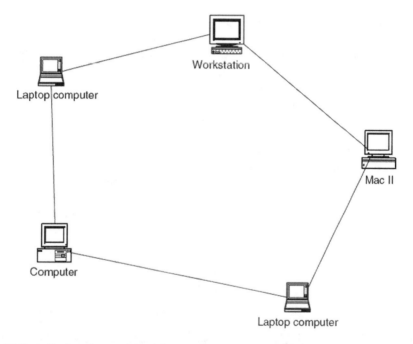

Fig. 11.3 A distributed network model

each other. This central computer, commonly called the master, must receive and forward all correspondence between any two or more communicating computers and devices. All other computers in the network are correspondently called dependent or surrogate computers. These surrogates may have reduced local resources, such as memory, and shareable global resources are controlled by the master at the center. The configurations are different, however, in the distributed network model, which consists of loosely coupled computers interconnected by a communication network composed of connecting elements and communication channels. However, in contrast to the centralized model, here the computers themselves may own their own resources locally or may request resources from a remote computer. Computers in this model are known by a string of names, including host, client, or node.

11.2.2 Computer Network Types

Computer networks, in any configuration centralized or distributed, come in different sizes depending on the number of computers and other devices in the network. The number of devices, computers or otherwise, in a network and the geographic area covered by the network determine the network type. There are, in general, three main network types: the local area network (LAN), a wide area network (WAN), and metropolitan area network (MAN).

11.2.2.1 Local Area Network
A LAN is a computer network with two or more computers or clusters of network and their resources connected by a communication medium sharing communication protocols and confined in a small geographic area such as a building, one floor of a building, or a few adjacent buildings. In a LAN, all network elements are in close proximity, which allows the communication links to maintain a higher speed and quality of data movement. Figure 11.4 shows a LAN.

11.2.2.2 Wide Area Network
A WAN is a computer network including one or more clusters of network elements and their resources, but in contrast to the LAN its configuration is not confined to a small geographic area: it can spread over a wide geographic area such as a region of a country, or across the whole country, several countries, or the entire globe, as does

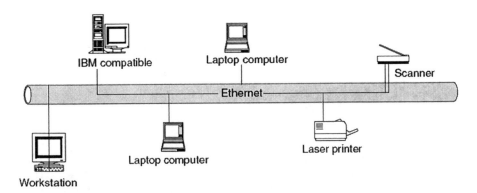

Fig. 11.4 A local area network (LAN)

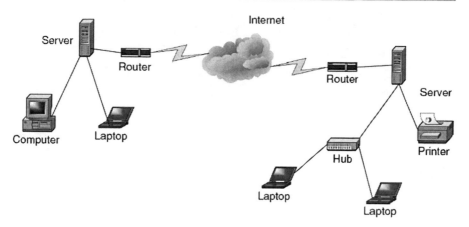

Fig. 11.5 A wide area network (WAN)

the Internet, which helps in distributing network services and resources to a wider community. Figure 11.5 shows a WAN.

11.2.2.3 Metropolitan Area Network

A metropolitan area network (MAN) is an unusual, and less often used, type of network that is intermediate between a LAN and a WAN. It covers a slightly wider area than the LAN but not so wide as to be considered a WAN. Civic networks that cover a city or part of a city are a good example of a MAN.

11.2.2.4 Mesh Network

A mesh network topology allows multiple access links between network elements, differing from other types of network topologies. The multiplicity of access links between network elements offers an advantage in network reliability because when one network element fails, the network does not cease operations; it simply finds a bypass to the failed element, and the network continues to function. The mesh network topology is most often applied in metropolitan area networks (MANs), also known as civic networks, that cover a city or part of a city. Figure 11.6 shows a mesh network.

11.3   Social Networks (SNs)

A *social network* is a theoretical network in which each node is an individual, a group, or an organization that independently generates, captures, and disseminates information and also serves as a relay for other members of the network. Individual nodes must collaborate to propagate the information in the network. The links between nodes represent relationships and social interactions among individuals, groups, organizations, or even entire societies.

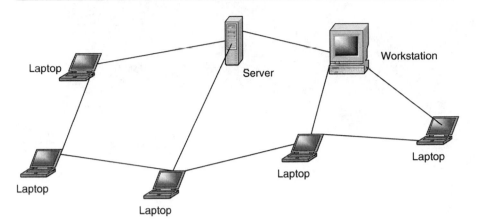

Fig. 11.6 Mesh network

The concept of social networking is not new. Sociologists and psychologists have been working with and analyzing social networks for generations. In fact, social networks have been in existence since the beginning of mankind. Prehistoric man formed social networks for different reasons including security, access to food, and social well-being.

Social networks begin with an individual reaching out to another individual or group for a social relationship of sorts that snowballs into a mesh of social relationships connecting many individuals or groups. In general, social networks come in all sizes and are self-organizing, complex, and agile depending on the nature of relationships in its links. As they grow in size, social networks tend to acquire specific elements and traits that make them different from one another. These traits become more apparent as the network increases in size. The type of social interactions, beliefs, and other traits usually limit the size of the social network. It is important to note that as the social network becomes large, it tends to lose the nuances of a local system; hence, if certain qualities of the network properties are needed, it is better to keep the size under control. Figure 11.6 illustrates three stages of development of a social network as it grows (Fig. 11.7).

11.4 Online Social Networks (OSNs)

Online social networks (OSNs) are social networks with underlining electronic communication infrastructure links enabling the connection of the interdependencies between the network nodes. The discussion in this chapter focuses on these OSNs. In particular, we focus on two types of online social networks:

- The traditional OSNs such as Facebook and MySpace: many of these can be accessed via mobile devices without the capability of handling mobile content

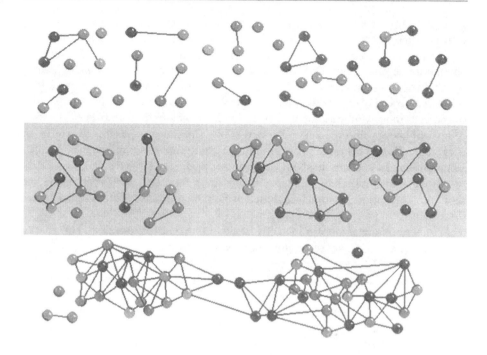

Fig. 11.7 Social network self-organizing configurations (http://en.wikipedia.org/wiki/ File:Network_self-organization_stages.png)

- The mobile OSNs (mOSNs): these which are newer OSNs that can be accessed via mobile devices and can handle the new mobile context

The interdependency between nodes in the OSNs supports social network services among people as nodes. These interdependencies as relationships among people participating in the network services define the type of OSNs.

11.4.1 Types of Online Social Networks

The growth of the OSNs over the years since the beginning of digital communication evolved through several types. Let us review the most popular types using a historical chronology.

Chat Network The chat network was born from the digital chatting anchored on a *chat room*. The chat room was, and still is, a virtual room online where people "gather" just to chat. Most chat rooms have open access, policies meaning that anyone interested in chatting or just reading others' chats may enter the chat room. People can "enter" and "exit" any time during the chats. At any one time several threads of the public chats may be going on. Each individual in the chat room is given a small window on his or her communication device to enter a few lines of chat contributing to one or more of the discussion threads. This communication occurs in real time, and whatever one submits to the chat room can be seen by anyone in the chat room. Chat rooms also have a feature wherein a participating individual can invite another individual currently in the public chat room into a private chat room where the two can continue with limited "privacy." To be a member of the chat room you must create a user name by which the members of the chat room will know you. Frequent chatters will often become acquaintances based on user names. Some chat room software allows users to create and upload their profiles so that users can know more about you via your profile.

Although chat rooms by their own nature are public and free for all, some are monitored for specific compliance, based usually on attributes such as topics under discussion.

With the coming of more graphically based online services, the use of chat rooms is becoming less popular, especially among young people.

Blog Network Another online social network is the bloggers network. "Blogs" are nothing more than people's online journals. Avid bloggers keep diaries of daily activities. These diaries sometimes are specific, on one thread of interest to the blogger, or a series of random logs of events during a specific activity. Some blogs are comment on specific topics. Some bloggers have a devoted following depending on the issues.

Instant Messaging Network (IMN) The IMNs support real-time communication between two or more individuals. As in chat rooms, each participant in the IMN must have a user name. To IM an individual, one must know that individual's username or screen name. The initiator of the IM is provided with a small window to type the message and the recipient is also provided with a similar window to reply to the message. The transcript of the interchange is kept scrolling up both users' screens. Unlike the chat room, however, these exchanges of short messages are private. As in chat networks, some IMNs allow users to keep profiles of themselves.

Online Social Networks (OSNs) The OSNs are a combination of all the network types we have already discussed and other highly advanced online features with advanced graphics. These social networks include Facebook, Twitter, Myspace, Friendster, YouTube, Flickr, and LinkedIn. As these networks grew from those we have already seen, many of the features of these networks are those we have already discussed. For example, users in these networks can create profiles that include their graphics and other enclosures and upload them to their network accounts. They must have a username or screen name. Also communication, if desired, can occur in real time as if one is using chat or IM capabilities. In additional to real time, these networks also give the user the delayed and archiving features so that the users can store and search for information. Because of these additional archival and search capabilities, network administrators have fought with the issues of privacy and security of users, as we see later in this chapter. As a way to keep user data safe, profiles can be set to a private setting, thus limiting access to private information by an authorized user.

11.4.2 Online Social Networking Services

An online social networking service is an online service accessible via any Internet-enabled device with the goal of facilitating computer-mediated interaction among people who share interests, activities, backgrounds, or real-life connections. Most online social network services consist of the following elements:

- User Profile
- Social or business links of interests
- Additional services

Currently, the most popular online social network services have categories that range among those based on friends, music and movies, religion, business, and many other interests. A sample of the current services in each of these categories follow.

- General and Friends-based Social Networks
  - Facebook
  - MySpace
  - Hi5
- Movie and Music Social Networks
  - LastFM
  - Flixster
  - iLike
- Mobile Social Networks
  - Dodgeball
  - Loopt
  - Mozes
- Hobby and Special Interest Social Networks
  - ActionProfiles
  - FanIQ
- Business Social Networks
  - LinkedIn
  - XING
  - Konnects
- Reading and Books Social Networks
  - GoodReads
  - Shelfari
  - LibraryThing

11.4.3 The Growth of Online Social Networks

OSNs have blossomed as the Internet exploded. The history and the growth of OSNs have mirrored and kept in tandem with the growth of the Internet. At the infancy of the internet, computer-mediated communication services such as Usenet,

ARPANET, LISTSERV, and bulletin board services (BBS) helped to start the growth of the current OSNs. Let us now see how these contributed to the growth of OSNs.

BITNET was an early world leader in network communications for the research and education communities and helped lay the groundwork for the subsequent introduction of the Internet, especially outside the U.S. [7]. BITNET and Usenet were invented around the same time in 1981 by Ira Fuchs and Greydon Freeman at the City University of New York (CUNY); both were "store-and-forward" networks. BITNET was originally named for the phrase "Because It's There Net," later updated to "Because It's Time Net" [1]. It was originally based on IBM's VNET *email* system on the IBM virtual machine (VM) mainframe operating system, but it was later emulated on other popular operating systems such as DEC VMS and *Unix*. What made BITNET so popular was its support of a variety of mailing lists supported by the *LISTSERV* software [2].

BITNET was updated in 1987 to BITNET II to provide a higher bandwidth network similar to the *NSFNET*. However, by 1996, it was clear that the Internet was providing a range of communication capabilities that fulfilled BITNET's roles, so CREN ended their support and the network slowly faded away [2].

Bulletin Board Services (BBS) A BBS is a piece of software running on a computer allowing users on computer terminals far away to log in and access the system services such as uploading and downloading files and reading the news and contributions of other members through e-mails or public bulletin boards. In "Electronic Bulletin Boards, A Case Study: The Columbia University Center for Computing Activities," Janet F. Asteroff [3] reports that the components of computer conferencing that include private conferencing facilities, electronic mail, and electronic bulletin boards started earlier than the electronic bulletin board (BBS). Asteroff writes that the concept of an electronic bulletin board began about 1976 through ARPANET at schools such as the University of California at Berkeley, Carnegie-Mellon, and Stanford University. These electronic bulletin boards were first used in the same manner as physical bulletin boards, that is, help wanted, items for sale, public announcements, etc. Electronic bulletin boards soon became, because of the ability of the computer to store and disseminate information to many people in text form, a forum for user debates on many subjects. In its early years, BBS connections were made via telephone lines and modems. The cost of using them was high, so they tended to be local. As the earlier form of the World Wide Web, BBS use receded as the World Wide Web grew.

Listserv Started in 1986 as automatic mailing list server software that broadcast e-mails directed to it to all on the list, the first Listserv was conceived by Ira Fuchs from BITNET and Dan Oberst from EDUCOM (later EDUCAUSE), and implemented by Ricky Hernandez, also of EDUCOM, to support research mailing lists on the *BITNET* academic research network [4].

By the year 2000, Listserv was running on computers around the world, managing more than 50 thousand lists, with more than 30 million subscribers, delivering more than 20 million messages a day over the Internet [4].

Other Online Services As time went on and technology improved, other online services supplemented, and always improved on, the services of whatever was in use. Most of the new services were commercially driven, and most of them were moving toward, and are currently on, the Web. These services, including news, shopping, and travel reservations, were the beginning of the web-based services we are enjoying today. As they were commercially driven, they were mostly offered by ISPs such as AOL, Netscape, and Microsoft. As the Internet grew, millions of people flocked onto it, and the web and services started moving away from ISP to fully fledged online social network companies such as Facebook, Flicker, Napster, Linked, and Twitter.

11.5   Ethical and Privacy Issues in Online Social Networks

Privacy is a human value consisting of a set of rights including solitude, the right to be alone without disturbances; anonymity, the right to have no public personal identity; intimacy, the right not to be monitored; and reserve, the right to control one's personal information, including the dissemination methods of that information. As humans, we assign a lot of value to these four rights. In fact, these rights are part of our moral and ethical systems. With the advent of the Internet, privacy has gained even more value as information has gained value. The value of privacy comes from its guardianship of the individual's personal identity and autonomy.

Autonomy is important because humans need to feel that they are in control of their destiny. The less personal information people have about an individual, the more autonomous that individual can be, especially in decision making. However, other people will challenge one's autonomy depending on the quantity, quality, and value of information they have about that individual. People usually tend to establish relationships and associations with individuals and groups that will respect their personal autonomy, especially in decision making.

As information becomes more imperative and precious, it becomes more important for individuals to guard their personal identity. Personal identity is a valuable source of information. Unfortunately, with rapid advances in technology, especially computer and telecommunication technologies, it has become increasingly difficult to protect personal identity.

11.5.1 Privacy Issues in OSNs

Privacy can be violated, anywhere including in online social network communities, through intrusion, misuse of information, interception of information, and information matching [5]. In online communities, intrusion, as an invasion of privacy, is a wrongful entry, a seizing, or acquiring of information or data belonging to other members of the online social network community. Misuse of information is all too easy. While online, we inevitably give our information to whomever asks for it to obtain services. There is nothing wrong with collecting personal information when it is authorized and is going to be used for a legitimate reason. Information routinely collected from online community members, however, is not always used as intended. It is quite often used for unauthorized purposes, and hence is an invasion of privacy. As commercial activities increase online, there is likely to be stiff competition for personal information collected online for commercial purposes. Companies offering services on the Internet may seek new customers by either legally buying customer information or illegally obtaining it through eavesdropping, intrusion, and surveillance. To counter this, companies running these online communities must find ways to enhance the security of personal data online.

As the number and membership in online social networks skyrocketed, the issues of privacy and security of users while online and the security of users' data while offline have taken center stage. The problems of online social networking have been exacerbated by the already high and still growing numbers, especially of young people, who pay little to no attention to privacy issues for themselves or others. Every passing day, there is news about and growing concerns over breaches in privacy caused by social networking services. Many users are now worried that their personal data are being misused by the online service providers. All these privacy issues can be captured as follows [6]:

- Sharing of personal information with all OSN users:
    - Users in the network give out too much personal information without being aware who might wrongly use that information. Sexual predators are known to use information from teenagers on these networks. Currently, many of the OSNs are working with law enforcement to try to prevent such incidents [5]. Information such as street address, phone number, and Instant Messaging names are routinely disclosed to an unknown population in cyberspace.
    - Ease of access to OSNs. Currently it is very easy for anyone to set up an account on any one of these networks with no requirements for specific identifications, which can lead to identity theft or impersonation [5].
    - Privacy threats result from placing too much personal information in the hands of large corporations or governmental bodies, allowing a profile to be produced on an individual's behavior on which decisions may be made that are detrimental to that individual [5].
    - Updating profiles with current activities poses a great threat, for example, updating your profile informing people of your whereabouts.
- Lack of precise rules by the OSNs on who should use which data.
- Leakage of private information to third parties:
    - On many of these networks, information altered or removed by a user may in fact be retained or passed to third parties [5].
- Interlinkages in OSNs. In their paper "(Under)mining Privacy in Social Networks," Monica Chew, Dirk Balfanz, and Ben Laurie of Google, Inc. point to three distinct areas where the highly interlinked world of social networking sites can compromise user privacy [7]:
    - Lack of control over activity streams: An *activity stream*, according to the authors, is a collection of events associated with a single user including

changes a user makes to his or her profile page, the user adding or running a particular application on the social networking site, news items shared, or communication with friends. Activity streams may compromise a user's privacy in two ways:

- A user may not be aware of all the events that are fed into their activity streams, in which case the user lacks control over those streams.
- A user may not be aware of the audience who can see their activity streams, in which case the user lacks control over that audience.

- Unwelcome linkage: *Unwelcome linkage* occurs when links on the Internet reveal information about an individual that they had not intended to reveal. Unwelcome linkage may occur wherever graphs of hyperlinks on the World Wide Web are automatically created to mirror connections between people in the real world. Maintaining separation of individual activities and different personae is important in OSNs.
- Deanonymization of users through merging of social graphs. OSN sites tend to extract a lot of personally identifiable information from people such as birth date and address. With this information, it is possible to de-anonymize users by comparing such information across social networking sites, even if the information is partially obfuscated in each OSN.

As the growth in online social networks continues unabated, the coming in the mix of the smart mobile devices is making the already existing problems more complex. These new devices are increasing the number of accesses to OSNs and increasing the complexity of the privacy issues, including, in addition to those already noted in the traditional (OSNs) [8], the following:

- The presence of a user. In contrast to the most traditional OSNs, where users were not automatically made aware of the presence of their friends, most mobile OSNs (mOSNs) now allow users to indicate their presence via a "check-in" mechanism, whereby a user establishes their location at a particular time. According to Krishnamurthy and Wills [8], the indication of presence allows their friends to expect quick response, and this may lead to meeting new people who are members of the same mOSN. Although the feature of automatic locate by oneself is becoming popular, it allows leakage of personal private information along two tracks: the personal information that may be sent and the destination to which it could be sent.
- location-based tracking system (LTS) technologies that are part of our mobile devices. This is a feature that is widespread in the mobile environment. However, users may not be aware that their location can be made known to friends and friends of friends who are currently online on this mOSN, to their friends in other mOSNs, and to others, which may lead to leakage of personal information to third parties.
- interaction potential between mOSNs and traditional OSNs. According to Krishnamurthy and Wills [8], such connections are useful to users who, while interacting with an mOSN, can expect some of their actions to show up on

traditional OSNs and be visible to their friends there. However, much of their personal information can leak to unintended users of both the traditional OSNs and the mOSNs.

In addition to almost free access to a turn of personal data on OSNs, there is also a growing threat to personal data ownership; for example, who owns the data that were altered or removed by the user which may fact be retained and/or passed to third parties. This danger was highlighted when, in June 2011, a 24-year-old Austrian law student, Max Schrems, asked Facebook for a copy of all his personal data. Facebook complied, sending him a CD containing 1200 pages of data, including his likes, "friend" and "defriend" history, and chat logs. But before that, Schrems had deleted some of the data returned to him from his profile, yet Facebook had retained his information. Of course Schrems filed 22 individual claims against Facebook for €100,000 ($138,000) for retaining data deleted by users, in the case *Europe v. Facebook* [9].

Fortunately, users are beginning to fight for their privacy to prevent their personal details from being circulated far widely than they intended them to be. For example, take Facebook's 2006 News Feed and Mini Feed features, designed to change what Founder and CEO Mark Zuckerberg called Facebook's old "encyclopedic interface," where pages mostly just list information about people, to the current stream of fresh news and attention content about not only the user but also the user's friends and their activities [10]. The first, News Feed, brought to the user's home page all new activities on all friends and associate links, including new photos posted by friends, relationship status changes, people joining groups, and many others, thus enabling the user to get an abundance of information from every friend's site every day.

Although these features adhered to Facebook's privacy settings, meaning that only people whom a user allowed to view the data were able to see them, this still generated a firestorm from users across the world. More than 700,000 users signed an online petition demanding the company discontinue the feature, stating that this compromised their privacy [11]. Much of the criticism of The News Feed was that it gave out too much individual information.

Online social networks, just like their predecessor cyberspace communities, are bringing people together with no physical presence to engage in all human acts that traditionally have taken place in a physical environment that would naturally limit the size of the audience and the amount of information given at one time. As these cyber-communities are brought and bound together by a sense of belonging, worthiness, and the feeling that they are valued by members of the network, they create a mental family based on trust, the kind of trust you would find in a loving family. However, because these networks are boundary less, international in nature, they are forming not along well-known and traditional identifiers such as nationalities, beliefs, authority, and the like, but by common purpose and need with no legal jurisdiction and no central power to enforce community standards and norms.

11.5.2 Strengthening Privacy in OSNs

As more and more people join OSNs and now the rapidly growing mOSNs, there is a growing need for more protection to users. Chew et al. suggest the following steps are needed [7]:

- Both OSN and mOSN applications should be explicit about which user activities automatically generate events for their activity streams
- Users should have control over which events make it into their activity streams and be able to remove events from the streams after they have been added by an application
- Users should know who the audience of their activity streams is and should also have control over selecting the audience of their activity streams
- Both OSN and mOSN applications should create activity stream events that are in sync with user expectation

Other suggestions that may help in this effort:

- Use secure passwords.
- User awareness of the privacy policies and terms of use for their OSNs and mOSNs.
- Both OSNs and mOSNs providers should devise policies and enforce existing laws to allow some privacy protection for users while on their networks.

11.5.3 Ethical Issues in Online Social Networks

Online social communities are far from the traditional physical social communities with an epicenter of authority in which every member pays allegiance to the center with a shared sense of responsibility. This type of community governance with no central command, but an equally shared authority and responsibility, is new, and a mechanism needs to be in place and must be followed to safeguard every member of the community. But these mechanisms are not yet defined, and where they are being defined, it is still too early to say whether they are effective. The complexity, unpredictability, and lack of central authority is further enhanced by these aspects:

- *Virtual personality*: You know their names, their likes and dislikes. You know them so well that you can even bet on what they are thinking, yet you do not know them at all. You cannot meet them and recognize them in a crowd.
- *Anonymity*: You work with them almost every day. They are even your friends; you are on a first-name basis, yet you will never know them. They will forever remain anonymous to you and you to them.
- *Multiple personality*: You think you know them, but you do not because they are capable of changing and mutating into other personalities. They can change into as many personalities as there are issues being discussed. You never know which personality you are going to meet next.

These three characteristics are at the core of the social and ethical problems in online social networks in particular and cyberspace in general; the larger and more numerous these communities become, the more urgent the ethical concerns become. With all these happening in online social network, the crucial utilitarian question to ask is what is the best way and how can we balance the potential harms and benefits that can befall members of these online social networks and how if possible to balance these possibilities. Of late, the news media has been awash with many of these online ills and abuses, and the list is growing:

(i) *Potential for misuse*

Online social networks offer a high degree of freedom that is being misused by a growing number of users. Cases abound of these incidents with tragic endings including suicide, especially in young people.

(ii) *Cyberbullying, cyberstalking, and cyber-harassment*

Cyberbullying, cyberstalking, and electronic harassment are relatively common occurrences and can often result in emotional trauma for the victim. They are, unfortunately, becoming a common form of abuse on online social network sites such as Facebook and MySpace, especially to youth. Cyberbullying is defined as use of Internet services and mobile technologies such as web pages and discussion groups, as well as instant messaging or SMS text messaging, with the intention of harming another person. Cyberstalking or cyber harassment on the other hand is defined as the use of the Internet or other electronic means to stalk or harass an individual, a group of individuals, or an organization. It may include false accusations, monitoring, making threats, identity theft, damage to data or equipment, the solicitation of minors for sex, or gathering information for harassment [12].

Because of the nature of cyberspace's telepresence, anonymity, lack of allegiance of users, and the non-existence of central governance, there are no limitations as to what individuals can post when online and how toxic those posts can be. Individuals, therefore, take it as if they are given the power to post offensive remarks or pictures that could potentially cause a great amount of emotional pain, oftentimes leading to teen suicide. Cases are growing of these kinds of activities, some of which are tragic. Bullying statistics show that cyberbullying is a serious problem and alarmingly common among adolescents and teens. According to cyberbullying statistics from the i-SAFE foundation [13]:

- More than half of adolescents and teens have been bullied online, and about the same number have engaged in cyberbullying.
- More than one in three young people have experienced cyberthreats online.
- More than 25 % of adolescents and teens have been bullied repeatedly through their cell phones or the Internet.
- Considerably more than half of young people do not tell their parents when cyberbullying occurs.

As these statistics indicate, the number of teen suicides attributable to cyberbullying is on the rise.

(iii) *Risk for child safety*

Problems with online social networks are not only limited to misuse of the sites and cyberbullying, they also include real threats to children whether cyberbullied or not. There is growing exploitation of children in online social networks. The latest figures show that about 1 million children under 16 years of age use Bebo, and 600,000 minors are on MySpace [14]. With these numbers, the potential for child abuse online is growing. The networking sites say they are making it possible for users to report abuse, although those reports usually go to the site administrators rather than the authorities. Governments around the world are taking steps, at least to better understand the problem and find some solutions.

Discussion Topics

- How do we balance these harms and benefits, reducing one and increasing the possibility of the other?
- How do we protect individuals and how do we handle the issue of consent?

(iv) *Psychological effects of online social networking*

The rise in the use and membership of online social networking has resulted in a dramatic rise not only in the numbers of online social networks but also in the number of users. With the rise in the number of users is also a rise in the number of users with problems. More and more people, especially teenagers, are spending an excessive amount of time on the Internet in general and on social networking sites in particular, which has led researchers to classify Internet addiction as a new clinical disorder [15].

According to Neville Misquittaa in "Psychiatry and Society in Pune," the most common predictors of excessive use of social networking are these [16]:

- *Extroverted and unselfconscious* individuals spend more time on social networking sites and their usage tends to be addictive.
- *Shy people* also like Facebook and spend more time on it. However, they have few Facebook "friends."
- *Narcissistic personalities* also have high levels of online social activity. They are recognized online by the quantity of their social interactions, their main photo self-promotion, and the attractiveness of their main photo.

(v) *Free speech*

What types of speech are protected once one is in an online social network? Although the National Labor Relations Act protects workers from being fired for "protected concerted activity," which prevents workers from being fired for collective action while allowing companies the right to fire workers for individual actions they take against the company, when it comes to online social networking, the issues are still murky and there is still uncertainty as to the boundaries of what types of speech is protected in online social networks. This fuzziness is illustrated by the Pembroke Pines Charter High School case in which Katherine Evans, who was a senior at Pembroke Pines Charter High School in Florida in 2007 when she created a group on Facebook called, "Ms. Sarah Phelps is the worst teacher I've ever met."

Peter Bayer, the principal of Pembroke Pines High, suspended Evans for 3 days and removed her from her Advanced Placement classes for violating the school's rules against "cyberbullying" and "harassment" of a staff member, according to court documents. Evans sued the principal in his individual capacity, alleging that her First Amendment free speech and 14th Amendment due process rights were violated.

In a ruling that followed, in **Bayer v. Evans**, U.S. Magistrate Judge Barry L. Garber of Miami declined Evans's request for an injunction barring the principal from keeping the student's discipline in school records. However, the judge denied qualified immunity for Bayer, holding that Evans's speech was protected under the First Amendment and that the principal should have known he was violating a clearly established right by disciplining Evans [17].

This ruling, as do other recent rulings, speaks volumes about the ethics of social networking and schools and is indicative of the haziness of the legal boundaries of free speech in online social networks.

Discussion Topics Should teachers be allowed to befriend students on sites such as Facebook? Should students blog about their teachers while on an online social network?

11.6   Security and Crimes in Online Social Networks

Online crimes, in tandem with the growth of computing and telecommunication technologies, are one of the fastest growing types of crimes and they pose the greatest danger to online communities, e-commerce, and the general public. An *online crime* is a crime like any other crime, except that in this case, the illegal act must involve either an Internet-enabled electronic device or computing system either as an object of a crime, an instrument used to commit a crime, or a repository of evidence related to a crime. Also, online crimes are acts of unauthorized intervention into the working of the telecommunication networks and/or the sanctioning of authorized access to the resources of the computing elements in a network that lead to a threat to the system's infrastructure or cause a significant property loss. The International Convention of Cyber Crimes and the European Convention on Cyber Crimes both list the following crimes as online crime [1]:

- Unlawful access to information
- Illegal interception of information
- Unlawful use of telecommunication equipment
- Forgery with use of computer measures
- Intrusions of the Public Switched and Packet Network
- Network integrity violations
- Privacy violations
- Industrial espionage
- Pirated computer software
- Fraud using a computing system
- Internet/e-mail abuse
- Using computers or computer technology to commit murder, terrorism, pornography, and hacking

11.6.1   Beware of Ways to Perpetrate Crimes in Online Social Networks

As we pointed out in Chap. 9, if we have to fight online crimes, we have to first learn how they are perpetrated. Earlier, we noted that online crimes are defined in a variety of ways, reflecting the many different ways these crimes are perpetrated. Some of the most common ways are through system penetration and denial of service attacks.

11.6.1.1   System Penetration

System penetration is the most widely used approach to committing online crimes. A system penetration is a process of gaining unauthorized access to a protected system's resources: the system may be automated or not. Penetration attacks always compromise the integrity of the resources of a system. Most penetration attacks are not accidental; they are preplanned and proceed with a coordinated reconnaissance. The goal of the reconnaissance is to acquire the following lead information on the targeted system:

- IP addresses of all hosts or selected hosts in the victim network
- Accessible UDP and TCP port numbers
- The type of operating system(s) used on all hosts or selected hosts in the network

There are two types of reconnaissance: passive and active. In a *passive reconnaissance*, the attacker gathers freely available system information, mostly from an open source. A typical passive reconnaissance can include physical observation of buildings housing the system, dumpster diving near the target system, collecting discarded papers and system computer equipment in an attempt to find equipment or data that may include personal identifying data such as usernames and passwords which will lead them to gain access to the company system. It also includes using other information-gathering techniques like eavesdropping on employee conversations, social engineering, and packet sniffing. Some common sources and tools used when looking for open source information legally include these [2]:

- A company website
- Electronic data gathering, analysis, and retrieval (EDGAR) filings (for publicly traded companies)
- Network news transfer protocol (NNTP) USENET newsgroups
- User group meetings
- Business partners
- Dumpster diving
- Social engineering

Active reconnaissance on the other hand involves collecting information about a target system by probing that system or neighboring systems. A typical active reconnaissance involves port scanning to discover vulnerable ports through which to enter the system, probing firewalls and system routers to find ways around them, and other methods. Some of the tools used in active host reconnaissance include these:

- NSLookup/Whois/Dig lookups
- SamSpade
- Visual Route/Cheops
- Pinger/WS_Ping_Pro

11.6.1.2 Distributed Denial of Service

Another approach used by perpetrators of online crimes is the *denial of service*, an interruption of service of the target system. This interruption of service occurs when the target system is made either unavailable to users through its disabling or destruction. Denial of service can also be caused by intentional degradation or blocking of computer or network resources. These denial of service attacks are commonly known as *distributed denial of service* (DDoS) attacks because they attack hosts in a network.

Similar to penetration attacks (e-attacks), DDoS attacks can also be either local, where they can shut down LAN computers, or global, originating thousands of miles away on the Internet. Attacks in this category include these [1]:

- *IP spoofing*. A forging of an IP packet address such as the source address, which causes the responses from the destination host to be misdirected, thus creating problems in the network. Many network attacks are a result of IP spoofing.
- *SYN flooding*. Using a three-way handshake protocol to initiate connections between a malicious (spoofed) source nodes and flood the target node with too many connection requests, thus overwhelming it and bringing it down.
- *Smurf attack*. The intruder sends a large number of spoofed ICMP Echo requests to broadcast IP addresses. Hosts on the broadcast multicast IP network then respond to these bogus requests with reply ICMP Echo, significantly multiplying the number of reply ICMP Echoes to the hosts with spoofed addresses.
- *Buffer overflow*. The attacker floods a carefully chosen field such as an address field with more characters than it can accommodate. These excessive characters, usually executable malicious code, when executed may cause havoc in the system, effectively giving the attacker control of the system.

- *Ping of death.* The attacker sends IP packets that are larger than the 65,536 bytes allowed by the IP protocol, knowing that many network operating systems cannot handle this, leading to the possible freezing or eventual system crash.
- *Land.c attack.* In which the land.c program sends TCP SYN packets whose source and destination IP addresses and port numbers are those of the victims.
- *Teardrop.c.* In which the attacker causes a fragmentation of TCP packets to exploit the reassembling process that may lead to the victim to crash or hang.
- *Sequence number sniffing.* In which the intruder takes advantage of the predictability of sequence numbers used in TCP implementations to sniff the next sequence number to establish legitimacy.

11.6.2 Defense Against Crimes in Online Social Networks

Although there are systems that are randomly attacked, most victim systems are preselected for attack. Because of this, we can defend systems against online attacks. An effective defense plan consists of prevention, detection, and analysis and response.

11.6.2.1 Prevention
Prevention is perhaps the oldest and probably the best defense mechanism against online crimes. However, prevention can only work if there is a strict security discipline that is effectively enforced and must include the following:

- A security policy
- Risk management
- Vulnerability assessment
- Use of strong cryptographic algorithms
- Penetration testing
- Regular audits
- Use of proven security protocols
- Legislation
- Self-regulation
- Mass education

Let us discuss some of these. More details may be found in Sects. 5.3 and 8.3.

11.6.2.2 A Security Policy
A security policy is a critical and central document in an organization security effort that spells out in great detail how the organization manages risk, controls access to key assets and resources, and implements policies, procedures, and practices for a safe and secure environment [3]. A security policy usually also spells out what resources need to be protected and how the organization can protect such resources. It is a living document and sometimes controversial. There are as many opinions on the usefulness of security policies in the overall system security picture as there are

security experts. However, security policies are still important in establishing an organization's security guidelines such as these:

- *Hardware and software acquisition and installations in the organization.* For example, if a functioning firewall is to be configured, its rule base must be based on a sound security policy.
- *User discipline.* All users in the organization that connect to a network, such as the Internet, must do so in conformity to the security policy.

A security policy is unique for each organization, covers a wide variety of topics, and serves several important purposes in the organization's security cycle. Because of this, the following carefully chosen set of basic steps must be established and carefully followed in the construction of a viable implementable and useful security policy:

- Determining the resources that must be protected and for each resource drawing a profile of its characteristics
- Determining, for each identified resource, from whom the resource must be protected
- Determining, for each identifiable resource, the type of threat and the likelihood of occurrence of such a threat
- Determining, for each identifiable resource, what measures are needed to give it the best protection
- Determining what needs to be audited
- Determining and defining acceptable use of system resources such as e-mail, News, and Web
- Considering how to implement and deploy security protocols such as encryption, access control, key creation, and distributions and wireless devices that connect on the organization's network
- Providing for remote access to accommodate workers on the road and those working from home, and also business partners who may need to connect to the organization's network via a VPN

11.6.2.3 Vulnerability Assessment

As is risk assessment, vulnerability assessment is the process of identifying and quantifying vulnerabilities in a system. A *vulnerability* in a system is an exploitable weakness in the system. As we saw in Sect. 8.3, this is a two-part process; we need to first identify all system vulnerabilities and then develop strategies to mitigate the effects of these vulnerabilities. The rest of the steps usually taken are similar to those in Sect. 8.3.

11.6.2.4 Use of Strong Cryptographic Algorithms

Cryptography is a Greek word meaning "secret writing." It was used to describe the art of secret communication. As shown in Figs. 4.1 and 11.8, cryptographic system consists of four essential components [1]:

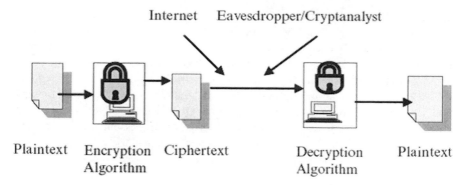

Fig. 11.8 Symmetrical encryption

- Plaintext: the original message to be sent
- A cipher: consisting of mathematical encryption and decryption algorithms
- Ciphertext: the result of applying an encryption algorithm to the original message before it is sent to the recipient
- Key: a string of bits used by the two mathematical algorithms in encrypting and decrypting processes

Cryptographic technologies are today being used increasingly to fight off massive invasion of individual privacy and security, to guarantee data integrity and confidentiality, and to bring trust in global e-commerce. In fact, cryptography has become the main tool for providing the needed digital security in the modern digital communication medium. Its popularity is a result of its ability to guarantee authorization, authentication, integrity, confidentiality, and non-repudiation in all communications and data exchanges in the new information society.

11.6.2.5 Penetration Testing

One of the core security techniques for safeguarding the security of an organization's system is a periodic penetration test of the system. The test may be outsourced for it to be more authentic, or it could be carried out inhouse, so long as one has competent personnel to do it. The process of penetration testing actively evaluates an organization's system resources and information in real time looking for design weaknesses, technical flaws, and vulnerabilities in the system: this can be done on a regular basis or with a scheduled timeframe. The possible outcomes of the test vary depending on the focus of the test.

Penetration testing may also focus on the security of information on the organization network by doing tests such as document grinding, privacy of information review, and intelligence scouting. If the organization supports wireless technology, this component must also be tested. No penetration testing can be complete without testing social engineering, communication within and outside the organization, and the physical security within the organization. Finally, physical testing may require testing access to the facilities, monitoring the perimeter and alarm systems, and an environment review.

11.6.2.6 Regular Security Audits

A penetration testing of an organization system is a focused look at the security holes in the system's resources such as firewalls and servers, whereas a security audit is a systematic, measurable, and quantifiable technical assessment of the organization security and the security of its system. Management usually requests security audits to gain knowledge and understand the security status of the organization's system. From the audit report, management may decide to upgrade the system through acquisition of new hardware and software. In "Conducting a Security Audit: An Introductory Overview," Bill Hayes suggests that a security audit should answer the following questions [4]:

- Are passwords difficult to crack?
- Are there access control lists (ACLs) in place on network devices to control who has access to shared data?
- Are there audit logs to record who accesses data?
- Are the audit logs reviewed?
- Are the security settings for operating systems in accordance with accepted industry security practices?
- Have all unnecessary applications and computer services been eliminated for each system?
- Are these operating systems and commercial applications patched to current levels?
- How is backup media stored? Who has access to it? Is it up to date?
- Is there a disaster recovery plan? Have the participants and stakeholders ever rehearsed the disaster recovery plan?
- Are there adequate cryptographic tools in place to govern data encryption, and have these tools been properly configured?
- Have custom-built applications been written with security in mind? How have these custom applications been tested for security flaws?
- How are configuration and code changes documented at every level? How are these records reviewed and who conducts the review?

If genuine and trustful answers are given to many of these questions, a realistic security status of the organization's system emerges.

11.7   Proven Security Protocols and Best Practices in Online Social Networks

There are hundreds of security protocols to meet the needs of organizations trying to improve their system security. There are so many of them, some open source and others not, that they pose a problem to security professionals to choose a really good product. The security personnel must strive to come up with a list of the best protocols and best practices to suit the system. Some of these protocols include the following.

11.7.1 Authentication

Authentication is the process of validating the identity of someone or something. It uses information provided to the authenticator to determine whether someone or something is in fact who or what it is declared to be. The process usually requires one to present credentials or items of value to the authenticating agent to prove the claim of who one really is. The items of value or credential are based on several unique factors that show something you know, something you have, or something you are [1]:

- *Something you know.* It may be something you mentally possess like a password, a secret word known by the user and the authenticator. This technique of authentication is cheap but has weaknesses, such as memory lapses.
- *Something you have.* It may be any form of issued or acquired self-identification such as SecurID, Activcard, or any other forms of cards and tags. This authentication technique is slightly safer.
- *Something you are.* These are individual physical characteristics such as voice, fingerprint, iris pattern, and other biometrics.

Besides these, there are other forms of authentication using a variety of authentication algorithms. These authentication methods can be combined or used separately, depending on the level of functionality and security needed. Among such methods are password authentication, public key authentication, anonymous authentication, and remote and certificate-based authentication.

11.7.2 Access Control

Access control is a process of determining how access to the system's potential resources can be provided to each of the system users. Because a system, especially a network system, may have thousands of users and resources, the management of access rights for every user per every object may become complex. Several control techniques and technologies have been developed to handle this problem; they include access control matrix, capability tables, access control lists, role-based access control, rule-based access control, restricted interfaces, content-dependent access control, and biometrics.

11.7.3 Legislation

Ever since the start of noticeable computer technology misuse, governments and national legislatures around the world have been enacting laws intended to curb the growth of these crimes. The report card on these legislations has been mixed. In some cases, legislation as a form of deterrent has worked and in others it has been a failure. However, we should not lose hope. Enforceable laws can be productive.

11.7.4 Self-Regulation

Perhaps one of the most successful forms of deterrence has been self-regulation. A number of organizations have formed to advocate parents and teachers to find a way to regulate objectionable material from reaching the children. Also families and individuals, sometimes based on their morals and sometimes based on their religion, have made self-regulation a cornerstone of their efforts to stop the growing rate of online crimes.

11.7.5 Detection

Although it is easy to develop mechanisms for preventing online crimes, it is not so easy to develop similar or effective techniques and best practices to detect online crimes. Detecting online crimes constitutes a 24-h monitoring system to alert security personnel whenever something unusual (something with a nonnormal pattern, different from the usual pattern of traffic in and around the system) occurs. Detection systems must continuously capture, analyze, and report on the daily happenings in and around the network. In capturing, analyzing, and reporting, several techniques are used including intrusion detection, vulnerability scanning, virus detection, and other ad hoc methods.

11.7.6 Recovery

Recovery is a process preceded by a process of analysis, which involves taking as many data as possible gathered during the last intrusion and analyzing these for patterns that can be used in future for a response, for detection, and for prevention. Recovery requires the use of all available resources to first mitigate the problem in progress, then to recover whatever can be recovered and use it to build on new data in place of or to replace the destroyed data.

Exercises

1. What are the differences between online social networks and online communities?
2. Discuss the social problems of online social networks.
3. An ecosystem is a localized group of interdependent organisms together with the environment that they inhabit and on which they depend. How do you relate this to online social networks?
4. Discuss privacy issues that apply in your online social ecosystem.
5. Discuss five modern online crimes.
6. Discuss strategies that can be used to effectively eliminate (if possible) online social network crimes.
7. If you were to write a framework to prevent cybercrimes from online social networks and indeed from all online spaces, what would be in it?

8. Is cryptography all we need to secure computer network and protect information?
9. Why is cryptography failing to protect digital systems and information? What do we need to do?

References

1. Kizza JM (2005) Computer network security. Springer, New York
2. Newman D, Whitaker A (2006) Penetration testing and network defense: performing host reconnaissance. Cisco Press, Indianapolis http://www.ciscopress.com/articles/ article. asp?p = 469623&seqNum = 1&rl = 1
3. Tittel Ed Understanding security policies. http://www.informit.com/articles/article. asp?p = 25041&rl = 1
4. Hayes B Conducting a security audit: an introductory overview. http://www.ecurityfocus. com/infocus/1697
5. Kizza JM (1999) Ethical and social issues in the information age. Springer, New York
6. Robert F (2000) News track: age and sex. Commun ACM 43(9):9
7. Chew M, Balfanz D, Laurie B, Google, Inc (2008) (Under)mining privacy in social networks. http://w2spconf.com/2008/papers/s3p2.pdf
8. Krishnamurthy B, Wills CE (2008) Characterizing privacy in online social networks. WOSN'08, August 18, 2008, Seattle, Washington, USA, http://www.ccs.neu.edu/home/cbw/5750/papers/bala-privacy.pdf
9. Schroeder S (2013) Facebook facing $138,000 fine for holding deleted user data. http://mashable.com/2011/10/21/facebook-deleted-data-fine/
10. Colgan B (2006) Facebook News Feed feature inspires student ire. The Wesleyan Argus CXLI(2)
11. Arrington M (2006) New facebook redesign more than aesthetic. Tech Crunch
12. Wikipedia: cyberstalking. http://en.wikipedia.org/wiki/Cyberstalking
13. Cyber bullying: statistics and tips. I-Safe Foundation. https://auth.isafe.org/outreach/media/media_cyber_bullying
14. http://www.bullyingstatistics.org/content/cyber-bullying-statistics.html
15. Young K (1998) Internet addiction: the emergence of a new clinical disorder. Cyber Psychol Behav 1(3):237–244
16. Misquittaa N. Psychiatry and society in Pune. http://blog.pathfinderclinic.com/2011/02/social-networkingpsychological- effects.html
17. Walsh M. Court backs student on facebook page criticizing teacher. News Week, http://blogs.edweek.org/edweek/school_law/2010/02/court_backs_student_on_faceboo.html

Elastic Extension Beyond the Traditional Computer Network

12

Mobile Systems and Their Intractable Social, Ethical, and Security Issues

---

Learning Objectives

After reading this chapter, the reader should be able to

1. Learn the working of mobile systems.
2. Learn about the growth of mobile systems.
3. Understand the social issues in mobile ecosystems.
4. Understand security issues in mobile ecosystems.
5. Understand privacy issues in mobile ecosystems.
6. Learn the ethical framework applicable in mobile ecosystems.

12.1   Introduction

In the previous chapters, we discussed the new frontier for computer ethics. This new frontier includes cyberspace, virtualization and virtual reality, artificial intelligence, and online social networks. We discussed how the new basic infrastructure created has been and is being misused. We also discussed the crucial role Internet-enabled devices play in computer-mediated interactions essential in online social networks. What we did not do, however, is actually talk about the elastic extension and evolution of all these devices and technologies that are resulting in a phenomenal and dangerous environment.

In the past two decades we have witnessed a revolution of sorts in mobile communication systems spearheaded by the rapidly evolving technologies in both software and hardware. A mobile communication systems consists of two or more of the following devices, running specifically developed software to sustain, for a period of time, a wireless communication link between them: mobile telephone, broadly construed here to include devices based on Code Division Multiple Access (CDMA), Time Division Multiple Access (TDMA), Global System for Mobile

© Springer International Publishing Switzerland 2016   255
J.M. Kizza, *Ethics in Computing*, Undergraduate Topics in Computer Science,
DOI 10.1007/978-3-319-29106-2_12

Communications (GSM), and Wireless Personal Digital Assistants (WPDA) digital technologies and follow-ons, as well as satellite telephones and e-mail satellite technologies are bringing appliances. Mobile communication systems are revolutionizing the world today, shrinking the world to that held between two or more small handheld mobile devices. The rapid changes in communication technologies, revolutionary changes in software, and the growth of large and powerful communication network technologies all have eased communication and brought it to large swathes of the globe. The high-end competition between the mobile telecommunication operators resulting in plummeting device prices, the quickly developing smartphone technology, and the growing number of undersea cables and cheaper satellite technologies are bringing Internet access to almost every one of the global rural poor faster than many had anticipated.

12.2 Role of Operating Systems in the Growth of the Mobile Technology Ecosystem

Perhaps nothing has contributed more handsomely to the global digital communication revolution than the mobile operating system technology. The mobile operating system, commonly called the mobile OS, or just *mOS*, is an operating system that is specifically designed to run in a small compact environment found in mobile devices such as mobile phones, smartphones, PDAs, tablet computers, and other handheld devices. The mobile operating system is the software platform on top of which other programs, called application programs, can run on mobile devices. The mOS performs the same functionalities as its bigger brother that runs laptops and PCs. The differences, however, are in the size of the memory that an ordinary and modern operating system will need to perform those functions. In the case of mOS, we are talking small sizes for everything. In additional to running in limited everything, modern mOSs must combine the required features of a personal computer with touchscreen, cellular, Bluetooth, WiFi, Wi-Max, GPS navigation, camera, video camera, speech recognition, voice recorder, music player, near-field communication, personal digital assistant (PDA), and others [1].

Mobile operating systems are as crucial and central to the running and security of the mobile device as they are in the larger, less mobile devices such as PCs and laptops. When it comes to security-related issues, the mobile device is as secure as its operating system. So every mobile device integrates in its operating systems as many security features as it can possibly carry without sacrificing speed, ease of use, and functionalities expected by the consumers. Because most mobile operating system are similar in a number of ways to their older brothers, the operating systems in the PCs and laptops, which have seen and continue to see growing problems with security such as backdoors, spyware, worms, Trojans, and a growing list of others, mOS developers and other application third parties should not wait and solve these security problems using a knee-jerk reaction as occurred with PCs and laptop security. Probably quick preemptive measures could help safeguard the mobile device much more quickly.

12.3   Ethical and Privacy Issues in Mobile Ecosystems

Have you ever received an ad on your smartphone for an item on sale while you are in a shopping mall? Have you ever received a coupon for a few cents off an item in a store near you? These examples illustrate some of the benefits and risks of the location-based tracking system (LTS) technologies that are part of our mobile devices. There are three types of LTS technologies in use today [2]:

- *Global positioning systems (GPS):* Using a constellation of GPS satellites orbiting the earth, which broadcast messages on radio frequencies that consist of the time of the message and orbital information. A GPS receiver measures the transit times of messages from four satellites to determine its distance from each satellite, and thereby calculate its location.
- *Radiofrequency identification (RFID) tags:* An RFID tag consists of a microchip and an antenna with typical ranges in size between a postage stamp and a pager. Each tag stores a unique identification number. An active RFID tag, which has its own power source, can transmit identification information up to a mile away. A passive RFID tag, which is activated by an external source of power, can transmit information up to 20 or 30 ft [3].
- *Global system for mobile communication (GSM):* This system provides personalized services to cell phone subscribers based on their current locations. A GSM uses several methods to find the location of a subscriber, using the time taken by signals to travel between the subscriber's handset and the cellular network base stations. GSM signals emitted by cell phones in vehicles can automatically report their positions, travel time, traffic incidents, and road surface problems [4].

These LTS technologies are being used by merchants, law enforcement agencies, and almost everyone else who needs to know where you and your smart electronic device are. Although users of smart devices may not be aware of it, these technologies have huge ethical and privacy implications to users of these devices. In our discussion, let us focus on the security and threat to individual privacy, for even in public places individuals deserve some privacy, through the collection, aggregation and centralization of personal information, without user consent, and also on the absence of applicable laws. Use of LTS technologies can increase the risks to the privacy and security of individuals in the following ways [5]:

Privacy—Both LTS embedded in all smart mobile communication devices routinely transmit the location of an individual, many times providing information about the whereabouts of an individual without their consent. This action infringe on an individual's right to privacy, as we said earlier; even in public spaces, individuals must expect a certain degree of privacy. The information collected usually may be transmitted to a third party who may choose to do with the information as they please, without the device owner's consent.

Control—GPS systems have been used in a number of ways to help track individuals who, voluntarily or otherwise, need to be monitored: criminals on home arrest by wearing ankle devices and Alzheimer's patients to make sure they do not wander off. GPS systems are also used in a number of other transportation systems.

Hackers—When GPS data are collected and stored, they must be securely stored, otherwise a hacker can get to them, so that personal data become available to criminals.

Data Ownership—Who owns GPS data? Note that satellites used for GPS were created by the government to track military personnel. These same satellites are used to convey GPS information to drivers and third parties. Does the individual owning the GPS unit own the information? Or the government that created the satellite, or the third party who is gathering the data? If the government owns the information, it opens the door to the government being able to track your movements without your consent, and possibly without a warrant or reason.

Aggregation of LTS Data—We have seen that LTS systems collect data on individuals in different situations and circumstances. When do such data become an individual loss of privacy and when does this become a violation of that individual's privacy? It is ethically significant to understand the difference. Lin and Loui [6] observes that if data are collected from an individual in different situations, some of which may be in public places, and if those data are aggregated to derive new information about that individual, then this centralization of aggregated information of that individual violates the individual's moral right to privacy. Why is this the case, you ask? According to Rachels [7], and Wang and Loui [2], privacy is valuable because it provides a context for individuals to create and maintain a variety of human relationships that are eliminated by centralization of personal information.

Location-based tracking systems (LTSs) are increasingly used by businesses as well as government entities to track potential customers and criminals, and thereby to improve the business environments for businesses and to security of communities for governments. But keep in mind that LTSs cause loss of individual privacy whenever there is aggregation of individual information.

12.4   Security Issues in Mobile Ecosystems

As mobile devices, more importantly, smart devices that can do almost everything a computer can do and more, become ubiquitous, the risk for using them is increasing. They are increasingly holding and storing more private data, personal and business, and they are roaming in public spaces on public networks with limited security and cryptographic protocols to protect the data. In fact, the kind of security threats toward these devices is similar and probably more than that experienced by PCs and laptops in their heyday. The security threats to these mobile devices are comparable to, if not more than, those facing servers in that these devices can remain on without user attention and are always connected to a network. Also, because these devices have the ability to roam on several networks, there is a wider sphere of attack beset by geographic, legal and moral differences. Because of the high demand for global connectivity, especially in developing countries, service providers are responding with a zeal to consolidate networks and standardize communication protocols, thus making it easier for these devices to roam in large spaces and networks, creating fertile ground for attackers. The penetration trend of these smart mobile devices is not limited to faraway rural places but more scary is their rapid penetration on enterprise IT spaces where security is paramount for any device. This extension of smart devices into the enterprise IT spaces is a result of their popularity as they slowly replace the enterprise laptop as the enterprise mobile device. This change in turn is increasingly causing enterprise management to start focusing on their security issues. Although antivirus client applications have been available and security best practices have been in place for most high-level operating systems, this is not the case with small mobile devices. In his article "New Security Flaws Detected in Mobile Devices," Byron Acohido [8] reports the two recent examinations by Cryptography Research, the company that did the research, of mobile devices that revealed gaping security flaws. In one study, Cryptography Research showed how it is possible to eavesdrop on any smartphone or tablet as it is being used to make a purchase, conduct online banking, or access a company's virtual private network. Also, McAfee, an antivirus software company and a division of Intel, showed ways to remotely hack into Apple iOS and steal secret keys and passwords, and pilfer sensitive data, including call histories, e-mail, and text messages. What is more worrying is the reported fact that the device under attack would not in any way show that an attack is underway. Almost every mobile system user, and security experts and law enforcement officials, are all anticipating that cybergangs will accelerate attacks as consumers and companies begin to rely more heavily on mobile devices for shopping, banking, and working. So there is an urgent need for a broader array of security awareness of the community and actions by the community to assist in providing all users with the highest level of protection.

In their security report titled "2011 Mobile Threat Report," the Lookout Mobile Security, a smartphone security company [9], discusses security threats to mobile devices under four major areas: application, Web-based access, network, and physical environments. Major threats are encountered by mobile devices on a daily basis.

12.4.1 Application-Based Threats

For every mobile device, the biggest appealing feature is the ability to run thousands of applications (apps) to accomplish a variety of tasks. These applications are written by really unknown people with limited to no allegiance to anybody and taking no commands from anyone. The applications archiving companies like the Apple Store rarely have any security standards for these applications and rely, if at all, on checking for security requirements. So, downloadable applications present the greatest security issues for any mobile device that is capable of downloading software. Application-based threats, therefore, generally fit into one or more of the following categories [9]:

- *Malware* is software designed with the intent to engage in malicious behavior on a device. As we see later, malware can be used in a variety of ways, including identity theft and stealing of personal information from a mobile device.
- *Spyware* is designed with the intent to collect or use data without a user's knowledge or approval. We discuss this further in Sect. 12.5.
- *Functionality features* are the device's normal functionality features that reveal or threaten an individual's privacy. These features include the GPS location identification.
- *Vulnerable applications* is software that may have vulnerabilities that can be exploited for malicious purposes. Such software includes the device's operating system.

12.4.2 Web-Based Threats

Mobile devices, once on, are continuously roaming in public spaces on public networks with limited security and cryptographic protocols to protect them. In many cases, they are often constantly connected to the Internet for normal Web-based services. Under such circumstances, they are exposed to Web-based threats such as follows [9]:

- *Phishing scams* in which intruders use Web-based services to launch attacks on those devices connected to the Web to acquire information such as usernames, passwords, credit card details, and other private data of the device owner by the intruder masquerading as a trustworthy friend in an electronic communication such as e-mail and text.
- *Drive-by downloads* are similar to pop-ups written by scammers to automatically begin uploading a treacherous application as soon as the device visits a web page.
- *Other web exploits:* any one of the many web exploits discussed in Sect. 12.5 (following) is possible because scammers take advantage of vulnerabilities in a web browser or software that can be launched via a web browser to attack the mobile device.
- *Direct exploitation* is a threat to mobile browsers, some of them as code bases on mobile devices that malicious web pages can target, including the browser itself and image viewers, Flash, and PDF readers [5]:

12.4.3 Network Threats

As we have stated, once mobile devices are turned on, they immediately start looking for networks to connect on either cellular networks or the Internet. As we see in Sect. 12.5, a number of threats originate from these networks [5]:

- *Network exploits:* recall that mobile devices always network once turned on. Each one of these networks, including the Internet and Bluetooth, has their own exploits. (See more of this discussion in Sect. 12.5, following.)

12.4.4 Physical Threats

All the different classes of threats we have discussed so far are based on the nature and the functionality of the mobile device itself, but the physical threats are based on the size and the owner of the mobile device.

- *Lost or stolen devices:* the miniaturization of mobile devices affords more convenience for the user but the small sizes make them more susceptible to theft and being lost from the user. There are ways to wipe the device remotely, but very few users think of this immediately, giving the robbers enough time to acquire the data on it. In fact, there more mobile devices prone to these kinds of threats than any other we have seen so far.

12.4.5 Operating System-Based Threats

The last major category of mobile devices is that category based on the device's operating system. As has been observed by many security experts, while the threats originating from the device's operating systems are many, there are so far two windows of opportunities: one being that we have learned a lot from operating system security and vulnerabilities from their bigger brothers the PC and the laptops; and the second being that so far the domain is still relatively safer than the domain of the PCs and laptops, either because many would-be attackers have not yet acquired the script programming skills needed to develop and launch attacks, or that because most attacks in the PC and laptop domains are repeat attacks supported by large archives of malware and viruses; the mobile device domain has yet to develop extensive archives of these malware and viruses. So far, it is lack of expertise that is still helping. Also, most operating system threats are specific to the brand. So, in our discussion we make specific mention of the brand whenever possible.

- KDataStruct is a Windows Mobile (WM) operating system problem based on the vulnerability that in WM Microsoft placed all main system functions in one coredll.dll file so that developers do not have to include the code for functions in their own programs. They just call the coredll addresses of all the APIs it uses into memory space it is allocated. In so doing, an address to the list of modules is provided so that the address of the coredll can be determined. From here one can search through memory looking for the virtual address of the API wanted. This approach can open up the device for exploitation. This vulnerability is exploited by the virus WinCE.Duts.A.

- Pocket IE is another Windows vulnerability found in the small Internet Explorer, commonly known as Pocket IE (PIE), default Web Browser for the WM Oss. The PIE has all the vulnerabilities found in the standard IE for the big brother PCs and laptops. See all these vulnerabilities in Sect. 12.5.
- Jailbreaking is a process whereby a user can alter the phone's operating system to gain full access (or root access) to the operating system and allow applications not officially vetted by Apple's review policies. For example, JailbreakMe 3.0 for iOS devices is a nonmalicious web page that exploits two vulnerabilities to jailbreak a device [10].
- DroidDream is an Android malware that utilizes two exploits, Exploid and RageAgainstTheCage, to break out of the Android security sandbox, gain root control of the operating system, and install applications without user intervention [11–13].
- Update Attacks are a growing problem of using application updates as an attack method in the Android Market. A malware writer first releases a legitimate application containing no malware. Once they have a large enough user base, the malware writer updates the application with a malicious version [12].
- Malvertising is malicious advertising in which an attacker lures victims into downloading malware, especially on the Android Market. They rely on the fact that developers commonly use in-app advertisements to gain more users, so people are used to downloading apps via advertisements [12].
- Other threats include the Flowed shell model (iOS), Root Account (iOS), Static addressing (iOS), Static systems (iOS), and Reuse of Code (iOS).

12.5   General Mobile Devices Attack Types

Most mobile system attacks are launched against specific mobile devices or operating systems or applications. Most of these attack techniques are carryovers from the computer and computer networks, so they are not generally new in the arsenal of attacks. Over the years, we have learned specific methodologies the attackers use for success in their quest. The most common attack channels and techniques follow [1]:

12.5.1 Denial-of-Service (DDoS)

This technique is meant to unanticipated consequences to cause system disruption so that the device, the service, or the network on which the device is cannot complete the operation under way involving the device.

12.5.2 Phone Hacking

This is a technique used to intercept phone calls or voicemail messages, by accessing either the voicemail or text messages of a mobile phone without the knowledge or consent of the phone's owner. You may recall the News of The World phone hacking stories in the United Kingdom.

12.5.3 Mobile Malware/Virus

A mobile malware or virus is software that deliberately targets mobile phones or wireless-enabled PDAs.

12.5.4 Spyware

Spyware is a type of malware that automatically installs itself or in some cases is installed manually on computers so that it continuously or periodically collects information about a range or a single event, user, or application without the owner's knowledge.

12.5.5 Exploit

An exploit is software code that takes advantage of a bug, glitch, or vulnerability to cause unintended or unanticipated consequences to occur on computer software, hardware, or something electronic.

12.5.6 Everything Blue

This collection of malwares and spywares takes advantage of Bluetooth technology. Just like in any other wireless network, Bluetooth, with its ability to automatically connect with other Bluetooth-enabled wireless devices, has a number of security problems that are exploited. Bluetooth is now a basic feature of mobile devices. All mobile devices now have this feature embedded in them. Before Bluetooth, Infrared technology was used to transfer data and communication between any two wireless devices so long as they were within the line of sight. But Infrared hindered mean-ingful mobility of the devices, so Bluetooth technology came in to solve that prob-lem. Many Bluetooth devices offered the needed communication and mobility within the unlicensed band of radio waves without having to be in line of sight. Because of this, Bluetooth applications have emerged that allow peering of users with false security. Because this unlicensed radio band is under no regulation, it is more vulnerable to an array of security issues. Mobile devices operating within the Bluetooth range can be compromised easily as hackers can have easy access to data into these devices, even commanding them to do anything the hacker wants. Without exhausting them all, let us review the different categories of how hackers can infil-trate mobile devices using Bluetooth; then we discuss their mechanism briefly to make the end user aware of how vulnerable the user can be [16].

- Bluejacking is similar to spamming but in Bluetooth by sending unsolicited messages to a victim device, which opens up communication between the paired devices. Thus, the attacker can gain access to the victim device.
- Bluesnarfing is a form of Bluetooth hacking that can allow a hacker to gain access to the victim's device's contact list, text messages, e-mails, and other vital information. The hacker can even use a brute force attack, even if the device is invisible, to guess the victim's MAC address.
- Bluebugging is the type of attack like a Trojan horse where the hacker uses sophisticated attack techniques to gain control of a victim's mobile device. Once in control, the attacker can do anything with the mobile device.
- Bluetoothing is social engineering in Bluetooth wherein a hacker can use traditional social engineering tricks to masquerade as the legitimate user of the mobile device.
- BlueBumping is an attack involving two mobile devices pairing and setting up communication. The attacking device gets the victim to accept a connection for a trivial data exchange such as a picture, then uses that pairing to attack other services. While the connection is still open, the attacker requests a link key regeneration that it later uses to gain access to the victim device, thus getting full access to any of the services on the victim device.
- BlueChopping is an attack that targets the Bluetooth piconet (an ad hoc Bluetooth network linking other Bluetooth devices). It allows one *master* device to interconnect with many other active *slave* devices for disruption by spoofing one of the participating piconet slaves, leading to confusion of the master's internal state and thus disrupting the piconet.
- BlueDumping is the act of sniffing a Bluetooth device key exchange by forcing the Bluetooth victim mobile device to dump its stored link key. Before the sniff, the attacker needs to know the *BDADDR* of a set of paired devices. To get this, the attacker spoofs the address of one of the devices and connects to the other. Because the attacker has no link key, when the target device requests authentication, the attacker's device will respond with an 'HCI_Link_Key_Request_Negative_Reply,' which will, in some cases, cause the target device to delete its own link key and go into pairing mode [14].
- BlueSmucking is a Bluetooth Denial of Service attack that knocks out some Bluetooth-enabled devices immediately. It is carried out using the old "Ping of Death" but transformed to work in Bluetooth. On the L2CAP (echo request) layer there is the possibility to request an echo from another Bluetooth peer, to check connectivity, and to measure roundtrip time on the established link. This is possible in Bluetooth because the l2ping in BlueZ utils allows the user to specify a packet length that is sent to the respective peer, done by means of the **-s <num>** option [14].
- BlueSniffing is a Bluetooth version of war driving.

12.5.7 Phishing

Phishing in Bluetooth devices uses the same attempt techniques in their big broth-ers, the PCs and laptops, in that it is intended to acquire information such as user-names, passwords, and credit card details and other private data of the device owner by the intruder masquerading as a trustworthy friend in an electronic communica-tion like e-mail and text.

12.5.8 SMishing

Smishing is a social engineering crime like phishing in that it uses the mobile devices and texts as baits to pull in the mobile device owner to divulge private and sometimes personal information.

12.5.9 Vishing

Vishing is another criminal practice in the social engineering class resembling the last two. It mostly uses the mobile device phone features facilitated by Voice over IP (VoIP), to gain access to private personal and financial information from the public for the purpose of financial reward. The term is a combination of "voice" and phishing.

12.6   Mitigation of Mobile Devices Attacks

More and more people are now using some form of a data-carrying mobile device. The data on these devices are either personal or work related. Either way, this trend is growing. What is growing even faster and more worrying is the trend whereby a growing number of employers are increasingly using unmanaged personal devices to access sensitive enterprise resources and then connecting these devices to third-party services outside the enterprise security controls; this potentially exposes the enterprise-sensitive data to possible attackers, creating a growing security headache for sometimes underfunded and overworked security staff. The enterprise security team has to contend with a plethora of different devices running different operating systems or different versions of an operating system. According to the report "Mobile Devices Expose Company Data To Severe Vulnerabilities" by Mobilisafe, a Seattle-based mobile risk management company, small and mid-sized businesses (SMB) are more affected by this growing move. The report found the following [15]:

- SMBs are exposed to high severity vulnerabilities from the increasing levels of mobile devices used to access and download company data.

- SMB IT managers cannot keep up with the rate of discovery of severe vulnerabilities these devices bring to their corporate network.
- SMB IT departments lack a standardized approach to mitigate the risks from different types of mobile devices, as they do with laptops, desktops, and servers.
- Even though they feel exposed to mobile device security risk, SMBs do not think they have adequate tools to assess and mitigate these risks at a granular level.

So what needs to be done? There are several security protocols and best practices that can come in handy for such situations. According to Clint Adams [16], in the "holy trinity of mobile device management," there are three security components that must form the minimum security requirements for any mobile security management. These components are hardware encryption, remote wiping, and the ability to set a passcode policy. Therefore, those responsible for security in any enterprise that is intending to use mobile devices as one form of communication and corporate data access must pay attention to these three components of security. One good thing is that mobile device manufacturers and operating system developers have been paying increasing attention to these tenants, at least the first two. Because the pool of mobile device makers and mobile operating system developers is rather large, the task of ensuring that these three security tenants are adhered to by all in the company can be daunting. To somewhat lessen this task for a variety of companies and individuals, a new industry has sprung up. The mobile device management (MDM) system is a platform either from third-party or original mobile device manufacturers to support and help enterprises set up and enforce mobile security policies centrally. The MDM software secures, monitors, manages, and supports mobile devices deployed across mobile operators, service providers, and enterprises. MDM functionality typically includes over-the-air distribution of applications, data, and configuration settings for all types of mobile devices, including mobile phones, smartphones, tablet computers, ruggedized mobile computers, mobile printers, mobile POS devices, and others [17].

12.6.1 Mobile Device Encryption

Thus, it is important and probably a must, that when sensitive data are carried on either personal or business mobile devices, such devices must be encrypted. Encrypting a mobile device is meant to protect such data as the power-on and screensaver password, the SIM card, passwords to open apps or certain functions within apps such as logging into an e-commerce retailer account, confidential email, instant messages, SMS messages, and confidential data and medical files.

Mobile device encryption can be done in two different ways: application and hardware encryption.

12.6.1.1 Application Encryption

In securing mobile devices using applications, encryption protects the mobile device from attacks made on the host device, as well as across network connections end to end. There are many vendor solutions for this kind of encryption.

12.6.1.2 Hardware Encryption

Hardware encryption is encryption protocols embedded into the hardware by the original mobile hardware manufacturer. For example, Research in Motion (RIM), the manufacturer of BlackBerry, is well known and indeed currently takes first place in hardware encryption of the BlackBerry phones. On the BlackBerry, RIM combines strong Advanced Encryption Standard (AES) and Triple Data Encryption Standard (Triple DES) encryption with a strong mobile device management platform to provide a strong security stance for enterprise BlackBerrys. Its BlackBerry Enterprise Server (BES) and the BlackBerry devices provide a strong solution that can deliver encryption, remote wipe, and passcode policy enforcement [1]. Similarly, other mobile device manufacturers such as Apple, Goggle, and Microsoft have corresponding embedded encryptions either in their device operating systems, embedded SIM cards, or movable encryption SIM cards.

12.6.2 Mobile Remote Wiping

To remotely wipe data from a mobile device is one of the security techniques in the mobile device security bag of tricks. It offers the security IT managers the basic mobile device management capabilities to remotely wipe data from a lost mobile device. The remote wipe and other management features are both mobile device manufacturer and third party developed. Many are cross platform: Google's Apps Premier and Education Edition, which works for iPhones, Nokia E series devices, and Windows Mobile smartphones.

12.6.3 Mobile Passcode Policy

Because there is a plethora of different devices running different operating systems or different versions of an operating system, it is hard for the IT team to keep abreast of the many mobile device manufacturers and third-party vendor mobile security solutions. To cope with these problems, a security policy targeting the mobile devices in use is required.

A complete mobile security solution should include [18]:

- A firewall to secure the device from attacks and malicious code.
- A VPN to allow flexible means to ensure secure communications for any wireless data traffic.
- An authentication mechanism to ensure that unauthorized persons are not accessing the device if it is lost or stolen.
- Data encryption on the device to ensure that information is not stolen, either physically or electronically.
- Antivirus software to protect the device from viruses and malware.

12.7   User Role in Securing Mobile Devices

Although we are living in a time when doing without mobile devices in day-to-day personal communication and personal access to data is awkward, users must be aware that there are risks to the convenience afforded by these mobile devices. It is important to know that mobile computing devices can store large amounts of personal and sometimes sensitive data whose loss may cause problems to the owner or user. It is also important to know that it is easy to steal or lose those data. Furthermore, it is important to know that unless precautions are taken, an unauthorized person can gain access to the information stored on these mobile devices or gain access through these devices to other devices or data because these devices may provide access to other services that store or display nonpublic data. This access may be enabled because the mobile device contains passwords or security certificates and other information that may help to identify the device, its user, or its content. So, our role as users is to be vigilant and security aware.

Exercises

1. Discuss the steps you would take to protect your mobile device.
2. Search the Internet to find a company's security policy for its mobile devices. Suggest what you would change in that security policy to enhance security.
3. Study three remote wiping solutions and compare them.
4. Comment on the reasons for the rapid growth of the Android Operating System.
5. Recently, Apple found itself in a dispute with the FBI sparked off by the FBI's request to Apple to help unlock the cell phone, an iPhone 5C, the model used by one of the perpetrators of the 2015 San Bernardino attack. But the FBI was unable to unlock the iPhone due to its advanced encryption. So the FBI request for help from Apple, which refused to help, saying that doing so will undermine the security features of its products. Discuss the legal and security responsibilities of either party.
6. Discuss two main privacy concerns with LTS.
7. What is the difference between privacy loss and privacy violation?
8. When does privacy loss occur but privacy violation does not and vice versa?

Advanced Exercises

1. Study the Mobile Device Management platforms and discuss the solutions offered.
2. What does a typical MDM solution include?
3. List and discuss vendors of MDM
4. Discuss the Windows Mobile security model, Authentication Services, Credential Manager, Cryptography, and LASS application development and programming elements.
5. Discuss the iPhone Mobile Authentication system.
6. Discuss laws in place to protect individual privacy violation in LTS.
7. Give a thorough discussion of ethical issues in mobile systems.

References

1. http://en.wikipedia.org/wiki/Smartphone_operating_systems
2. Wang JL, Loui MC. Privacy and ethical issues in location-based tracking systems. http://students.cse.unt.edu/~ry0049/LP3.pdf
3. How radio frequency identification tags will help retailers, from supply chains to store shelves. MIT Technology Review, March 2004 [Online]. Available: http://www.technologyreview.com/computing/13509/. Accessed 2 Oct 2008
4. Hoh B, Gruteser M, Xiong H, Alrabady A (2006) Enhancing security and privacy in traffic monitoring systems. IEEE Pervas Comput 5(4):38–46
5. Ethical issues in GPS tracking. http://www.ehow.com/info_8432238_ethical-issues-gps-tracking.html#ixzz24naYTmrR
6. Lin D, Loui MC (1998) Taking the byte out of cookies: privacy, consent, and the web. Comput Soc 28(2):39–51
7. Rachels J (1995) Why privacy is important. In: Johnson DG, Nissenbaum H (eds) Computers, ethics & social values. Prentice Hall, Upper Saddle River, pp 351–357
8. Acohido   B   (2012)   http://www.enterprise-security-today.com/news/Mobile-Devices-Vulnerable-to-Attack/story.xhtml?story_id=0010003FAI65. Accessed 10 Apr 2012
9. 2011 mobile threat report. https://www.mylookout.com/mobile-threat-report
10. http://esec-lab.sogeti.com/post/Analysis-of-the-jailbreakme-v3-font-exploit
11. C-Skills (2010) http://c-skills.blogspot.com/search?q=exploid
12. C-Skills (2010) http://c-skills.blogspot.com/
13. Lookout Mobile Security Blog (2011) Android malware DroidDream: how it works. http://blogmylookout.com/2011/03/android-malware-droiddream-how-it-works
14. http://trifinite.org/trifinite_stuff_bluedump.html
15. Mobile devices expose company data to severe vulnerabilities. http://www.prnewswire.com/news-releases/mobilisafe-study-details-vulnerability-risk-to-company-data-forsmbs-146647805.html
16. Adams C. http://searchconsumerization.techtarget.com/tutorial/Mobile-device-security-overview
17. Wikipedia. http://en.wikipedia.org/wiki/Mobile_device_management
18. Komisky M. Mobile device security II: handheld operating systems. Bluefire. http://wwwdatamation.com/mowi/article.php/3575316/Mobile-Device-Security-II-Handheld-Operating-Systems.htm

Index

A

Access, 30, 32, 37, 66, 69–71, 74, 76, 79, 80,
83, 85, 96, 110, 113, 115–117,
119–123, 126, 128, 132, 152, 181, 182,
184, 186, 187, 190–192, 196, 203, 219,
223, 231–234, 236, 238–240, 244, 245,
247–251, 256, 259, 262–266, 268
Access control lists (ACLs), 250, 251
Accountability, 31, 40, 43, 46–47, 60, 221
Acquired immune deficiency syndrome
(AIDS), 217
Activism, 182, 183
African, 118
Alienation, 135, 142, 143
Altruism, 20
Analytical engine, 222
Anonymity, 35, 56, 57, 63–85, 187, 196–200,
223, 237, 241, 242
Anonymous, 56, 58, 67–69, 79, 241, 251
remailers, 56, 67
Appeals, 47, 50–52, 221, 261
ARPANET, 180, 236
Artificial intelligence (AI), 207–224, 255
Asimov, Isaac, 211, 212, 217
Assessment, 28, 32, 50, 137, 157, 185, 247,
248, 250
Association of Computing Machinery (ACM),
27–33, 159
AT&T Bell Laboratories, 131
Atheist, 2
Atomic Energy of Canada Ltd.
(AECL), 159
Authentication, 69, 71, 73–74, 218, 249, 251,
264, 268, 269
Autonomous agents, 210, 212
Autonomy, 40, 42, 44, 45, 76, 77, 79, 134,
209, 212, 213, 237

B

BAE Automated Systems Ltd., 152
Bhopal, India, 163
Biometric algorithm, 251
Biometrics, 251
Breach of contract, 169, 170
BTT, 97
Buffer overflow, 183, 246
Buyers' right, 107, 150, 165–166
Byzantines, 5

C

Canadian, 182, 183
Carpal tunnel syndrome (CTS), 143
Censoring cyberspace, 220
Censorship, 220, 221
Central Intelligence Agency (CIA), 223
Challenger, 57, 160–163
Cipher, 249
Ciphertext, 72, 249
Civil liberties, 14, 63–84, 127
Clone, human, 13, 17–18
Close circuit television (CCTV), 70
CNN, 183
Code
community, 42, 43
conduct, ethics, 3, 27, 42, 53, 212
executable, 90, 107, 109, 246
institutional, 42, 43, 53
local, 53
moral, 4–9, 11, 12, 14, 40, 43
object, 89, 90, 107, 109
penal, 12
personal, 42, 43, 53
professional, 42, 43, 47, 49–53
source, 89, 107

© Springer International Publishing Switzerland 2016
J.M. Kizza, *Ethics in Computing*, Undergraduate Topics in Computer Science,
DOI 10.1007/978-3-319-29106-2